THE BUSINESS OF GOLF
What Are You Thinking?

2016: The Fourth Edition

How to Create Value for Golfers and Enhance the Financial Performance of Your Golf Course

By

James J. Keegan, Strategist

JJ Keegan+

ISBN: 978-0-9846268-5-4

Library of Congress Control Number: 2013953827

Printed in the United States of America.

Table of Contents

Section 2—Tactical Planning 117

CHAPTER 7: Technology—The Foundation 119

CHAPTER 8: Financial Modeling 137

Section 3—Operational Execution 205

CHAPTER 12: The Playing Field 207

CHAPTER 13: Marketing, the Internet, and Social Media 223

CHAPTER 14: Game Time 245

Acknowledgments

Treat a man as he is, and he will remain as he is. Treat a man as he could be, and he will become what he should be.

Ralph Waldo Emerson

Vegetable or Fruit?

Is there a vegetable or fruit that is symbolic of one's career? I would suggest a tomato or watermelon might be such. From the outward appearance they appear as one but in slicing them open, they are filled with seeds. Those seeds represent all of the people that have guided, mentored, and provided motivation to one's career.

Writing about tomatoes may be apt for many may view me as "smashing the tomato" as an outsider to the golf industry. Associations and management companies serve as the bastions protecting the status quo. Change is adopted within the golf industry at a glacier pace.

I am appreciative to those who encourage and contribute to my challenging the conventional wisdom, for I am passionate about creating astute insights that provide meaningful value to golf course owners and their management teams. The results are that we have developed a Golf Executive Management System that will significantly guide every golf course owner and management team in enhancing the financial performance of their facility.

Professional Appreciation

A pleasant by-product of writing this book was that it facilitated reflection on the past 27 years in the golf industry of the many wonderful people I have met. The annual PGA Merchandise Show has almost become to me like a yearly class reunion.

I hardly know where to start to thank each person who contributed to my knowledge of the industry. I have come to realize that I am merely a secretary transcribing the thoughts and best practices of the brilliant minds within the industry.

Serving in this industry, I have been impacted by some amazing people whom I hold in deep admiration and respect: Peter Aeillo, Managing Partner, Kokanee Springs Resort; Eddie Ainsworth, Executive Director of the Colorado PGA Section; Justin Apel, Executive Director, Golf Course Builders Association of America; Joe Assell, PGA, President of GolfTec; Scott Atkinson, Managing Director, Play Golf Calgary; Chad Becker, General Manager, Three Creek Golf Course; Dr. Joseph Beditz, President and CEO, National Golf Foundation; Peter Bevacqua, CEO, PGA of America; Jeff Brauer, ASGCA; Jeff Calderwood, Chief Executive Officer, NGCOA—Canada; Jack Crittenden, Editor, Golf Inc.; David Clark, Editor, Golf Magazine; Graham Cliff, PGA, Colorado Golf Club; Kevin Collins, Managing Partner, Club at Ravenna; Jorge Croda, GCSAA, Southern Hills Golf Club; Sandy Cross, Senior Director of Diversity and Inclusion, PGA of America; Cindy Curtis, Former Assistant City Manager, City of Virginia Beach; Mike Cutler, PGA, Senior Vice President, Billy Casper Golf; Gordon Dalgleish, President, Perry Golf; Tim Eberlein, PGA Master Professional, Campus Director Golf Academy of America—Phoenix; Jim Fedigan, President, Jonas Software; Michael Fentress, PGA, Head Golf Professional, Kempsville Greens Golf Course; Jeff Foster, SVP New Media Group, Golf Channel; Steve Friedlander, Vice President—Golf, Pelican Hill and Oak Creek Golf Clubs; Eric Greytok, National Sales, Macrosorb Technologies; Jack Grum, Executive Vice President, Weather Trends International; Chad Hatch, Vice President, Bird Dog Equity; Cathy Harbin, President, OnCourse Operations; Doug Hellman, Senior Vice President, Kemper Sports Inc.; Dr. Brian Horgan, Associate Professor, Turf Management, University of Minnesota; Keith Kalny, Director of Golf Operations; Minneapolis Park and Recreation Board; Jay Karen, Chief Executive Officer, National Golf Course Owners Association; Brad Klein, Senior Writer, *Golfweek*; Michael Loustalot, President, ORCA; Evan Lowery, Senior Meteorologist, Weather Trends International; Rick Lucas, PGA, Director PGA PGM Program at Clemson University; Quentin Lutz, Co-Founder, The Outpost Club; M.J. Mastalir, President, Real

Estate Capital Corporation; Jayne Miller, Superintendent, Minneapolis Park and Recreation Board; Nick Mokelke, General Manager, Cog Hill Golf and Country Club; Karen Moraghan, President, Hunter Public Relations; Tim Moraghan, President, Aspire Consulting; Greg Nathan, Chief Business Officer, National Golf Foundation; Kevin Norby, ASGCA, Herfort-Norby; Joe Passov, Travel Editor, *Golf Magazine*; Warren Pitman, PGA, Golf Academy of America; Del Ratcliffe, PGA, President, Ratcliffe Golf Services; James E. Roschek, PGA, President and CEO, Municipal Golf Association of San Antonio; Kristine Schoonover, University of Wisconsin – Stout; Paul Schock, President, Bird Dog Equity; Randy Shannon, Director of Golf and Placements, Professional Golfers Career College; David V. Smith, CEO, Golf Projects International; Tom Stine, Co-Founder and Partner, Golf Datatech; Armen Suny, Suny Zokol Golf Design; Kyle Taggart, Vice President, Tag Team Design; Michael Vogt, CGCS, McMahon Group; Donna White, LPGA, Instructor, Keiser University College of Golf and Sports Management; and Andrew Wood, Founder, Legendary Marketing.

Professional Appreciation for Assistance with This Endeavor

Sharon Anderson, Jen Welsch, and the staff at Bookmasters were fabulous in editing and flawlessly completing the typesetting. Jostens does a marvelous job of printing. Robert Lane of Aspire Communications continues to design amazing book covers. Janna Keegan's "fresh eyes" were invaluable in the final review.

JJ Keegan+ has been very fortunate to have many excellent clients who we have celebrated and thanked in prior editions of this book. They made possible, by the inclusion of data and insights from the strategic, tactical, and operational reviews the principles presented herein. Since 2014, the following having contributed to our continuing research and testing and have validated the principles herein: Arroyo Trabuco, Bakker Crossings, Bemidji Town and Country Club, Carmel Clay County Parks, Carolina Country Club, City of Arlington, City of Becker, City of Brookings, City of Brooklyn Park, City of Durango, City of Grand Rapids, City of Greenville, City of Hot Springs, City of Litchfield, City of Louisville, City of Midland, City of Reno, City of Round Rock, City of South Bend, Club at Stoney Creek, Cog Hill Golf and Country Club, Colorado Golf Club, Cutter Creek Golf Club, Edgewood Golf Club, Fox Hills Golf Club, Golf Club at Ravenna, Golf Summerlin, Green Meadow Country Club, Kapalua Resort, Minneapolis Park and Recreation Board, Pacific Grove Golf Links, Prairie Club, Sioux Falls Regional Airport Authority, Southern Hills Golf Course, Talking Stick Resort, and University of Minnesota–Les Bolstad Golf Course.

During the past two years, we have conducted quarterly webinars comprising ten weekly conferences mentoring participants in conjunction with an Ed.D. Dissertation for Rick Lucas, PGA, Director of the Clemson University Professional Golf Management Program. Participants included: Alamo City Golf Trail, Baltimore Municipal Golf Corporation, City of Bloomington, City of Cedar Rapids, City of Charlotte, City of Columbus, City of Fort Worth, City of San Antonio, City of Virginia Beach, Crystal Mountain Resort, Fernie Golf and Country Club, Golf Club at La Quinta, Kokanee Springs Resort, Northstar Golf Club, Oak Creek Golf Club (Irvine Company), Pine Meadow (Jemsek Family), Play Golf Calgary, Thornberry Creek at Oneida (Oneida Nation) and Western Illinois University – Mussatto Golf Course. The templates that are referred to in this book were thoroughly tested and refined by this talented group.

Personal Appreciation for Those Who Have Influenced My Life

When all is said and done, what matters is family.

To Debra, my wife, my friend, partner, confidant, and cheerleader; you make a house a home, and your career finding others employment provides balance. May we reach the end together.

To my daughter, Janna Michaela. With your Master's Degree and fluency in five languages, your passion for the arts and your independence are to be celebrated.

To my brother Mark. Though we have taken vastly different paths, we have reached the same plateau from which, in silence, respect and admiration are mutually conveyed. Your continued evolution seeking expertise in photography and as a national field judge is impressive.

To my father who passed over ten years ago and mother who passed in 2015, their discipline and thoughtful conservative perspective is now appreciated, for they have ingrained in our family a spirit to pursue our passion.

Concluding Thoughts

Gratitude is not only the greatest of virtues but the parent of all the others.

Marcus Tullius Cicero

Attributions

Do or Do Not, There is No Try.

Yoda

Here Is How You Will Benefit

How does a writer measure success? Writing is a lonely sport. Hours are spent crafting words with alliterations and cadence to humor the writer and to ensure that the reader benefits from the research, insights, and perspectives offered. Long sentences are rewritten time and time again, with the hope of creating a single thought. When a client, reader, webinar participant, or caller sends an unsolicited comment, whether positive or negative, the circle of connection is complete, and each provides me valuable guidance.

Every day we strive to improve the profitability of our clients' golf courses. Our advice is delivered in many different ways; comprehensive strategic plans, targeted client engagements, teaching at Professional Golf Management programs, webinars, blogs, articles for leading golf industry magazines, social media, and by answering the frequently received telephone call in asking our viewpoint. These efforts are perfected as we fly over 100,000 miles per year, often to as many as ten countries and hundreds of cities and towns.

Are we making a difference? Change is tough. Excuses are easy to formulate. Perfection is not an attainable goal. Creating a consensus through inspired leadership is rare. It seems that our society has become one of self-entitlement in which critics abound—critics who highlight the flaws of any idea rather than offer an alternative.

But we are motivated by those who take precious moments of their time to send us an unsolicited comment or encouragement. A smattering of those e-mails are presented below, not to fan my pride, but to share the insights provided by readers who are the leaders in the golf industry. We hope their words fuel the motivation within you to adopt the suggestions contained herein for the benefit of your career and ultimately at facilities that you may have the opportunity to lead.

Industry Research Groups

The Business of Golf is an exhaustive work that brings the world of golf course management under one roof. I highly recommend it. **Joe Beditz, President & CEO, National Golf Foundation**

Jim Keegan is golf's answer to "Money Ball." **Greg Nathan, Chief Business Officer, National Golf Foundation**

How many times have you heard, "Boy, I'd like to run my golf course?" Well, before you do, or if you already do, you should work behind the counter in a pro shop, and read everything you can about the business. You can start with this book. It is well researched by someone who knows how to apply it to a broad range of golf course operations. **Tom Stine, Co-Founder Golf DataTech, LLC**

Outstanding Golf Course Operators

Jim Keegan's unique business and life experience have brought a new level of critical thinking to the golf industry. On the golf course, he may be a seven handicap, but his insights into the business side of the game are no less than "scratch." This book is about the business of golf; what the *Rules of Golf* are to playing the game. **Nick Mokelke, CCM, General Manager, Cog Hill Golf and Country Club**

Jim Keegan's comprehensive analysis of the golf business is a highly enlightening manuscript for the golf business person. Whether you are a 35-year operator like myself, or just getting started in the golf business, each chapter is packed full of useful insight that can be used TODAY to make your golf operation better. **Jim Roschek, PGA, President, Alamo City Golf Trail**

I finished reading your book last week and have been meaning to send you a note of congratulations. What an excellent book for every golf professional or anyone running a golf property in our business! It should be *a required book for all PGA members and apprentices.* I would have enjoyed a piece like this years ago when I first entered the golf business in 1975. The fundamentals illustrated could be used in any business, but certainly apply to the golf business. I assure you I will use the book as a reference almost daily and certainly during my staff and mentoring meetings. Congratulations on a tremendous resource guide to the business of golf. **Steve Friedlander, General Manager and PGA Professional, Pelican Hills Golf Course**

Your book is a very fun, informative read. Thanks so much for taking the time to write such a thoughtful, informative and valuable resource for the golf industry. It's easy to see that your insights are right on target, but actual application in the golf industry is sorely lacking. Your book is a "must-read" for anyone in the golf business. I can understand why Clemson wants to use it in the classroom. The knowledge the PGM students will gain from this exposure will be a HUGE benefit to them as they embark on a career in the golf industry. Participating in the Clemson Study was one of the best moves we made. Going through the steps outlined in "The Business of Golf: What Are You Thinking" was an eye-opening experience for us. We found many core areas where we had substantial room for improvement and came away from the process with a better understanding of our overall business. We have tweaked our business plan in a way that has already resulted in revenue improvement, and I am excited about our ability to continue to make positive changes based on what we learned. **Del Ratcliffe, PGA, President, Ratcliffe Golf Services, Inc.**

I just wanted to tell you how impressed I am with the book and all the time and effort you put towards the project. Obviously a labor of love and many years of dedicated service to the business. **John Cannon, President, Sunbelt Golf Corporation, Alabama's Robert Trent Jones Golf Trail**

It has been a pleasure working with you over the last couple of years. Your insight has been incredibly valuable, and the lessons learned will most assuredly go with me. **Terri Leist, Assistant Director & Golf Administrator at Columbus Recreation and Parks**

Golf Course Management Companies

Jim Keegan's inherent strength is his ability to recognize and understand the problems and challenges of a golf club operation, and then having the knowledge, discipline and work ethic to dive into the issues and come out on the other end with solutions. This book illustrates both his technique and his tenacity towards solving these problems. Very useful in these trying times! **Phil Green, President, OB Sports Golf Management**

Jim has consolidated years of experience, and visits to over 4,000 courses around the globe, into a comprehensive review and guide to the business of golf. More importantly, he shares the tools, techniques, and best practices he has developed and repeatedly implemented to decrease operating costs, drive revenues and improve customer service. Anyone interested in accomplishing any, or all, of these three objectives, is sure to find this book insightful and a valuable reference. **Stuart Hayden, Co-Owner, Strato Partners**

Well documented, well researched—much like a great manual on golf lessons. It is our goal to become a scratch golfer in the business of golf through the lessons contained in this book. **Jeff Levine, SVP of Daily Fee Properties for Arcis Golf**

Clients

Your insights and passion have made an enormous difference in the profitability of our municipal golf courses. In these troubled times, you have provided the leadership and returned our courses to profitability. Your commitment to lifelong learning is admirable and something I deeply admire. We are a better organization and individual professionals after spending time with you. **Cindy Curtis, Former Assistant City Manager, Virginia Beach**

You were too humble in your involvement with CGC. It was a total team effort with you included. I appreciate everything you opened our eyes to at CGC with your assessments. Thanks for hosting the webinar today. I thought it was very well done. I already have the next one booked on my calendar!!! **Graham Cliff, Head Golf Professional, Colorado Golf Club, Host of the 2013 Solheim Cup**

I would like to tell you how much you helped golf in Sun City here. You have given us a much-needed kick-start to making our courses better. Thank you. If you ever need a reference, I will be happy to give you a glowing one. **Joe O'Connell, Chairman of Golf Oversight, Sun City, LV**

We appreciate all the great work and insight that Jim has provided the club over the past few months. He has been a significant resource and wealth of knowledge to all of us. He is the best and hardest working consultant I have worked with over the years. Jim has helped us address many issues regarding club management, planning, and processes, which have provided us with an excellent foundation to move the club successfully forward. **Kevin Collins, Managing Partner, The Club at Ravenna**

Professional Golf Management

I am confident of one thing. For those who diligently read the book and studiously complete this case study, the vast knowledge gained will place you significantly ahead of your peers in being able to manage the profitability of a golf course. I believe students learn best by doing, and the case study has provided exercises and opportunity to grasp the essential JJ Keegan's formula concepts and their positive effects on financial performance. **Rick Lucas, PGA, MBA, Doctoral Student; Director, PGA Golf Management Program, Clemson University**

An excellent book, one of best I've ever seen on the subject. I would love to use it. Before this book, I always had to hunt and peck for what I could teach because there are NO golf textbooks! Love the book! **Ms. Kim Kincer, Director, Eastern Kentucky University, College of Business and Technology**

The book is fascinating reading. There is much for the UK golf industry to learn from this book. **Gary Jackson, Business Skills Development Manager, The PGA National Training Academy Ping House, The Belfry Sutton Coldfield, West Midlands B76 9PW**

Trade Publications

Reading this book has changed my view of how golf courses operate—and how they could operate. I've been looking at golf courses for 30+ years, but in the wake of Keegan's analysis I've already walked into clubhouses and onto courses and seen them very differently, with a much sharper eye for those vital moments of customer contact and business management that can make or break an operation. Golf has always been a great game; but as Keegan shows, it doesn't have to be a lousy business. Owners and operators who heed to finer points of this volume will have a heads up on the competition. **Bradley S. Klein, architecture editor of *Golfweek*, author of thousands of essays and five books on golf design and the golf industry**

Golf Management Software Vendors

Jim has managed to take such a multi-faceted subject as the golf industry and create an understandable benchmark with which any club can measure themselves and create realistic goals to become more successful. **Jim Fedigan, Chief Executive Officer, Jonas Software**

The Business of Golf provides a very structured look at the sophisticated metrics involved in running a successful golf course in challenging times. Along with thought-provoking anecdotes and ideas, the book provides the reader with a host of real-world solutions sure to improve the success of any operation. **Andrew Wood, Author, *The Golf Marketing Bible & CEO Legendary Marketing***

Industry Leaders

The component of a golf course that fails the quickest is the "crop." This book provides the guidelines necessary to ensure the golf course owner as the "leader of the band" can focus on the music and turn his back to the audience (primarily industry pundits) which mostly serves as a distraction. **Tim Moraghan, former USGA Agronomist, President Aspire Consulting**

In "The Business of Golf—What are you Thinking", Jim Keegan brings together the two very complex worlds of investing in and managing real estate and operating a going concern business. Golf courses are unique in this manner because they represent a company with an intensive use of real estate. Few books have gone as deep into both worlds and tied them together as neatly as Jim has. I've often thought of taking on this project and writing such a book myself, but Jim not only beat me to it, but he also did an excellent job. **Larry Hirsh, CRE, MAI, SGA, President—Golf Property Analysts**

In today's business of golf, this book is a must read to ensure you're on the right course. Jim Keegan splits the fairway in this approach to strategic planning! **Eddie Ainsworth, PGA, Executive Director, Colorado Section PGA**

James. You are a genius! Your brain can only be compared to another great one in Bro Hof, thank you. Your book is excellent; you know the business, and there are many things in the book that makes me smile! **Peter Nyberg, Managing Director/Klubbdirektör Bro Hof Slott Golf Club**

I wanted to thank you again for an excellent class. I have been sitting in GCSAA seminars for 20 years now, and your class was one of the best I have ever had the privilege to take. It is very evident that you are passionate about what you do and your delivery of the "why" was spot on. I look forward to the webinar and going over all of the material finding creative ways to implement these strategies at my club. **Jerry C. West, Director of Operations, Highland Cove**

You are becoming the Swiss Army Knife of Golf Consultants. When your course needs help, who you are going to call? Jim Keegan! **Robert Waldron, Investment Advisor, Leisure Investment Properties Group**

Concluding Thoughts

No one who achieves success does so without acknowledging the help of others.

Alfred North Whitehead

Introduction

A good plan today is better than a perfect plan tomorrow.

General George S. Patton

Warning

This book is not a mere narrative that one reads in a single sitting. Rather, it is designed as a textbook for understanding the "golf business." It is a reference book in which subsequent review is recommended for full absorption and proper application. Why?

The term "golf business" often seems like an oxymoron. Golf is a game—a fun one people play for a myriad of reasons. Those who work in the industry understand that golf is far more than a quiet, outdoor recreational pursuit. It is a challenging business in a competitive and unique working environment. Thus, grasping the concepts contained herein mandate a disciplined approach.

You now hold a roadmap for turning a recreational facility into a profit center—creating value for golfers on a foundation that enhances the financial performance of a golf course.

This book will guide you in creating a winning strategic blueprint for a golf course facility—a blueprint that will be ever-changing but will keep you on the path to success.

This book is also intended as a complement to the PGA of America's Professional Golf Management programs as follows:

- Level 1: Business Planning
- Level 2: Golf Operations

The seven-step technique and the accompanying analytical, financial and operational guides discussed in this book have been developed by crystallizing the facts, observations, and opinions I have gleaned mentoring golf courses over 25 years traveling more than 2.75 million miles on United Airlines visiting over 45 countries. The principles described herein have been vetted by leading golf course owners and management teams.

I am keenly aware of why a golf course exists, how it creates value for golfers, and what management and staff can do to offer a superior experience. There are things I have observed that are meritorious, things that can be learned, and things that any responsible golf course operator should want to emulate.

There also are many pitfalls that can, and should, be avoided for golf courses to reach their full potential.

Most people are too overwhelmed to discover and work with all the details. This book boils it downs, sums it up, and puts all the disparate data into an easy-to-follow plan.

This is a book about execution and was written for those looking to enhance their careers in the golf industry, ultimately lead a team in the managing of a golf course, or in the ownership thereof.

The Business of Golf

In theory, business is very simple. It is balancing supply against demand. By establishing the price that correctly balances the brand promise offered and the value delivered, net income is maximized.

Business can be made very complicated. The permutations of operating a successful golf course increase quickly when one considers the factors that shape supply (the number of golf courses) or those factors that influence demand (course conditioning, price, weather, service, and customer demographics and preferences).

In a perfect market, customers purchase products that satisfy their needs or desires at prices they determine to be the best value. Golfers purchase a round of golf for the price that creates the social status they seek, for the networking they want to achieve, for convenience to home or business, and for the recreational and leisure experience.

Unfortunately, capitalism is not about perfect markets. Inadequate information, undisciplined decision making, misleading marketing, and government intervention can create aggregate failure. The essence of capitalism is for the successful entrepreneur to gain a strategic advantage over competitors within an imperfect market.

In bridging the business of golf and the game of golf, as illustrated in the following chart, the goal of the course owner should be to blend superlative information, disciplined decision, and crisp execution.

Organizational Philosophy

Business of Golf

- Customer Loyalty
- Rate Management
- Merchandise
- Maintenance
- Labor Scheduling

Game of Golf

- Private Lessons
- Group Instructions
- Clinics
- Junior Programs
- Tournaments
- Outings
- Club Fittings

Lesson 1 – Why?

What makes golf such a fabulous entertainment, leisure, and recreational business opportunity? Every golf course in the world is unique. It is this uniqueness that provides an opening that can be leveraged to generate an economically viable business.

The foundation for every successful business is to attract and retain loyal customers. In the golf industry, it is requisite that each facility creates a vision that celebrates the distinctiveness of the golfer's experience.

We came to this belief based on watching a TED Talk by Simon Sinek: You can view this Top 10 Ted Talk at: http://bit.ly/dcDsbx.

In the video, Sinek asks, "Why is Apple so innovative year after year after year? Why was Martin Luther King able to lead the civil rights movement when there were others who suffered in the pre–civil rights era and who were also great orators? Why were the Wright Brothers the first to achieve controlled and powered man flight when other teams were more qualified and better funded?"[1]

He described the "golden circle: WHY?—HOW?—WHAT?" All companies and organizations on the planet know WHAT they do. They are easily able to describe their products and services. Some companies can explain HOW

1 http://www.ted.com/talks/ simon_sinek_how_great_leaders_inspire_action.html

they are different—their unique selling position. Few companies can articulate precisely WHY."

He concluded that successful business communicates from the inside out, illustrated here:

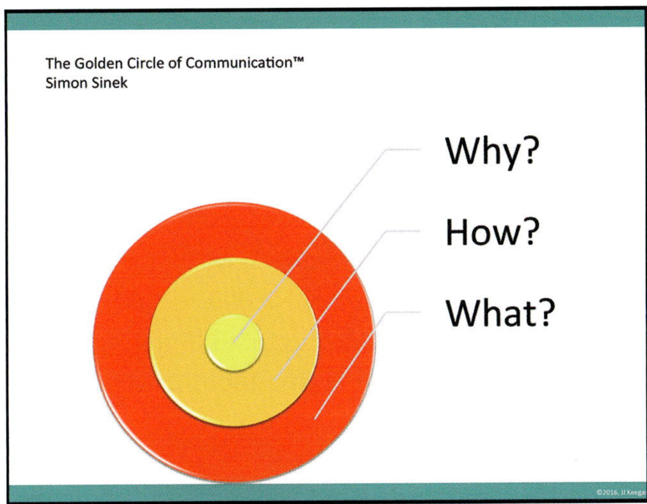

He postulates that "People don't buy WHAT you do; they buy WHY you do it."

Applying: Who? How? What?

If we apply the WHY? HOW? and WHAT? tenets of the process of creating a business plan, they clearly align:

First, the definitions. "Strategic," "tactical," and "operational" are three buzzwords in the business lexicon that make most people's eyes glaze over. Succinctly, they mean the following:

- **Strategic:** *culture*; vision, history, tradition, and governance.
- **Tactical:** *asset management*; comprising the facilities (golf course, clubhouse and other physical entities, finances, and human resources).
- **Operational:** *activities* (green fees, tournament, merchandise, food and beverage, and range) and *management* (leadership, staffing and scheduling, marketing, and customer interaction).

In a well-managed operation, every operational decision can be traced up to the tactical plan and then up to the strategic vision. To illustrate, would you expect valet parking at a low-end municipal golf course? Not hardly. Would you expect bottled water, free range access, ball repair tools, and towels at a golf course charging more than $200? Very likely.

These tools—strategic vision, tactical planning, and operational execution—blend in relative proportions to create a profitable formula.

The Formula for Success

The creation of a strategic plan requires work. To ease and accelerate the development of a winning formula for a golf course, we have designed a seven-step process (JJ Keegan+ WIN™—what's important now formula):

This seven-step process in this book is the "critical path" that moves you from strategy to tactics to execution.

Although the course's location and the impact of weather are uncontrollable factors, the integration of technology, benchmarking the financial performance of the course to industry metrics, the architectural and agronomy practices, operations—the assembly line of the golf experience, and the customers can all be managed to boost profitability.

The following is an overview of each of these steps.

Strategic

1. **Geographic Local Market Analysis.** Seven key numbers accurately forecast the potential of a golf course: MOSAIC Profile, ethnicity, age, income, golfers per 18 holes, prime time green fee, and slope rating within 10 miles of the golf course are predictors for 90% of all golf courses. Only resorts escape precise classification based on these factors.

   Assembling this data represents a competitive market review. (Chapter 5)

   The **key questions** to be answered are: Are the MOSAIC Profile, age, income, ethnicity, and population density sufficient to sustain the golf course? Does the demographics indicate that there is there sufficient demand to meet the available supply? How many golfers per 18-holes are there within the competitive local market? Where does your course rank as to its financial potential amongst the 15,204 golf courses in the United States?

2. **Strategic: Weather.** The axiom that "if rounds are up, it's because of good management, and if rounds are down it's because of inclement weather" is a standard joke, but golf is an outdoor sport. Experts estimate that over 90% of rounds are played when the temperature is between 55 and 90 degrees. Monitoring the number of playable golf days in a year compared to a 10-year trend allows an analyst the opportunity to differentiate clearly between the impact of weather and the impact of management on a course's performance. (Chapter 5)

   The **key questions** to be answered are: What impact has weather played on rounds vs. management policies? Are there sufficient playable days to generate a return on the proposed investment? Has weather forecasting been fully leveraged? Are the season passes appropriately priced based on the number of playable days, how frequently the golfer plays, and discount desired.

Tactical

3. **Technology—The Foundation.** The aggregation of data on which a business can be analyzed is dependent upon having an integrated technology solution, properly installed and fully utilized by the staff. Ascertaining if the tee sheet is incorporated into the POS system, the size of the customer database, the efficacy of the website, whether proactive e-mail and text messaging marketing is occurring , and the extent to which social media has been adopted accurately reflect the successful implementation of technology.

   Unfortunately, there may never in the history of man have been more money invested with such a small return as there has been in the acquisition of golf management systems. (Chapter 7)

   The **key questions** to be answered are: How effectively has an integrated golf management solution been deployed to create the collection of data required? Is the customer database correctly segmented? Is the website design informational or transaction focused?

4. **Yield Management, Key Metrics, Financial Modeling and Course Valuation**. The valuable research data of the National Golf Foundation, Golf Datatech, Club Benchmarking and ORCA Reports is contrasted to a facility's performance to determine opportunities for improvement. Statistics such as course utilization, revPAT, revPAR, EBIT, technology ROI, cost per round, staffing levels, capital budgets, and deferred expenditures are compared to those of local and regional courses. (Chapters 8, 9, 10, 11)

   The **key questions** to be answered are: Have accurate financial models that support proactive decision-making been developed? What debt service can the golf courses cover? Is there a gap between the potential fees charged and clientele's disposable income base?

Operational

5. **Facilities and Maintenance Review.** A golf course is a living organism. It is only designed as intended by the architect on the day it opens. Primary constraints include annual renovation expenses and the equipment required to maintain a course. Comparing the available equipment to industry standards and identifying deferred capital benchmarks provides valuable information. (Chapter 12)

The **key questions** to be answered are: What is the proposed style of the golf course? Are the design, agronomic and turf practices, and equipment levels compatible with the vision for the facility? Is there a gap between the potential fees charged and clientele's disposable income base?

6. **Management, Marketing, and Operational Review.** The entrance to the clubhouse, staffing, organizational structure, merchandising, food and beverage, advertising, marketing, and public relations are evaluated and compared to the industry's best management practices. (Chapters 13 and 14)

   The **key questions** to be answered are: Will the value provided equal or exceed the associated fees? Are the proper operating procedures going to be consistently deployed through each step of the "assembly line of golf"? What are the additional programs that could be added to bolster revenues and are the marketing strategies properly aligned with the customer's preferences and the experience offered? Are the staffing levels appropriate to provide the level of customer service desired.

7. **Customers: Learning Their Preferences and Loyalty.** By utilizing a golf course's database, purchasing an e-mail file of local golfers, and employing electronic survey tools, enlightening insights can be obtained. Why aren't the golfers in your area playing more? What are the motivating price points in your region? What is your course's brand image? You'll never know the answers if you don't ask the questions.

   Fifteen percent of the customers generate 60% of the revenues; 25% produce 80% of the income, and many daily fee golf courses have at least 50 clients who spend more than $4,000 annually. Although only half the golfers who played a course one year will return the next, identifying your core customers provides the foundation for your marketing program. (Chapters 15 and 16)

   The **key questions** to be answered are: Who are your core customers and how much do they spend? What is the annual retention rate? What are the barriers to increased play, what is the golfer's perceived value, and what is the primary reason one course is selected over another? How loyal are customers? What are the key loyalty drivers that create satisfaction? What recommendations do they have to improve the experience? What is the financial referral impact of promoters vs. detractors?

This seven-step formula creates a tapestry of sound principles and common-sense solutions for the golf course operator. By following that critical path, you will overcome the barriers to operating a fiscally sustainable golf course

Analytical, Financial and Operational Guides

Beyond the book as a supplemental resource, a comprehensive set of analytical, financial and operational guides have been developed that are highlighted below:

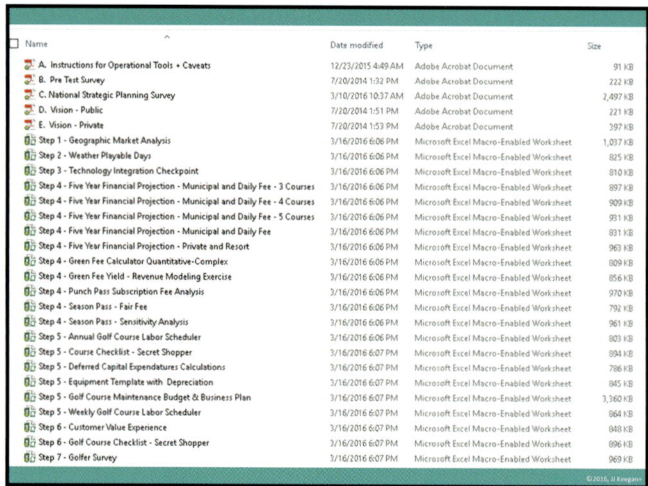

Name	Date modified	Type	Size
A. Instructions for Operational Tools + Caveats	12/23/2015 4:49 AM	Adobe Acrobat Document	91 KB
B. Pre Test Survey	7/20/2014 1:32 PM	Adobe Acrobat Document	222 KB
C. National Strategic Planning Survey	3/10/2016 10:37 AM	Adobe Acrobat Document	2,497 KB
D. Vision - Public	7/20/2014 1:51 PM	Adobe Acrobat Document	221 KB
E. Vision - Private	7/20/2014 1:53 PM	Adobe Acrobat Document	397 KB
Step 1 - Geographic Market Analysis	3/16/2016 6:06 PM	Microsoft Excel Macro-Enabled Worksheet	1,037 KB
Step 2 - Weather Playable Days	3/16/2016 6:06 PM	Microsoft Excel Macro-Enabled Worksheet	825 KB
Step 3 - Technology Integration Checkpoint	3/16/2016 6:06 PM	Microsoft Excel Macro-Enabled Worksheet	810 KB
Step 4 - Five Year Financial Projection - Municipal and Daily Fee - 3 Courses	3/16/2016 6:06 PM	Microsoft Excel Macro-Enabled Worksheet	897 KB
Step 4 - Five Year Financial Projection - Municipal and Daily Fee - 4 Courses	3/16/2016 6:06 PM	Microsoft Excel Macro-Enabled Worksheet	909 KB
Step 4 - Five Year Financial Projection - Municipal and Daily Fee - 5 Courses	3/16/2016 6:06 PM	Microsoft Excel Macro-Enabled Worksheet	931 KB
Step 4 - Five Year Financial Projection - Municipal and Daily Fee	3/16/2016 6:06 PM	Microsoft Excel Macro-Enabled Worksheet	831 KB
Step 4 - Five Year Financial Projection - Private and Resort	3/16/2016 6:06 PM	Microsoft Excel Macro-Enabled Worksheet	963 KB
Step 4 - Green Fee Calculator Quantitative-Complex	3/16/2016 6:06 PM	Microsoft Excel Macro-Enabled Worksheet	809 KB
Step 4 - Green Fee Yield - Revenue Modeling Exercise	3/16/2016 6:06 PM	Microsoft Excel Macro-Enabled Worksheet	856 KB
Step 4 - Punch Pass Subscription Fee Analysis	3/16/2016 6:06 PM	Microsoft Excel Macro-Enabled Worksheet	970 KB
Step 4 - Season Pass - Fair Fee	3/16/2016 6:06 PM	Microsoft Excel Macro-Enabled Worksheet	792 KB
Step 4 - Season Pass - Sensitivity Analysis	3/16/2016 6:06 PM	Microsoft Excel Macro-Enabled Worksheet	961 KB
Step 5 - Annual Golf Course Labor Scheduler	3/16/2016 6:06 PM	Microsoft Excel Macro-Enabled Worksheet	803 KB
Step 5 - Course Checklist - Secret Shopper	3/16/2016 6:07 PM	Microsoft Excel Macro-Enabled Worksheet	894 KB
Step 5 - Deferred Capital Expendatures Calculations	3/16/2016 6:07 PM	Microsoft Excel Macro-Enabled Worksheet	786 KB
Step 5 - Equipment Template with Depreciation	3/16/2016 6:07 PM	Microsoft Excel Macro-Enabled Worksheet	845 KB
Step 5 - Golf Course Maintenance Budget & Business Plan	3/16/2016 6:07 PM	Microsoft Excel Macro-Enabled Worksheet	3,360 KB
Step 5 - Weekly Golf Course Labor Scheduler	3/16/2016 6:07 PM	Microsoft Excel Macro-Enabled Worksheet	864 KB
Step 6 - Customer Value Experience	3/16/2016 6:07 PM	Microsoft Excel Macro-Enabled Worksheet	848 KB
Step 6 - Golf Course Checklist - Secret Shopper	3/16/2016 6:07 PM	Microsoft Excel Macro-Enabled Worksheet	896 KB
Step 7 - Golfer Survey	3/16/2016 6:07 PM	Microsoft Excel Macro-Enabled Worksheet	969 KB

They are available for purchase as a separate downloadable resource at www.jjkeegan.golf.

The Audience

In writing a book, the first question is: Who is the audience? That was easy. While this book has value for the 34,000+ golf courses around the world and its over 50 million golfers, the United States has a competitive advantage in the depth of statistical information that is available to help frame the successful plan. Thus, those likely to receive the greatest value from reading this tome are:

Category	Target Audience
Golfers (United States)	24.1 million
Industry Personnel	2 million
PGA Professionals	26,500
Golf Course Owners	12,500+
PGM Students	1,000
Multi Course Operators	200
State Golf Course Associations	71

Not everything in these pages fits the needs of each potential reader, but hope fully everyone will find it interesting, and there will always be some nugget that makes you say, "Wow, I didn't know that."

The greatest benefit from this book will be derived by those not satisfied with the status quo, but for those committed to positive change—those who seek to improve their current operating methods, for the benefit of the game and their course. It is not for the average manager. As Yogi Berra says, "The average person is average." Golf courses, to survive, must be raised to something higher.

My Goal

As author Anna Quindlen stated, in a speech given at the University of Denver's "Pen and Podium Series," "I hate writing. I love having written."

I feel the same way. This has been an arduous process, but one that has been, for me, very worthwhile. As I wrote, I was often reminded of the folly of Hlade's Law, "If you have a difficult task, give it to a lazy man—he will find an easier way to do it." I have honestly found that the cliché, "If you desire to master a subject, teach it" is right. Having invested a good portion of my life assimilating this knowledge and undertaking the necessary research, committing the resulting thoughts to paper is clearly the hardest thing I have ever done; not getting a BBA, not earning an MBA, not passing the CPA exam, but writing this book.

As human beings, we process information in three primary ways: through verbal skills, through images, and through intuition. Of these processes, the most powerful is the image. Words have opposites; images do not. Therefore, my goal was to present as many pictures—tables, charts, graphs, and photos—as possible.

Golf represents what is best about our society. Nearly all of the 24 million who play the game represent ideal role models. In my 60 years of playing the game, I can think of very few people whose company I did not enjoy during a round of golf.

Ensuring that each golf course uses best practices to balance the business of golf with the game of golf adroitly is the goal of this book.

Key Points to Remember

1) Watch the Simon Sinek YouTube video: http://www.ted.com/talks/simon_sinek_how_great_leaders_inspire_action.html
2) Create your personal "WHY?" statement.
3) Define the "WHY?" statement for your golf course. Each golf course is unique. Each course serves a different role. Each course attracts a different kind of golfer. Who is your customer? Clue—"everyone" is not the answer.

Concluding Thought

A poor idea well written is more likely to be accepted that a good idea poorly written

Isaac Asimov

Tell me and I'll forget. Show me and I'll remember. Involve me and I'll understand.

Confucius

SECTION 1

Strategic Vision
Chapters 1 through 6

To create a strategic plan, a broad vision must be first defined. In Chapters 1 through 6, we progressively narrow the focus on the uncontrollable factors that influence the financial success of a golf course.

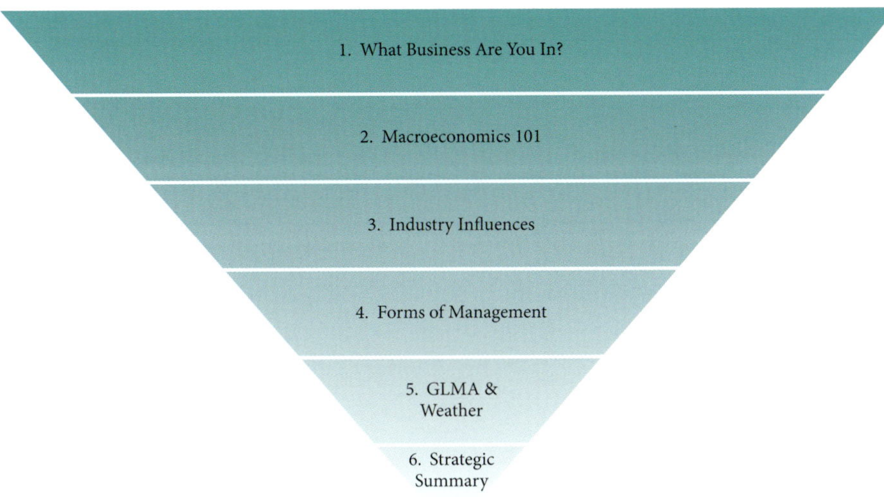

An understanding of what a golf course can't directly control frames one's ability to create a plan that can be successfully executed.

If you don't know where you are going,
you might wind up someplace else.

Yogi Berra

The chains of habit are too late to be felt
until they're too heavy to be broken.

Blaise Pascal

Chapter 1

What Business Are You In?

"It isn't the mountains ahead to climb that wear you out; it's the pebble in your shoe."

Muhammad Ali

Chapter Highlights

This chapter will introduce the first strategic elements that help you decide what role your business provides the golfer.

Is your facility meant to be the entry door to the game for the masses, a park to entertain the taxpaying citizens, a forum for business people to meet and greet, a private enclave, or a resort that attracts a certain clientele?

What is the economic, societal, and business impact of golf in your area? What are the opportunities to grow the game? What are the barriers to increasing play?

The mantra that golf is a business in which an investment return is required is a fundamental precept on which the entire strategic planning process is based.

This chapter is the first of four that discuss the environmental factors, which are often beyond the control of the golf course owner.

Golf: For Whom

Who is the most important person in the golf industry? It is the customer.

In developing a strategic plan, intimately understanding the demographics of those interested participants is essential.

In the United States, those that golf attracts is reflected in the following chart:

	2016[1]			2012[2]
Category	All	Core	Occasional	All
Age	41.4	47.9	35.7	41.5
Household Income	$96,236	$98,097	$88,600	$85,700
Annual Rounds	19.3	34.2	2.7	18.6
All Golfers Age 6+ (millions)	24.1	12.7	11.4	25.7
% Male	76.1%	79.3%	71.6%	80.7%
Notes:[3] There are some pundits that believe that in the United States only 22.1 million play golf. See Chapter 3 regarding cautions expressed about data accuracy from third party sources.				

Note that in contrast to those who play golf, in the United States, the median household income is $52,747 with an average age of 36.9. This is quite a difference from the typical golfer. What is of concern from the chart above is that from 2012 to 2016, the increase in household income from $85,700 to $96,236 further creates an impression that golf is a sport of the well-to-do.

Those numbers define the greatest challenge facing golf—where is the influx of new, younger golfers and how do we retain existing customers? It is your ability, if you are a golf course owner or manager, to address and solve those issues that will ultimately determine your success in the business of golf.

1 National Golf Foundation, "Golf Participation Report in the United States," 2015 Edition, pp. 4–6.

2 National Golf Foundation, "Golf Participation Report in the United States," 2012 Edition, p. 6.

3 http://ngfdashboard.clubnewsmaker.org/Newsletter/1q4qa5rz8no1sl9b7u4wlc?a=5&p=2389923&t=410871

Part of the game's allure is that golf is an elitist sport and, therefore, unlikely to be adopted by the masses. In 1899, Thorsten Veblen wrote, "Golf is a game of the leisure class."[4]

That stereotype continues to be reinforced by the media as illustrated by a CNBC story labeling golf as one of the nine pricey sports of the wealthy. Golf was included in the list along with "dressage, yachting, croquet, figure skating, polo, pheasant hunting, snowboarding, and horse racing."[5]

However, to pigeonhole the customer base and the industry within such a narrow definition as elitist dismisses the opportunity that exists, for golf is a great game and the business of golf can generate a sizeable investment return for those who manage well.

That sentiment is supported by 2016 research by the National Golf Foundation which concludes:

> "Golf's overall reach is impressive. One out of three Americans—about 95 million—played golf on a golf course or alternate venue, watched on TV or read about it in 2015. The interest is there.
>
> While participation growth remains difficult to achieve, with the recession in the rearview mirror and an exciting new wave of young players in front of us, there are good reasons to be optimistic about future growth if emphasis continues to be placed on converting more beginners into a committed golfer."[6]

Golf's Appeal is Far Different Than What is Perceived

Golf is a lifestyle choice.

Golf attracts those who like to spend to spend time outdoors, enjoy light exercise, and remove their minds from day-to-day cares.

---

4 Thorsten Veblen, *Theory of the Leisure Class* (Oxford, Oxford University Press), 1899. http://en.wikipedia.org/wiki/The_Theory_of_the_Leisure_Class. Veblen argued that, while sports could be advantageous to the community, the true reason for the popularity of sports were their usefulness as means of displaying conspicuous leisure.

5 http://money.msn.com/investing/9-pricey-sports-of-the-wealthy

6 http://ngfdashboard.clubnewsmaker.org/Newsletter/1q4qa5rz8no1sl9b7u4wlc?a=5&p=2389923&t=410871

In 2012, the National Golf Foundation (NGF) reported that the reasons those who are primarily attracted to golf are because of following:

Why We Play	Not and Fringe	Casual	Hooked and Nuts	Average
Time outdoors	43	54	63	53
Social aspect	33	46	53	44
The exercise	32	44	48	41
Ball striking	23	40	59	41
The challenge	18	36	66	40
The courses	20	28	52	33
Stress relief	19	36	43	33
Mental game	10	23	39	24
Values of the game	9	23	39	24
The competition	6	13	34	18
Keeping score	6	10	35	17
History & traditions	6	9	27	14
Practicing	5	9	26	13

So despite all the commercials you see about longer, straighter, fewer strokes and despite the PGA Tour, the Golf Channel, and the plethora of talk shows focused on championship golf, those features are motivating factors for only a small segment of amateur golfers who play.

Welcome to the Entertainment Business

The future success of the golf business is premised on creating an enjoyable recreational experience.

Many within our industry have lost sight of this fact, having become seduced by the "game" of golf at the expense of the "business" of golf. Many individuals in the golf business presume that everyone who plays golf is like them, watching golf on TV, and enjoying learning, practicing, and playing. These individuals believe that financial success will be assured by teaching golfers to play better on more challenging courses and by selling game improvement equipment.

However, the new driver that promises greater distance, the new course heralding the ultimate test, the eye-grabbing video technology that offers to change your swing forever—these appeal to only 15% of those who play.

Eighty-five percent of individuals who play golf don't have a handicap—the benchmark that measures ability and interest. Seventy percent drink alcohol, principally beer, while playing. Thirty-three percent of a course's revenue is from tournaments and outings, which primarily represent golfers who are playing in corporate or charity events. This may well be their single annual visit on a course.

Who is the "real" golf consumer? The "real" golf consumer is the recreational player—an everyday average Joe or Jo, who wants to challenge the course, drink beer, have some conversations and forget the client complaints of that morning or the hectic week at work.

Golf is not principally about competition, athletic challenge, or individual accomplishment. Golf is simply entertainment, and golf courses are like theme parks—no two courses are identical, and each one offers a different thrill ride every time you play.

In 2015, we conducted numerous consumer studies for clients. This process of understanding their customers' hopes, desires, and needs is an evolutionary process and usually includes up to 25 questions per survey. We asked "What is your average score for 18 holes?" adding the choice: "Don't keep score. I merely play for fun and recreation." The figure shown here shows those results.

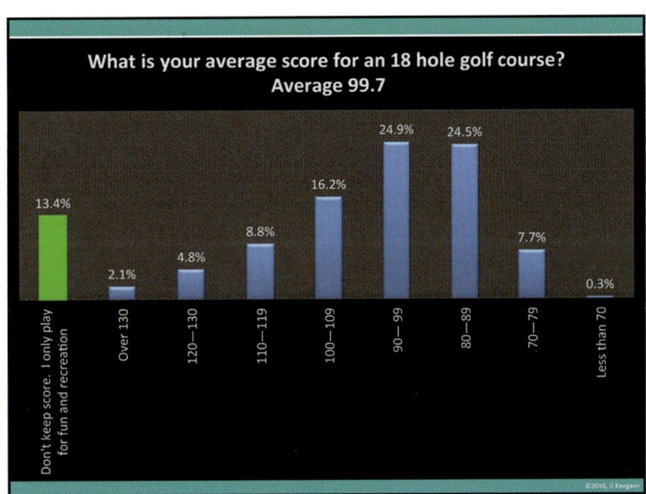

We were surprised that 13.4% of players representing over 62 million rounds don't even keep score. Note that the USGA reports that the average men's score is 92[7], and the women's is 110.[8]

Therefore, the success for the vast majority of golf courses is measured by how much fun the customer has. There is an awakened realization in 2016 as to this fact by golf course architects, equipment manufacturers, superintendents, and frontline golf course personnel.

---

7 http://www.usga.org/handicapping/articles_resources/Men-s-USGA-Handicap-Indexes/

8 Ibid.

That begs the following question in the short term: Should the industry better identify, communicate, and serve its existing customers or reach out to attract active players to growth the game?

The short-term answer is that the golf industry should focus on its current core customers. By engaging them, the game will grow as they introduce their family, friends, and associates to golf for fun, entertainment, and the lifestyle that this great game offers.

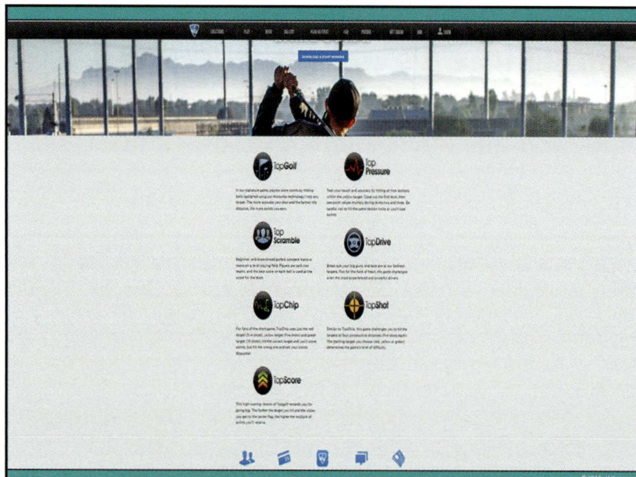

The long-term answer, however, may be found in a current phenomenon, where parking lots are full and the wait to play can exceed two hours: Topgolf.

The banner reads, "The Ultimate Venue for Fun – Golf skills are not required to have fun at Topgolf. Food & drink menu, 200+ HDTVs and addictively fun games provide something for everyone!"[9]

Will Topgolf be the entry door for the masses to enter the game? Perhaps not the masses, for Topgolf is more akin to bowling than golf, but its impact will certainly be beneficial.

What is a lesson for current operators?

A 4½" Circular Hole Comes in Many Different Shapes

Golf courses come in all flavors. The following chart shows the diversity of venues available.

9 http://topgolf.com/us/

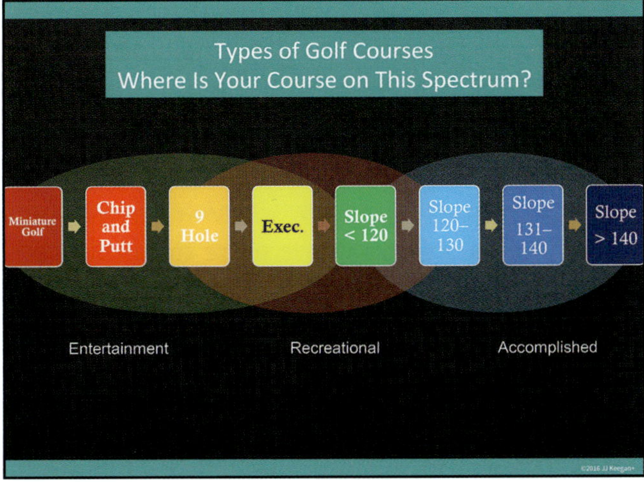

Industry statistics are lacking on the demographics of those attracted principally to each of the different alternatives.

What we do know from the consumer surveys we conduct is that the desired length of a golf course amongst the vast majority of golfers is clear.

We asked, "What is the average length of course you prefer?" Men prefer courses that are 6,040 yards long, as shown below. Women responded with a preferred length of 4,920 yards.

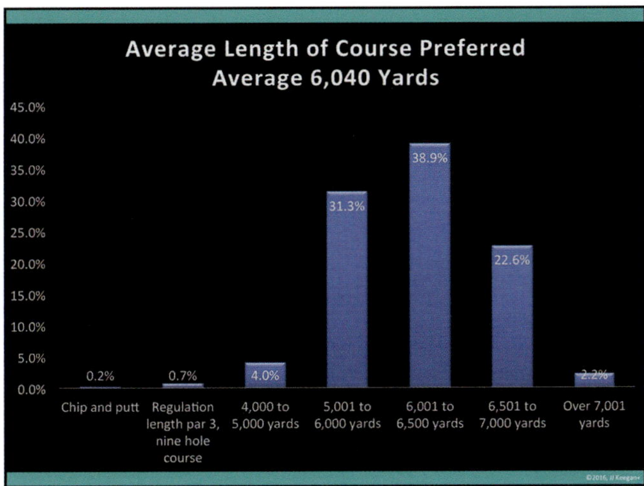

Arthur Little, who is a staunch supporter of women's golf (http://www.golfwithwomen.com), believes that the right length of a golf course for a woman who has an average club head speed of 65 mph is 4,200 yards. He also believes that to attract women to the game, the golf course has the responsibility to create a course of the right length, encourage a more flexible format that eliminates stroke and distance penalties, and de-emphasize scoring while still highlighting the importance of maintaining a course that can be enjoyed by both men and women.

With the objective of helping golfers have more fun on the course, the PGA, in combination with the USGA, launched a campaign titled "Tee It Forward." The objective was to encourage golfers to play a course that is aligned with their driving distance.

The results are impressive[10]:

- 85% of golfers found playing more enjoyable with TEE IT FORWARD.
- 56% felt they played faster.
- 93% are likely to use it again.
- 56% stated they were likely to play golf more often knowing they could TEE IT FORWARD.

Thus, for the majority of golfers, easier is better than harder, which provides a lesson for all responsible for the daily setup of a golf course. Have you ever heard someone say, "I just played one of my best rounds of golf ever! This game is boring." Not me.

What I have heard frequently is "That course was insanely hard, I lost a lot of balls, I didn't have any fun, and I am not coming back here."

So how then does a golfer pick which course to choose?

Why Do Golfers Choose One Course Over Another?

In surveys, we ask, "What is the primary reason you choose one course over another?" The results are very consistent, as shown here:

10 *Divot Magazine*, "Expo Issue 2013—Tee It Forward PGA Colorado Section," p. 12.

Starting in early 2015, we noticed that "pace of play," which historically ranked fifth to seventh, soared to the second or third spot in every survey conducted. Conditioning and price also remain important criteria today.

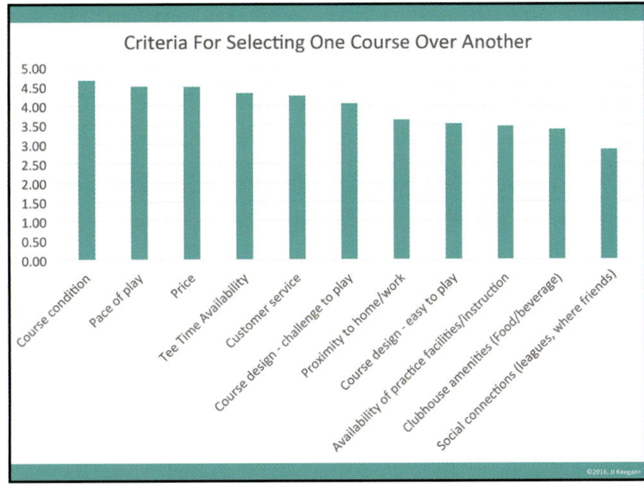

This emphasis on pace of play is both a perceived and real constraint to increased play. To further explore the impact of time, we asked in surveys conducted in 2015 and 2016, "What are the primary barriers that prevent you from playing golf more often?"

In responses from California to Florida, the results are nearly identical. Overwhelming majorities cite either no barriers or time as the primary constraint to playing more golf, as illustrated in the chart shown here.

No barrier is a troubling answer as it implies demand for golf is satiated. Regarding time, it, not money, has become our scarcest commodity limiting the growth of the game.

Today, individuals have more demands on their time. Lifestyles have changed. All of these factors have a direct impact on golf.

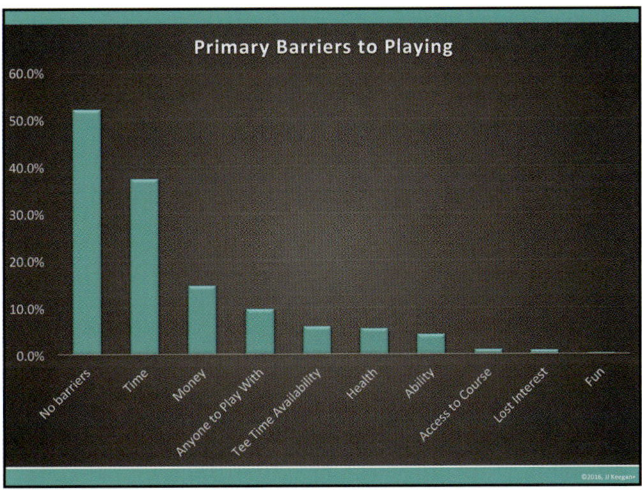

How then do we create an experience to attract and retain golfers? It first starts by recognizing the challenges and barriers that currently are adversely impacting the business.

An Industry That Is Stabilized

The industry faces many challenges:

- The heart of the golf industry's woes lies within the average golf course owner's inability to execute consistently, providing a customer experience that equals or exceeds the price, ensuring value.
- Few in the golf business realize that they are principally in the entertainment and leisure industry.
- Supply will continue to exceed demand for the foreseeable future in many parts of the United States. Within the Top 100 core statistical areas (the large cities), although demand equals or exceeds supply, golf course operators cite oversupply as an excuse for their lack of performance.
- Operating a golf course is a small business endeavor.
- Revenue generation programs targeting age, gender, or ethnic segments have little short-term impact.
- The attitude and the aptitude of most course staff can be enhanced.
- Many golf courses that are losing money make tactical changes that lead to strategic failure.
- Technology (websites, tee-time reservation systems, point of sale, e-mail tools, social media, accounting) is an investment that often produces a low return due to insufficient training and improper use.
- There are few golf courses willing to participate in industry initiatives to benchmark the financial performance of their facility against direct competitors and national standards.
- Golf course owners' marketing efforts are more reactionary than proactive.
- Many courses believe marketing solely comprises offering tee times at a discount, participating in coupon books, and utilizing last-minute, online, third-party vendors to liquidate inventory.
- Few courses identify or retain successful core customers.

- Few courses identify defectors and attempt to re-solicit their business.
- Many golf courses are in need of renovation but lack the required capital and are unable to secure debt financing.

If you focus on just the private club market, the challenges expand:

- Declining guest and member spending have driven revenue declines.
- Waiting lists have turned to resignation lists, impacting transfer fee income.
- Dues are at the top of the market, with increases not keeping pace with rising costs.
- Assessments, as they rise to cover operating expenses, accelerate attrition.
- Deferred maintenance is mounting.
- The club's nonprofit tax status limits outside play to 15% of gross revenue.
- Large, inefficient clubhouses are becoming out-of-date.
- The drinking and driving laws have adversely impacted beverage revenues.
- Competition from championship premium public courses is providing viable alternatives.

The list of challenges is endless. It can become overwhelming. No golf course plans to fail, but many simply fail to plan.

Why does this occur? The common thread in virtually every troubled company is the lack of disciplined management. As Napoleon Hill stated, "85% of all failures result from not having a clear purpose." Failure comes from management creating expectations that exceed the asset base, as measured by the capital assets and the investment made in human resources.

Today's operators of facilities find themselves in a difficult environment. What are their options?

The Assembly Line of Golf

Each golf course operation is a series of interconnected processes, the end product of which is a challenged, entertained, and satisfied customer. Every game is a “story,” and you can create a place for your customer to tell it. Course personnel, just like those who work at Disneyland, should be viewed as “cast members,” with roles to play to meet and exceed customers’ expectations.

The following table illustrates the “Assembly Line of Golf:”

The Assembly Line of Golf

Touch Point	Municipal	Daily Fee	Military	Resort	Private Club
Reservations					
Club Entrance					
Bag Drop					
Locker Room					
Pro Shop					
Cart					
Range					
Starter					
Course					
Beverage Cart Attendant					
Half Way House					
Cart Return					
Locker Room					
Bar/Restaurant					
Likely # of Points of Contact	9	12	8	12	14

Depending on the type of golf course, the number of opportunities to favorably impress a golfer can vary from 9 to 14. As expected, the higher the price per round of golf, the greater the number of anticipated touch points a golfer will experience.

Excellence is shown in many ways, but consistent attention to detail is one of the discriminating marks of a golf course. By understanding and exceeding your customers’ unique needs and desires, customer loyalty can be created and financial success achieved.

Retention is critical to enhancing revenue. Opportunities to impress (or entertain) your customers are limited, and you must create interest (preferably something that differentiates your course from others) that causes them to return.

Retention starts by realizing what golf is not. It is not a game that starts at 1 and leads through 18 holes in which there are typically four par 5’s, ten par 4’s, and four par 3’s.

Thus the exclusive private club, the high-end daily fee course, or exclusive resorts are likely to take advantage of many opportunities and continued efforts to enhance the overall impression.

Everyone's life experience is different and thus in attracting and serving it is important to communicate a vision as to "WHY" that can resonate and attract loyal customers.

Strategic Vision—The Aim of Your Golf Operation

A golf course owner should have a clear vision of its strategic plan. Is the strategic vision for Seminole, Sand Hills, Pebble Beach, Reynolds Plantation, Cog Hill, Bethpage, and Crandon Park the same? Not even close. Although each of these facilities has a superior golf course, their revenues, the depth and breadth of their customers, their management, their customer experience, and their projected investment return vary widely.

What remains common among these facilities is that before the first shovel of dirt was turned, each had a vision, perhaps only in the mind of the owner, as to how the facility would evolve, the niche it would serve, and the experience that it would create.

In golf, every course is unique. No two provide the same experience. But rather than be satisfied with your "uniqueness," it is important that you understand how your facility is different, how your patron's life experiences vary, and how you can capitalize on those differences.

The first key to increasing the net income of a golf course is to understand the big picture. Is your facility meant to be a platinum, gold, silver, bronze, or steel golf course?

The chart shown here highlights some of the important distinctions between the classifications.

Definition of Market Segments

	Platinum	Gold	Silver	Bronze	Steel
Vision	Rolls-Royce	BMW	Volvo	Chevrolet	Hyundai
Examples	Pine Valley, NJ Cypress Point, CA	Cherry Hills, CO Pebble Beach, CA	TPC Clubs Bay Harbor, MI	Lakewood, CO Bethpage, NY	Brookhaven, TX City Park, Anywhere
Cost	Over $250 per round	$175 to $500 per round	$75 to $200 per round	$50 to $100 per round	$50 or less
Carts	Caddies Mostly	Caddies + Electric Carts	Caddies Rare: Electric Carts plus Pull Carts	Electric or Gas Carts plus Pull Carts	Gas Carts plus Pull Carts
Access	By Invitation	Waiting List	Available	Seeking	Open Access
Style	Formal	Professional	Relaxed	Very Casual	Loose
Social Status	Generational Wealth	Upper Class	Upper Middle Class	Middle Class	Anyone

Other criteria to differentiate the experience might include whether the course is ranked in national magazines, the architect, championships hosted, slope, conditioning, cart policies, amenities provided, customer touch points, cell phone usage, dress code, smoking, other activities, use of computers, tipping policies, gift policies, whether reciprocity is granted, gender/ethnicity barrier whether express or implied, whether members hold multiple memberships at other clubs, and whether the facility attracts individuals who are first-time members or golfers.

Delineations, while arbitrary, serve as points of conversation in which a strategic vision can be determined.

Successful, storied golf clubs all have one thing in common: a rigid discipline to adhere to the strategic vision for the club. The centerpieces of a strategic plan are the vision and mission statements that guide all decisions regarding the operation of the facility. These statements serve as a lighthouse, providing a frame of reference for the owner, membership, management, and staff. By defining its vision, the golf course can align its infrastructure, facilities, and the operational policies and procedures to match the service ideals envisioned through innovative thinking as illustrated below:

As Lao Tzu stated, "The journey of a thousand miles begins with a single step." Let us begin.

Key Points to Remember

1) A golf course is a venue that creates entertainment for the purpose of generating a profit.
2) Who is the targeted customer, what experience will be provided, and at which price point are three factors that need to be ascertained.
3) The industry is undergoing many challenges.
4) The customer's leisure time is being constricted.
5) A course owner needs to carefully reflect on who is the target market.
6) The creation of a strategic plan will provide a definitive roadmap and benchmarks to achieve financial success in the operation of the golf course.

Concluding Thought

A path without obstacles usually leads nowhere.

Defalque's Observations

The hardest thing to open is a closed mind.

Admed Kathrada

Chapter 2

The Macroeconomics of the Golf Business

In order to properly understand the big picture, everyone should fear becoming mentally clouded and obsessed with one small section of truth.

Zun Xi

Chapter Highlights

Before a vision statement can be created, it is necessary to understand the environment in which the golf course operates.

Because daily operations are so focused on the details, it is important to frame the industry within which your business operates. While you may believe your facility is unique, there are parallels between golf courses and their associated customer bases world-wide.

This chapter focuses on golf around the world. As you read, ask yourself, "What is each course doing that is different from your current focus?" and "What can we learn from their successes and failures, and how can we apply that knowledge?"

The Universe Defined

In 2015, the R&A published "Golf Around the World" (www.randa.org). The four-year project created a definitive database of all golf courses: 34,011 in 206 countries as highlighted here:[1]

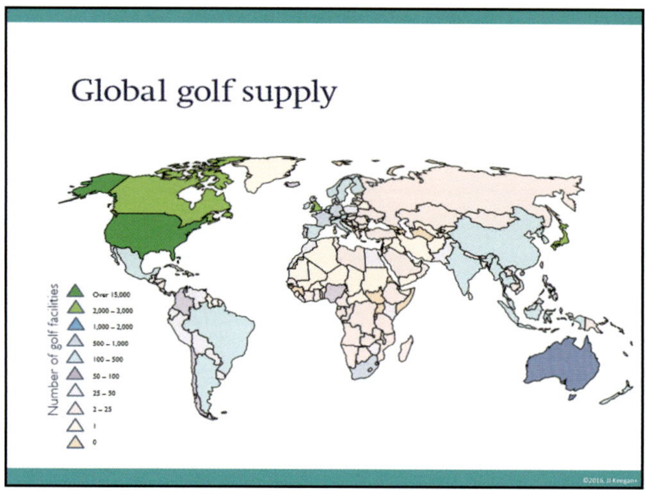

The vast majority of the facilities (79%) are located in Australia, Canada, England, Japan, and the United States.

Interestingly, 71% of the courses are open to the public. As reported, growth is occurring in China, Egypt, India, Mexico, Morocco, and Vietnam.[2] Since publication of the report, "China's Communist rulers have turned against the exclusive sport of golf with the government saying nearly 70 "illegal" courses have been closed, seemingly enforcing a decade-old ban for the first time."[3]

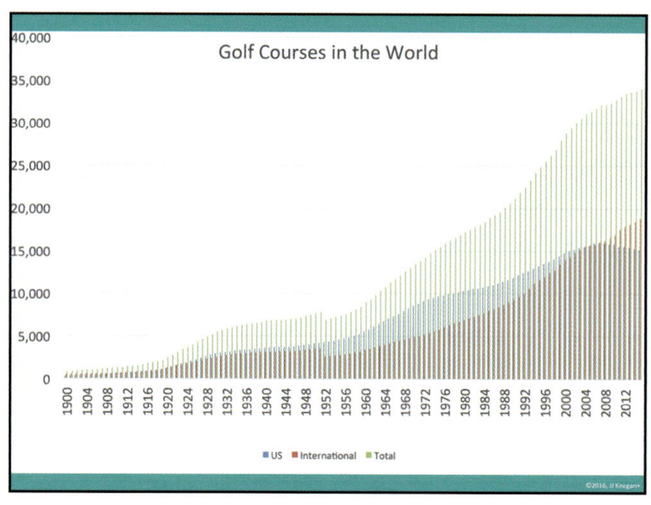

The growth of the game has now become international. From 1920 until 2004, there were more golf courses in the United States than the rest of the world combined as shown here.

1 R&A, "Golf Around the World – 2015," p. 4.

2 National Golf Foundation, "Golf Around the World—International Database Project," April 2013, slides 13 and 16.

3 http://sports.yahoo.com/news/china-closes-66-illegal-golf-courses-032913376--golf.html

Same Sport—Different Trends?

What is more important than the actual number of golf courses is whether the business practices of those "international courses" vary significantly from those of U.S. courses and what trends will shape the future of golf both internationally and domestically.

Andrew Satori, KPMG–Hungary, has done some just fabulous research (www.golfbenchmark.com) in analyzing the financial performance of golf courses worldwide, as highlighted in the following tables.[4]

Country	Courses	Playable Days	Golfers	Rounds	Gross Revenue
Africa – North	43	*	8,900	20,400	$1,256,850
Africa – South	450	346	150,000	33,575	$1,317,273
Caribbean	142	354	*	18,450	$1,720,000
China	300	*	~1,000,000	*	*
Europe – Central	908	235	673,868	19,964	$1,478,960
Europe – Eastern	135	249	45,000	9,637	$536,019
Europe – North	900	234	931,000	19,472	$919,161
Europe – Western	1,128	340	774,864	26,600	$1,725,010
Holland	192	361	361,000	37,500	$2,128,000
India	186	336	100,000	30,303	$190,000
Japan	2,350	320	9,000,000	39,999	$5,100,000
Middle East	20	359	16,900	40,237	$6,700,000
United Kingdom	3,084	357	287,000	30,500	$1,377,880
South America	561	330	117,600	13,500	$1,200,000
International Benchmarks	10,399	318	12,466,132	26,645	$2,032,692

* Data not available.
Note: It is thought that there are over 50 million who play golf in the world though no formal surveys have been conducted.

There are some striking parallels and some vast differences. As shown in the chart above the average number of rounds played, and gross revenues are similar to U.S. facilities. In the chart below, the initiation fees, annual dues, green fees and staffing vary from US courses:

4 KMPG–Hungary, "Golf Benchmarking Survey, 2006–2012."

Country	Initiation Fee	Annual Dues	Green Fee	Staff – Full Time	Staff – Seasonal
Africa – North	$325	$847	$77	45	14
Africa – South	$447	$596	$32	42	6
Caribbean	$7,880	$2,839	$129	*	*
China	$50,000	$2,750	$161	258	0
Europe – Central	$4,619	$1,598	$74	9	5
Europe – Eastern	$2,435	$919	$49	27	5
Europe – North	$867	$572	$56	6	5
Europe – Western	$8,599	$2,136	$75	22	2
Holland	$931	$1,197	$73	*	*
India	$1,865	$112	$18	48	10
Japan	$15,000	$3,600	$73	40	23
Middle East	$1,460	$3,741	$134	188	0
United Kingdom	$3,108	$1,091	$66	14	7
South America	$2,108	$1,349	$52	32	4
International Benchmarks	$7,640	$1,731	$76	62	6

* Data not available.

Note: It should be noted that for each country an individual analysis was performed by KPMG. For the purposes of this book, we extracted the data from each report, with full attribution to KPMG. Our goal was to highlight the financial performance of 18-hole golf courses. Readers should refer to www.golfbenchmark.com to review the source data for these charts.

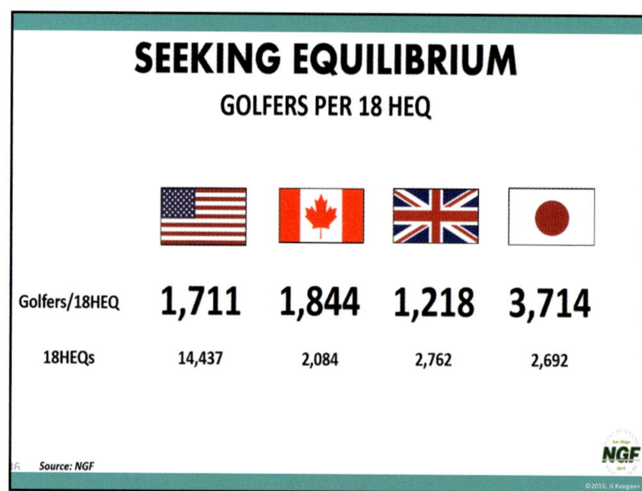

Significant differences also exist beginning with the participation rates. In most countries it is below 1%. Even in the United Kingdom, the participation rate is only 2.1%. In contrast, the participation rate in the U.S. is 8.3%. More importantly, as it reflects the demand vs. supply equilibrium, is the number of golfers per 18 hole equivalent reflected here:[5]

5 National Golf Foundation, "State of the Golf Industry," April 2015, slide 36.

There are many other differences:

1. Of the courses in Central Europe, 44% are not operated for profit.
2. Golf in China is limited to the truly elite.
3. The participation of females is far greater outside of the United States. The European Golf Course Owners Association released player statistics in March 2016[6] noting that women represented 32% of golfers whereas in the United States the female participation rate hovers around 24%. Female participation was particular highest among those countries that were not part of the original British Empire, such as Sweden, Norway, and Denmark.
4. Management of the golf course outside the United States is far less outsourced to third-party firms.
5. In nearly all countries outside the United States, members play the majority of rounds. For example, in North Africa, outside play comprises only 11% of play. The U.S. concept of "daily fee" or "municipal" is rarely in evidence internationally, except in India, where 43% of the courses are owned by the military.
6. The water cost for golf courses in the Middle East would bankrupt most U.S. golf courses. Each golf course in the Middle East spends approximately $500,000 annually to pump about 750,000 gallons of water daily.
7. In most countries, an 80-rounds-per-day statistic is considered busy, while in the United States courses average about 90 rounds per day open.

Though golf became an Olympic sport in 2016 reflecting its growing International presence, an HSGC report caution includes that "There are risks here for a sport which is associated with affluence. In a world in which inequality is moving up the political agenda and resources such as land are becoming more contested, golf will need to learn the language of inclusion and sustainability."[7]

This represents a significant warning for the future of golf operations in the United States. But what is the economic impact of golf?

---

6 European Golf Course Owner's Association, "*Europe Player Stats 2014–2015,*" p. 1.

7 Ibid., p. 9.

U.S. Economic Impact Study

The most recent study, as reported by Golf 20/20, measured golf's impact on the United States at $68 million as shown below.[8]

Golf's Economic Impact

Size of the U.S. Golf Economy by Industry Segment in 2000, 2005 and 2011 ($ millions)

Core Industries	**2000**	**2005**	**2011**
Golf Facility Operations	$20,496	$28,052	$29,852
Golf Course Capital Investment	$7,812	$3,578	$2,073
Golfer Supplies	$5,982	$6,151	$5,639
Endorsements, Tournaments & Associations	$1,293	$1,682	$2,045
Charities	$3,200	$3,501	$3,900
Total Core Industries	**$38,783**	**$42,964**	**$43,509**
Enabled Industries			
Real Estate	$9,904	$14,973	$4,745
Hospitality/Tourism	$13,480	$18,001	$20,555
Total Enabled Industries	**$23,384**	**$32,974**	**$25,300**
TOTAL GOLF ECONOMY	**$62,167**	**$75,939**	**$68,809**

Note: Columns sum based on rounding of individual estimates. Numbers also have not been adjusted for inflation but are expressed as nominal dollars.

As would be expected, the impact of the recession which started in 2007 shrank golf's economic impact from $76 million in 2005.

While the superficial observer might feel that there was a direct correlation between the number of golf course closings and the reduction in golfers during that time frame, a closer look indicates that it was new course construction and the slowdown in real estate associated with golf course facilities that had the largest impact.

Golf courses are usually classified as daily fee, municipal, resort, or military. Within the NGF Charter Facility database, there is an internal coding that categorizes the golf courses as reflected below. Such classification provides a more informative light on why the slowdown occurred:

8 http://golf2020.com/media/31526/2011_golf_econ_exec_sum_sri_final_12.17.12.pdf, p. 5.

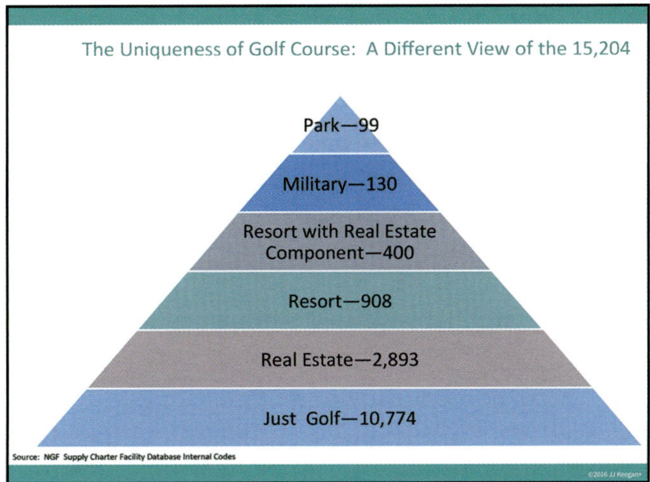

Golf courses affiliated with real estate represent 19.02% of all golf courses in the United States. But there is a silver lining in that dark cloud.

The role of golf in competing for the consumers' entertainment capital is highlighted by the following table presented in the World Golf Foundation Golf 20/20 report.[9]

Description	Amount
TV broadcasting, cable, and other subscription broadcasting	92.4
Motion pictures and videos	83.1
Golf (core industries)	43.5
Spectator sports (baseball, basketball, football, hockey, etc.)	33.1
Other amusement (skiing, fitness and recreational centers, bowling, etc.)	32.3
Performing arts	15.1
Note: Amounts given in billions.	

The Multiplier Effect of Golf's Economic Impact

As most economists appreciate, golf has direct as well as indirect and multiplier effects on the overall U.S. economy. For example, for every dollar spent by a golf facility for goods and services, other businesses derive economic benefit. The wages paid to golf course employees are spent by them for living expenses.

9 http://golf2020.com/media31526/2011_golf_econ_exec_sum_sri_final_12.17.12.pdf, p. 6.

In 2011, the $68.8 billion impact generated by the golf industry translated into a total economic impact, calculated by SRI International, an independent non-profit research institute, as follows:[10]

- $176.8 billion for the U.S. economy, including the indirect and induced economic impacts stimulated by golf sector activity;
- 1.98 million jobs; and
- $55.6 billion of total wage income.

As a comparison, in Canada, "The game of golf accounts for an estimated $11.3 billion of Canada's Gross Domestic Product (GDP), which includes:

- 29.6 billion for the Canadian economy, including the indirect and induced economic impacts stimulated by golf sector activity;
- 341,794 jobs; and
- $7.6 billion in household income."[11]

Interestingly, in Canada, "the revenues generated directly by golf courses and their facilities and stand-alone driving and practice ranges ($4.7 billion) rivals the revenues generated by all other participation sports and recreation facilities combined ($4.8 billion)."[12]

Golf's Place as an Individual Sport

Golf's core industries compete well against other forms of entertainment. Of the 24.1 million participants, shown on the next page,[13] each spends $1,850 annually, or 1.97% of a golfer's median household income.

The chart on the next page shows the National Sporting Goods Association's data that there are only 23.7 million golfers in the United States in 2012.[14] Others believe that there are only 22.1 million golfers in the United States.

10 Ibid., p. 7.

11 http://golf2020.com/media/12784/economicimpact_golfcanada_2009_execsummary_en_issuedaug17_09_25.pdf, p. 1.

12 Ibid., p. 2.

13 National Golf Foundation, "Demand Database," March 26, 2016.

14 National Sports Golf Association, "2011 Participated Ranked by Percent Change."

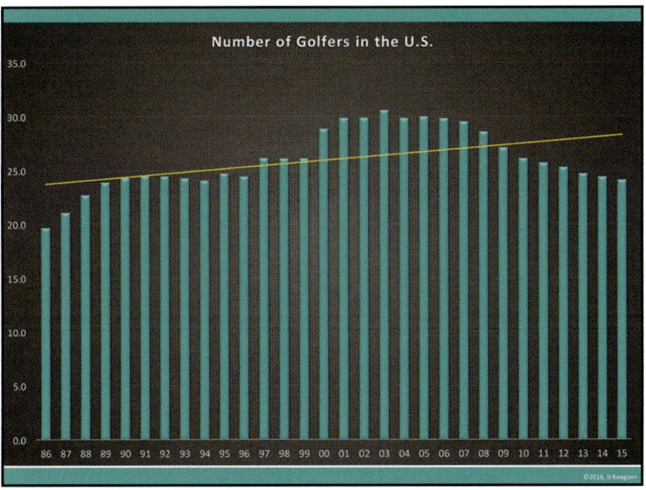

Why the difference?

The task of assembling empirical data is really difficult. Respondents often inflate their responses on consumer surveys. Rather than indicating how much they played or spent, their responses are reflective of how they had intended to play or wished they had played.

Gathering data from golf courses has become easier with the advent of golf management information reporting systems during the past decade. But though the accuracy of data is improved, its precision remains sorely lacking.

What is the solution? In an industry that lacks vital benchmarks, it would be far preferable if research studies identified the degree of confidence indices and margins of error. It would be far preferable, for example, to publish consumer spending if it was labeled 80% confidence with a 20% margin of error, rather than have no data at all. Wouldn't it be better to know that consumer spending was between $700 and $900 or $1,400 and $1,800 than to not have any benchmark at all? We believe so.

The naysayers will highlight that golf has lost 21.3% of its customer base from its high point in 2003 of 30.6 million golfers. That trend has also been experienced as rounds are down 16% in Australia, 9% in Canada, 17% in Sweden, and 15% in the United Kingdom, as illustrated in the next figure:[15]

15 National Golf Foundation, "Big Questions on Golf's Participation," April 2013, slide 4.

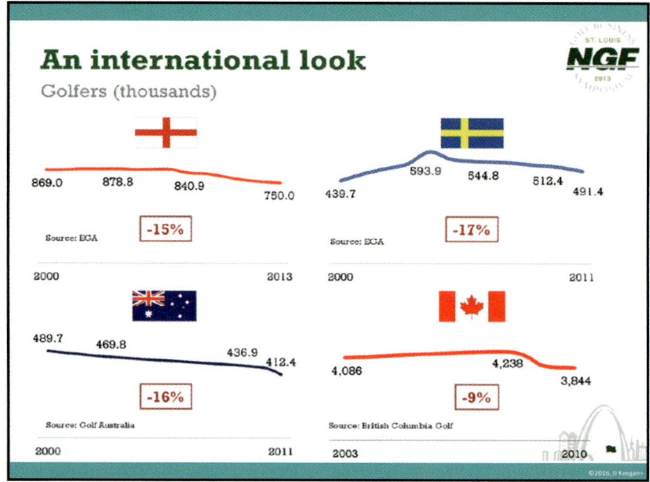

But is the problem with the decline in participation just with golf or is there a bigger societal issue that is impacting all individual sports?

The participation rates for all individuals sports has fallen significantly over the last five years as reported by the U.S. Physical Activity Council:[16]

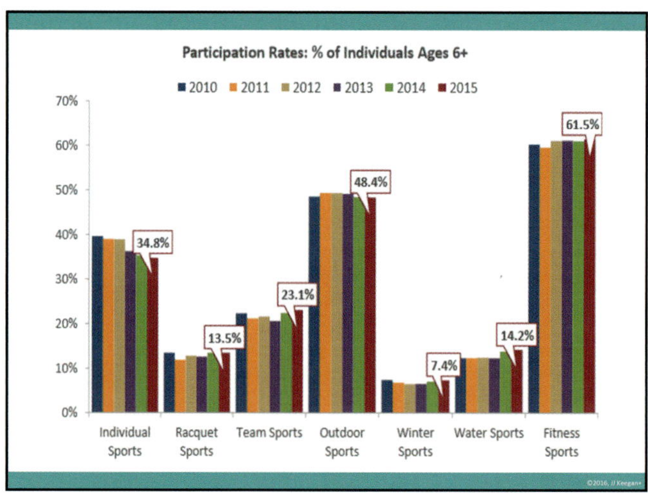

Of the seven categories, individual sports which include golf is the only one that declined. Racquet, team, outdoors, and winter sports remain consistent in participation over the last five years. Only water and fitness sports (think aerobics, the gym, tai chi, yoga, etc.) have increased.

16 Physical Activity Council, "2016 Participation Report," p. 7.

It should be noted that individual sports, as defined by the Physical Activity Council, include the following[17]: Triathlon (Traditional/Road, Non-Traditional/Off-Road), Adventure Racing, Golf, Boxing (Fitness, Competition), Martial Arts, MMA (Fitness, Competition), Other Combat Training, Bowling, Ice Skating, Roller Skating (2×2 Wheels, In-Line), Skateboarding, Archery, Shooting (Sports Clays, Trap/Skeet), Target Shooting (Rifle, Handgun), and Trail Running.

Thus, the decline in golf participation is consistent with all individual sports.

The Tertiary Effects of a Decrease in Demand

The industry believes that the source of golf's woes in the United States is attributable to the fact that the supply of golf courses exceeds the demand. Viewed from a macroeconomic perspective, that conclusion is correct.

The following chart highlights golfers per 18 holes and indicates the declining number of golfers per 18 holes over the past two decades.

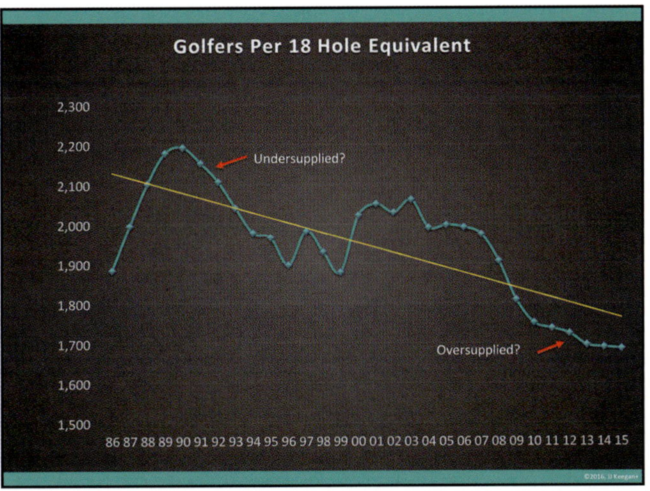

We are confident however, that a golf course operator sincerely believes that it is impossible for the golf industry to have ever been undersupplied. It is easy to side with that argument because golf courses as a whole have historically operated at less than 60% of capacity. Hotels and airlines have utilization benchmarks at 80%, and the utilization of golf courses pales in comparison.

17 Physical Activity Council, "2016 Participation Report," p. 23.

The increase in supply coupled with stagnant demand has created a reduction in the number of rounds played at each facility.

The seriousness of the oversupply of golf courses in the United States is suggested by the following:

	Category	Number
Facilities	Golf Facilities	15,204
Rounds	Rounds Played – NGF Demand Model	465,794,000
	Rounds Played/Facility	30,636
Utilization Benchmarks	Current Utilization	52.00%
	Leisure Industry Benchmark	80.00%
	Excess Capacity	28.00%
Target Round	Target Rounds/Facility	39,214
Courses Required for Supply/ Demand to Be Balanced	Number of Facility Required	11,878
Excess Courses	Potential Excess Number of Facilities	3,326
Percent of Excess	Percent Number of Facilities Oversupplied	21.88%

Although some may question whether it is operationally realistic for a course to achieve 80% of capacity every playable day, clearly, to some extent, there are simply too many golf courses in the United States for all of them to be financially sound.

But here is the rub—not every golf market is oversupplied. The extent to which the golf in a major metropolitan market is possibly oversupplied would be far different than that measure in a rural part of the United States. To presume an equal distribution of golfers in relationship to the supply in each market would be fallacious.

The following are some industry benchmarks:

1. There are 1.4 golfers per household. The 17,094,510 golfing households in the United States form the basis for calculating that there are 24,130,020 golfers.
2. In the United States, 8.3% of the population plays golf. Interestingly, with the growth in the African American (1.4 million golfers), Asian American (1.1 million golfers), and Hispanic American (3.2 million golfers) communities at a rate faster than the Caucasian segment (18.4 million golfers), golf participation in the United States is likely to continue to decrease for the foreseeable future.

3. Avid golfers represent 26.8% of all golfers.
4. There are 464 avid golfers and 1,711 golfers per 18 holes.

If one examines the number of golfers within the major metropolitan markets, you might conclude that the Top 100 core-based statistical areas in the United States are vastly undersupplied, as illustrated in the following table:

	Nation	**Top 100 Core-Based Statistical Areas (CBSA)**	**% in Top 100 CBSA**	**Remaining USA**	**% in Non–Top 100 CBSA**
Households	17,084,510	11,392,810	66.69%	5,691,700	33.31%
Rounds	465,794,000	293,535,000	63.02%	172,259,000	36.98%
Rounds per Household	27.26	25.76		30.26	
Courses	15,204	7,193	47.31%	8,011	52.69%
Rounds/ Course	30,636	34,912		20,415	−15.71%
Golfers > Courses			15.71%		−15.71%

It is hard to believe that although 66.69% of all golfing households live within the Top 100 core-based statistical areas in the United States, only 47.31% of the nation's golf courses are located in those areas.

The Top 100 core-based statistical areas are shown here.

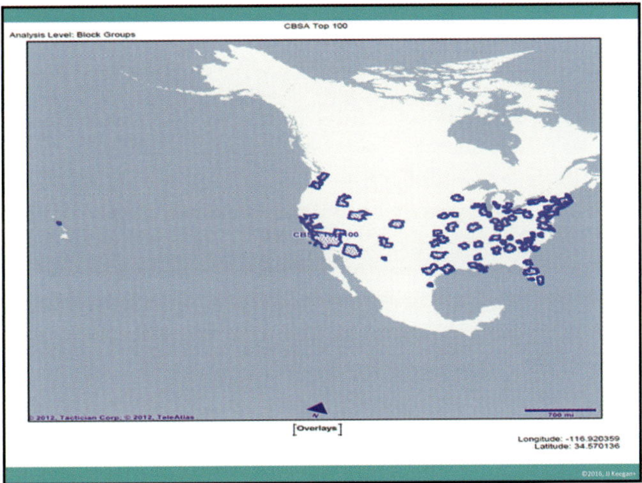

This is where a trap lies for the researcher and author. An irresponsible journalist will take one statistic, blow it out of proportion, and challenge all of the findings when merely one statistic is paradoxical.

The quote that would be taken out of context would be "Golf in the

Top 100 core-based statistical areas is undersupplied by 15.71%." No one in the industry would present that fact as truth for many reasons, including self-denial, and also because they may realize to some extent that their course's economic underperformance is attributable to management and not to uncontrollable factors. The journalist would become culpable by implying that the author was calling for more new course construction.

Such is not the case here. What it does mean is that golf courses located within the Top 100 CBSA might have more price flexibility than has been historically perceived. If a golf course were to raise its rates, golfers in a densely populated market have fewer courses to choose from; thus course revenues are likely to rise.

In buying or selling a golf course, a premium might be associated with a course in a densely populated area beyond the normal revenue multiple, and a high discount will probably be accorded a course in a less populated area; its ability to produce a superior experience becomes challenged by a small potential revenue base.

What about the reverse, when those non–Top 100 CBSA would be considered to be oversupplied by 15.71%?

In a market that is overcrowded, it becomes increasingly hard to differentiate, as price often becomes a dominant factor that seduces the owners into believing that volume of rounds, not yield per round, is more important. Such markets fall prey to third-party providers who build their success, in my opinion, on desperate inferior providers seeking some revenue stream to stay afloat.

Thus, golf operators who emphasize volume over yield per round have a flawed concept.

Caught in the Death Spiral?

From a microeconomic viewpoint, it can be simply stated that the reduction in the number of golf course closing is occurring at a slower pace than the decrease in the number of golfers as reflected below.

However, for the first time since 2012 when favorable weather stimulated rounds, in 2015, we have seen a positive upturn in the number of rounds per facility. Is that trend sustainable?

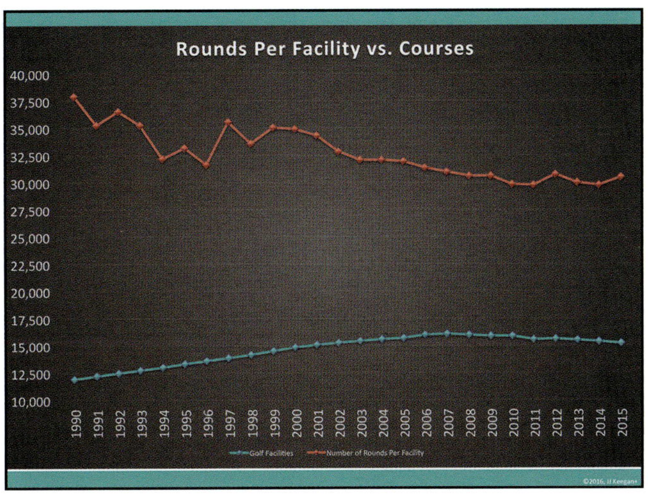

The Future of Golf: When Will Demand Equal Supply?

The National Golf Foundation in the 2016 Symposium held in Chicago forecast when supply and demand are likely to be in balance, illustrated here.

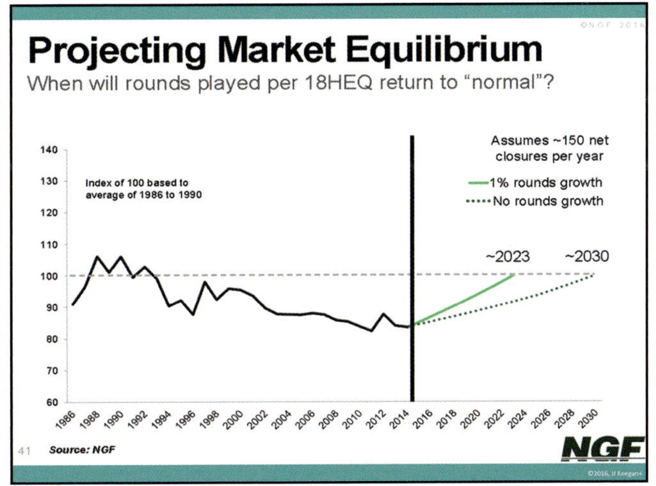

To reverse the downward cycle, two scenarios were presented: (1) no rounds growth but continued net closures of 150 courses per year, or (2) 1% rounds growth with the continued net closures forecast. The growth might come from:

- Millions of high-interest golfers who want to play more (for example, Generation X and Y who are now in their prime working and family-rearing years).

- Millions of former golfers who are open to trying again (for example, people who were turned off by slow play, embarrassing situations, or cost of entry).
- Millions of never-evers who want to start (recent NGF research shows that 4% of 200 million never-evers are very or somewhat interested in playing golf).

We believe that the number of golfers leaving the game is higher than new entrants or those returning after a hiatus and is the source of leakage. We speculate that a contributing factor is those core and avid golfers are playing less frequently, migrating into the category of merely an occasional golfer as shown here:

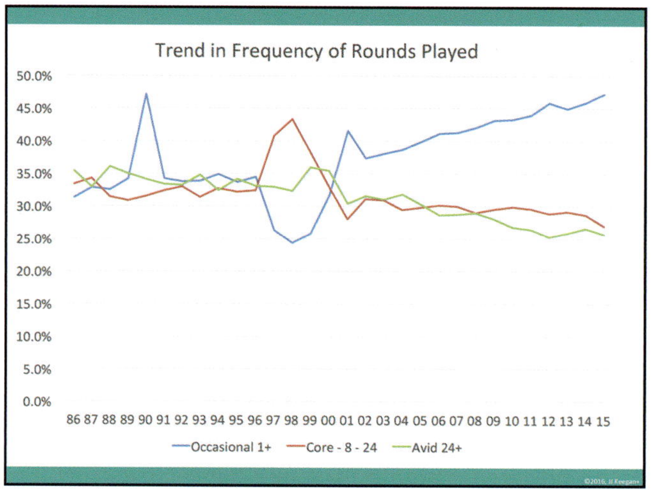

Thus, challenges lie ahead in the short-term for the golf industry.

Is There Hope?

There are some quick fixes that should address the game's primary barriers.

- **Time**—Create more opportunities for alternative forms of play (Stableford scoring, Scrambles among families, reward pace of play, emphasize range programs for the severely time-compressed).
- **Money**—Find creative ways to make frequency more affordable (don't discount, but pay for volume; offer couple or family rates; offer season passes only on a restricted basis during the slowest playing times, usually

weekdays from noon to 3). Also, educate the aspirational golfers; encourage them to practice more with the latest equipment.

- **Skill**—Facilities should focus on playable options with multiple tees, easier pin positions, and eliminating those elements of "penal architecture" found within their courses. Course renovations should emphasize "fun" over difficulty.

More importantly, there are some trends that bode well for the future of golf. If one examines closely the average rounds by age chart presented earlier, there is a bubble from 6 to 22 years where the various programs, i.e., Get Golf Ready and PGA Junior Golf League, are having a positive impact.

Increases in rounds from baby boomers is a distinct possibility. There is clearly a correlation between the age of the golfer and the number of rounds played, as shown here:[18]

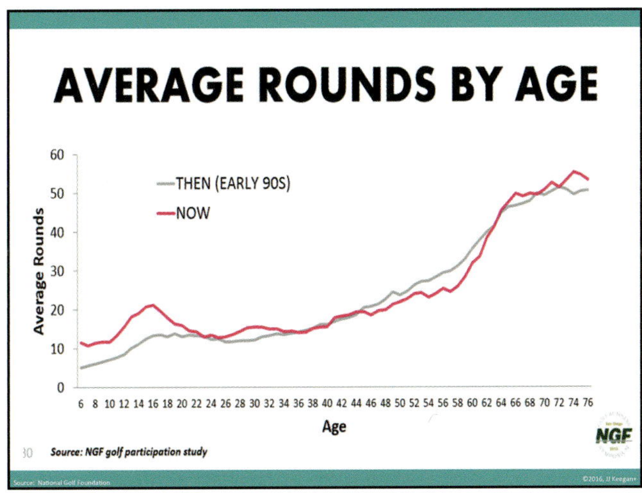

There are many initiatives for women and the emphasis on pace of play to create rounds are healthy indications for a successful future.

Although few new golf courses are being built, golf course renovations are becoming in vogue. With such, it is now perceived that architecturally, shorter is better than longer, easier is preferred over hard, brown must become the new green, and firm must be the new fast. The luscious mannered courses featured weekly on the TV should become the exception—not the rule.

18 National Golf Foundation, "2015 State of the Industry, The NGF Perspective," slide 30.

All of these developments are positive. What follows is the formula to address these woes permanently. For the golf course creating a strategic plan, the economic and environmental factors present a gloomy picture. It is vitally important that a golf course owner has a clear delineation, as reflected in its vision statement, as to its course's market niche.

Key Points to Remember

1) The number of golf courses in the world, based on a National Golf Foundation survey, is over 34,000.
2) Growth of the game is international, not U.S. based.
3) Supply for golf in the United States exceeds demand by 10%.
4) The number of individuals who play golf in the United States continues to fall.
5) If you are located in a top 100 core-based statistical area, evaluate if you have the leverage to increase your rates.
6) For those golf courses located in less populated areas, understanding the value provided to the consumer in relationship to the price charged will be fundamental to the facility's profitability.

Concluding Thought

It is impossible to begin to learn that which one thinks one already knows.

Epictetus

As the world becomes more and more complicated, our minds are trained for more and more simplification.

Nassim Nicholas Taleb

Chapter 3

The Players
Associations and Equipment Manufacturers

We are inclined to believe those we do not know because they have never deceived us.

Samuel Johnson

Chapter Highlights

The golf industry is segmented into three sectors: the game of golf, the business of golf, and the media, principally television entertainment.

The distinctions, while very clear, often become confused as the plethora of associations, golf courses, and companies jockey for space within the arena of golf. Many have morphed from the purpose for which they were formed to become diverse organizations operating within at least two sectors.

This chapter concentrates on the trade associations that influence the business of golf: the National Golf Course Owners Association, the National Golf Foundation, the Professional Golfers' Association of America, and the United States Golf Association. The role of leading equipment manufacturers in attracting golfers to the game also is examined.

Why is this information important to the golf course owner? Golf Associations and equipment manufacturers influence golfers. Their efforts promote entrance to the game and perhaps also create barriers.

Can You Separate the Game of Golf from the Business of Golf?

What purpose would it serve if there were rules to define a game and no one played? What would happen if golf courses were built and no one came because engaging in the activity wasn't fun? Would anyone choose to participate if the tools of the game, the equipment, didn't enhance their ability to play the game?

Do we take for granted that people will always want to play golf? Perhaps so.

What is more important? Should we protect the history of game founded over 450 years ago as perceived by today's historically sensitive golfers? Or should we allow the game to evolve based on a changing society's desire for recreation? And, as in every other major sport, should there be a set of guidelines for the professionals and a different set of guidelines for amateurs? There is no clear agreement on this matter, but the enjoyment of many and the financial fortunes of some are dependent on the results of the debate.

At its core, if people are engaged in an activity that doesn't serve their self-interest, they will not continue to do it for long.

Golf represents a cocktail of three components:

The Game of Golf

The actual origins of golf can be traced:

> "… to a region in eastern Scotland known as the Kingdom of Fife in the early 1400s. The ball was a pebble, and players used existing dunes and rugged terrain as their courses.
>
> Handcrafted clubs and balls followed, and by the middle of the 15th century, golf was so popular in Scotland, King James II had to outlaw the sport to get the men of Scotland ready for an impending battle with England.
>
> In the 16th century, golf's popularity spread in England thanks to the support of King Charles I. Mary Queen of Scots helped spread the popularity in France during her studies there. In 1744,

> the Gentlemen Golfers of Leith, an area in the northern section of Edinburgh, formed the first golf club to promote an annual competition.
>
> St. Andrews, often incorrectly credited as being the birthplace of golf, became in many ways a symbolic home for golf. After Leith's rules, the Society of St. Andrews Golfers was formed, with its rules and a tournament to crown its champion."[1]

From those meager beginnings, golf is now enjoyed by over 50 million people worldwide. As the game evolved, associations were formed to foster its growth.

Some associations were formed to define the rules of the game; these included The Royal and Ancient (1754) and the United States Golf Association (1895). Like the clubs formed at Leith and St. Andrews, state golf associations in countries around the world were formed to crown champions. Some were "open competitions," and others narrowed the competition by gender, age, or ability; hence the need for the formulation of a handicap system.

The game of golf comprises "hitting a ball that weighs no more than 1.620 ounces (45.93 grams) with a diameter not less than 1.680 inches (42.67 mm), performing within specified velocity, distance, and symmetry limits into a series of 18-holes, 4¼ inches wide over varying terrain with obstacles created by nature and by humans."[2]

The Business of Golf

The business of golf would be defined as the sale of "anything" related to the game of golf, such as memberships, green fees, cart rental, equipment, merchandise, food, and beverage, etc.

If one were to create an organization chart of the "Business of Golf" it might resemble this:

1 http://www.golflink.com/facts_5034_was-golf-invented.html

2 http://en.wikipedia.org/wiki/Golf_ball

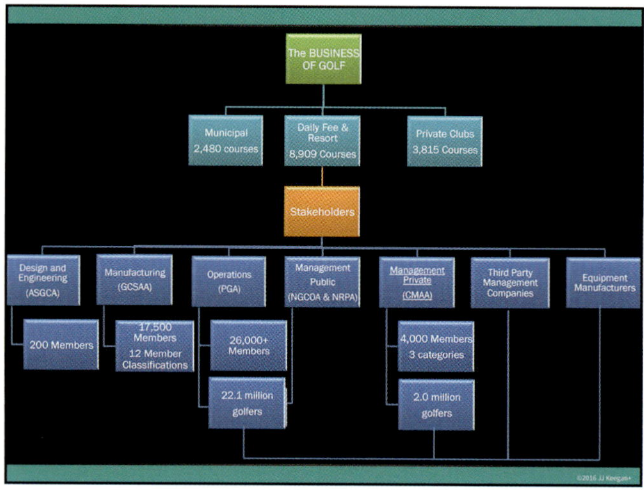

The game of golf attracts, the business of golf fulfills.

The Entertainment of Golf

But there is a third equally influential component that generates over $2 billion for the golf industry—watching the game of golf. Entertainment is big business.

INVOLVEMENT IS MULTI-DIMENSIONAL

Participation in the last 12 months	Total (MM)	Non-Golfers (MM)
Golf on a golf course	25	--
Golf at a driving range	15	5
TopGolf	4	2
Screen Golf (Indoor simulator)	4	2
Mini-golf	22	16
Video game(s)	56	46
Watched golf	81	60
Read about golf	27	17

15 *Source: NGF golf participation study* Groups are not mutually exclusive NGF ©2016, JJ Keegan+

It is estimated that as many people watch golf on television as play the game. For the individuals who watch, golf serves simply as entertainment. The PGA Tour, the LPGA Tour, and the USGA are the principal associations focused on filling this niche.

Golf as entertainment is widespread as it is very multi-dimensional, as illustrated here.[3]

Balancing Competing Interests

Industries are formed and evolve to serve consumers. All industries exist through the invisible hand of capitalism, where the ebb and flow of individual self-interests compete against the welfare of the community in the aggregate.

3 National Golf Foundation, "2015 State of the Golf Industry," slide 15.

Such is also the case within the golf industry—the lack of a unified vision. Creating a consensus as to what serves the mutual welfare between the game of golf, the business of golf, and golf as an entertainment product would be difficult to achieve.

Every major professional sport from the National Football League to Major League Baseball to the National Basketball Association all have one thing in common—a commissioner who balances the interests of the owners, the players, and the fans. Rules are changed annually based on reviews by the competition or the rules committees to ensure player safety, equity, and fan enjoyment.

Such is not the case with golf.

You Need a Scorecard

Six associations or foundations have the most influence over the business of golf. They are:

Association	Headquarters	Focus	Mission Statement
Golf Course Superintendents Association of America, founded in 1928 (GCSAA)	Lawrence, Kansas	Superintendents	Dedicated to serving those responsible for maintaining the golf course by advancing their profession, and enhancing the enjoyment, growth, and vitality of the game of golf.
National Golf Course Owners Association, founded in 1979 (NGCOA)	Charleston, South Carolina	Course Owners and Operators	To enhance the lives of golf course owners by making their business more profitable, more efficient, better managed, and more stable.
National Golf Foundation (NGF)	Jupiter, Florida	Industry Research	To help golf businesses succeed by providing marketing, research, customer targeting, and other consulting services.

Association	Headquarters	Focus	Mission Statement
Professional Golfers' Association of America, founded in 1916 (PGA)	Palm Beach Garden, Florida	Professional Golfers	Experts in growing, teaching and managing the game of golf.
The Royal and Ancient Golf Club (R&A)	St. Andrews, Scotland	Clubs, Courses, Rules	The International governing body of golf outside U.S. and Mexico.
United States Golf Association (USGA)	Far Hills, New Jersey	Clubs, Courses; conducts US Open, US Women's Open, US Senior Open, 10 National Amateur Championships, and the State Team Championships	U.S. governing body of golf in the United States, its territories, and Mexico.

No single association claims leadership in the golf business. These associations serve in ways that blend (sometimes smoothly, sometimes awkwardly) to support the business of golf. Some have an implied monopoly power in their domain; others seek that influence.

Of these associations, those doing most of the heavy lifting with respect to the business of golf are the National Golf Foundation (providing research), the National Golf Course Owners Association (representing the owners' investment interests), and the PGA of America (providing qualified staff to play, teach, and manage the business end of the game).

The role of the USGA promotes and conserves the true spirit of the game as embodied in its ancient and honorable traditions. It acts in the best interests of the game for the continued enjoyment of those who love and play it.[4] The USGA conducts amateur and open championships that generate substantial revenue and provide great entertainment. It offers a handicapping system that affiliated golf course owners and PGA pros administer. It also guides golf course owners through its green section, and it tests equipment to ensure compliance with the rules.

Under the leadership of Mike Davis, the USGA has recently become very concerned about the sustainability of golf. It is conducting symposiums on the pace

4 http://www.usga.org/content/usga/home-page/about.html

of play and, with the America Society of Golf Course Architects, sponsoring site reviews to ensure that golf courses are sustainable.

Just as golf is a gentlemanly sport, the business of golf has a competitive aspect as golf associations often subtlety protect and respect each other's loosely defined territories.

What Is the Role of These Associations: To Educate or to Lead?

One of the great benefits of these trade associations is that they can influence an industry by representing their members' more enlightened interests.

A diverse range of professional talents is found within these organizations—from the very skilled and progressive to the bureaucratic and turf-protecting. If they fulfill their charter by serving the narrow interests of their members but adversely impact an industry, then are they good stewards of the game?

At its core, what are the essential components required for the golf industry to thrive?

The industry would include individuals who:

- Are financially sound, providing recreational entertainment to their customers and stable employment for their management and staff. (NGCOA)
- Understand the business of golf and can maximize the investment return of the facility. (NGCOA/CMAA)
- Understand the game of golf and can provide the instructions and programs to enhance the customer's enjoyment. (PGA)
- Can create, maintain, and enhance the grounds on which the customers play. (GCSAA)
- Provide guidelines by which individuals can compete. (R&A and USGA)

In theory, these roles could be provided by a single association. In reality, the lines are blurred as individuals and associations perform, on occasion, tasks within each of the core components required for the successful operation of a golf facility. However, is the golf industry served well in the following examples?

1. A golf course owner who has **financial resources** but lacks the business skill to maximize the investment return at a golf course or to teach the game chooses not to hire a general manager or a PGA professional to assist him.
2. An individual who **understands the business of golf** but not the game of golf fails to retain qualified personnel to fill that void, thereby reducing the investment return received by his employer.
3. An individual who is **skilled in the game of golf** but assumes the responsibility for managing the business of golf while lacking skills in finance, human resources, and maintaining the facility's physical assets.
4. An individual who **creates the standards for the industry** but so narrowly defines the guidelines that they effectively create deterrents for the masses embracing the activity as participants.

We all like to classify individuals and associations into well-defined categories to give us a frame of reference. That provides security so that when advancing our personal interests, we understand the motivations of those with whom we interact.

Associations have evolved based on self-interest. But they have evolved citing a familiar mantra, "for the good of the game." That begs the questions, "Good for whom?" and "How do golf course owners protect their investment in this industry from the associations that exist within it?"

Who Are the Real Players?

If there is any lesson to be learned by the golf course owner, though we all preach the values of the recreational aspects of the game, it is that, within the golf industry, money = power and power = influence.

The following table presents the industry's principal trade associations, their roles, and a financial snapshot of their operations.

Association	Date	Employees	Assets	Fund Balance	Revenue	Expenses
PGA Tour	December 31, 2013	744	2,159,258,857	922,282,526	1,075,044,778	1,040,493,604
PGA of America	June 30, 2014	Not Disclosed	383,128,725	295,983,359	82,252,120	90,563,475
United States Golf Association	November 30, 2014	433	392,860,711	392,860,711	175,879,735	165,120,368
World Golf Foundation	December 31, 2013	137	82,555,714	44,623,418	40,889,932	36,014,427
Ladies Professional Golf Association	December 31, 2013	110	45.978,450	10,373517	102,669,736	101,669,736
Golf Course Superintendents Association of America	December 31, 2013	93	21,962,998	11,272,975	12,090,072	12,628,900
National Recreation and Park Association	June 30, 2014	63	10,672,816	6,261,733	13,496,937	13,118,153
National Golf Foundation	December 31, 2013	34	5,169,067	4,734,125	1,762,841	1,662,550
Club Managers Association of America	October 31, 2014	43	4,081,061	(1,080,339)	8,732,381	8,542,088
National Golf Course Owners Association	December 31, 2014	13	4,027,041	2,597,172	3,232,453	3,270,453
Source: The financial data for all associations were obtained from http://www.guidestar.org						

Note that many of the associations, such as the PGA and the USGA, post their financial statements on their respective websites. Those financial statements show a far greater financial strength than other sources because investments and other non-operating income are included in those statements. Some of the associations also operate for-profit corporations.

The financial performance of the PGA Tour, the PGA of America, the USGA, and the LPGA are impressive. Only the PGA Tour revenues match those of the leading equipment manufacturers. TaylorMade-Adidas Golf reported net sales of $1.022 billion;[5] Callaway reported $885 million,[6] while Acushnet Company (Titleist and Footjoy) sales were $1.5 billion.[7]

What Initiatives Are Making a Difference?

In 2015, various entities agreed to collaborate to grow, protect, and perpetuate the health of the game by endorsing the six initiatives shown here:

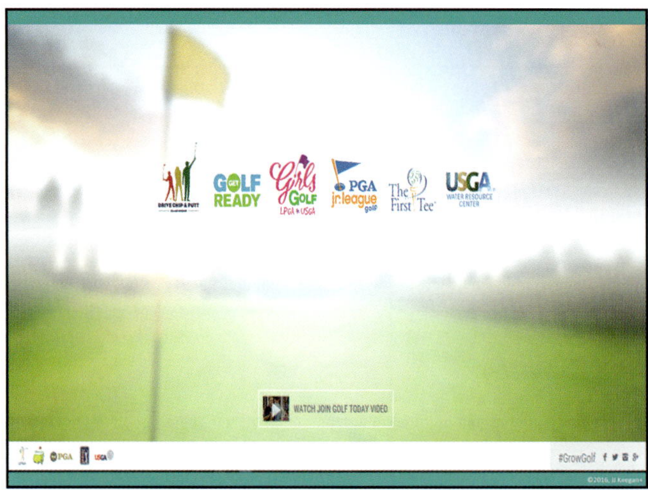

A summary of these initiatives follows[8]:

> Drive, Chip, and Putt is a joint initiative founded in 2013 by the Masters Tournament, the United States Golf Association, and the PGA of America. Drive, Chip, and Putt is a free junior golf development competition aimed at growing the game, focusing on the three fundamental skills employed in golf by tapping the creative and competitive spirits of girls and boys ages 7–15. Across the country, thousands of kids played in approximately 250 qualifying events, winnowing down the group to 80 boys and girls who will convene at Augusta National on Sunday before the Masters to play in the finals.

5 http://www.golfchannel.com/news/equipment-insider/taylormade-golf-sales-drop-28-2014/

6 http://www.marketwatch.com/investing/stock/ELY/financials

7 http://www.sginews.com/EMS_Base/EMS_Excerpt.aspx?tTargetUrl=/Content/acushnet-company-fy14-revenues-up-4-operating-margin-down.aspx

8 http://www.pga.com/news/pga/golf-industry-enters-new-era-collaboration-keep-growing-game

Get Golf Ready offers adults five lessons for $99. Over the six-year history of this program, Get Golf Ready has attracted 358,000 students through the more than 4,400 GGR-certified facilities across the country.

LPGA-USGA Girls Golf introduces the game to girls up to 14 years old. It has continued to get more girls involved in the game. LPGA-USGA Girls Golf has grown from 4,500 girls per year in 2010 to an estimated 50,000 girls per year in 2015.

PGA Junior League Golf is for boys and girls ages 7–13 playing a 9-hole Scramble in three-hole segments. It saw a 500% growth from 2012 (1,500 kids) to 2013 (9,000 kids). In 2014, the numbers nearly doubled (1,425 teams and 17,500 kids) compared to 2013 (740 teams and 9,000 kids). Estimates are that 100,000 girls and boys will participate by 2020.

The First Tee introduces young people to the game and the values inherent to it. It reached more than 4.1 million young people in 2014, the most since its inception in 1997. Since the program's inception through 2014, more than 10.5 million young people have participated in The First Tee programs. Programs are delivered at golf courses and in elementary schools and youth centers. In 2013, Scott Langley became the first participant of The First Tee to become a PGA TOUR member.

USGA Water Resource Center commits to sustainability shared industry-wide to support the long-term health of the game by delivering solutions to address key barriers to participation. It is focused on four key factors: the costs associated with the game, the time it takes to play the game, the overall quality of the golfer, and resource management, particularly water.

The Positive Impact: One Example

These programs are having a positive impact on the business of golf.

Get Golf Ready in 2015 offered programs, as shown below, on 2,628 golf courses attracting 107,485 students:[9]

9 Golf 20/20 – PGA of America, "2015 Get Golf Ready Annual Report," slide 2.

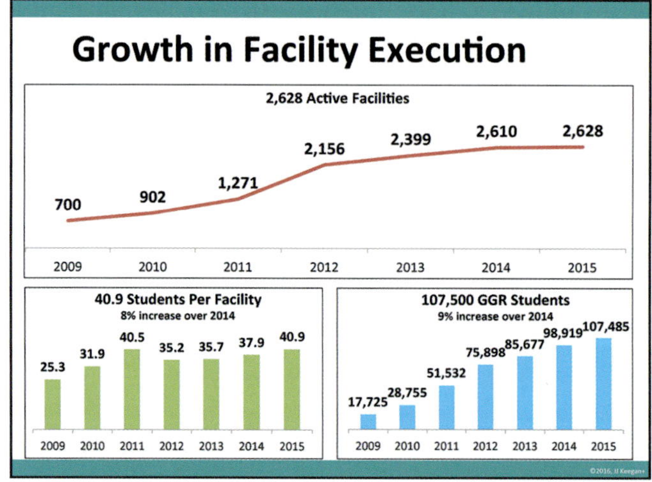

What is exciting is that the participants were 66% female, 24% minority, 39% had never played, and 97% indicated the program exceeded their expectations.

The program started in 2009. The average spending of a first-year participant is $1,032. In 2015, $353 million in revenue was generated from Get Golf Ready, and since inception the total revenue from this program exceeds $1 billion.[10] That is awesome!

GCSAA: Brown Is the New Green—Not So Fast

Which is the most important of all the trade associations? In my opinion, it is the Golf Course Superintendents Association of America. Its members create the "product" that we all enjoy. Their members have scientific training from some of the finest universities.

The educational programs offered by the GCSAA are vastly superior in depth and breadth to the information presented by any other organization.

How their members haven't made it from the maintenance buildings to the boardroom escapes me. Well, it may be because they prefer working with things rather than people, and that has defined their career path. However, they hold the key to the future success of the golf industry in "manufacturing" a product that produces consumer satisfaction.

10 Golf 20/20 – PGA of America, "2015 Get Golf Ready Annual Report," slide 7.

David Kohler is the chief operating officer of Kohler Enterprises, which owns four fabulous golf courses and an amazing hotel—The American Club, in Wisconsin. In a meeting a couple of years ago with the president of the GCSAA, Kohler made a great impression stating:

> "You can't change what consumers desire and want. Consumers say they support water conservation; we develop incredibly efficient shower headers and faucets, and the consumer reaction is they don't like the reduced water pressure."

The lesson? While the industry says green must become brown, and the firm must become fast, it is unrealistic to think consumers will change their desire for luscious turf and the finest in playing conditions. That trend will start when TV broadcasts of golf tournaments reflect golf courses with more economically sustainable playing conditions.

Equipment Manufacturers

Many people in the industry believe that equipment manufacturers, perhaps inadvertently, reinforce through their advertising the idea of golf as an elitist sport.

Equipment manufacturers sell over $5 billion annually.[11] They invest untold millions in research development and advertising. But it seems that with the arcane and technical product descriptions used, making informed decisions on what club is right for each golfer is all but impossible. If you read the equipment reviews in *Golf Magazine* and *Golf Digest*, confusion is often the result, not clarity.

Need proof? Look at the ads certain manufacturers run on television. Their engineers and designers are touted as modern-day Isaac Newtons, complete with algorithms dancing whimsically around their heads. To think that the average golfer understands the technical nuances of design is folly. Following is an example of the exact product description from the March 2016 Golfsmith online catalog:

11 The Futures Company for HSBC, "Golf's 20/20 Visin: The HSBC Report," 2012, p. 4.

Callaway XR Driver[12]

Speed is everything, and it's the driving force behind the Callaway XR Driver. That means speed comes from an aerodynamic crown, from the R-MOTO face, from a maximum shaft load, and the list goes on and on. Callaway traveled down a new path to make a driver that's a proving ground for these great technologies. If it increases speed, it's in XR Driver, and that's why it's Callaway's fastest titanium driver ever.

Speed from Speed Step Crown To reduce drag and maximize speed through the swing, Callaway put in a Speed Step Crown and combined it with an optimized aerodynamic head shape. Everything about this driver is optimized for aero efficiency, which is critical to add speed with less drag.

Speed from R-MOTO Face Technology Callaway increased ball speeds across the face by reducing 10% of the face weight to make it thinner. R-MOTO leads to more energy efficient energy transfer all over the face, allowing Callaway to put the center of gravity (CG) 17% lower where most golfers want it, therefore delivering a higher moment of inertia (MOI).

Speed from Maximum Shaft Load The shaft is a key component to speed, that's why the XR Driver comes stock with the new Project X LZ. It produces maximum shaft load during the downswing loading zone for greater energy transfer to the ball.

OptiFit Adjustability Choose from eight different lofts and lie configurations to find the perfect launch for your ball flight. When you get the right launch conditions, you get more distance.

The process of selecting the right equipment is daunting. From that description, could you tell whether that club was best for your game? Probably not. Shouldn't it be easy to find the "perfect" club? It isn't.

I ponder whether many golfers abandon their search for new clubs because there are so many choices, and they can't differentiate among the various clubs. Where there are confusion and doubt, there is delay. And when equipment purchases are delayed, the growth of the industry is slowed.

---

12 http://www.golfsmith.com/product/30153290/callway-xr-driver

Although all club makers maintain that PGA Professionals and off-course store representatives should educate and custom-fit golfers, such practices violate rule number one of the basic principles of Marketing 101: The customer doesn't like to look stupid and thus, if the answer isn't obvious to them, they will rarely ask a question because they don't want to appear to be an idiot.

We yearn for simplicity, yet the golf industry gives us complexity.

The Historical Role of State Golf Associations

State golf associations, which are private 501(c)(3) nonprofit organizations, are principally governed by volunteers representing distinguished members of the community from a cross section of golf courses and are usually weighted to the more prestigious golf clubs. In addition to conducting as many as 40 tournaments per year, the associations also sponsor rules seminars, calculate course ratings, provide a handicap and tournament management software service, and assist in the redistribution and implementation of USGA policies, programs, and championships.

For those on the periphery, there is often confusion about the differing roles of the USGA, the PGA, and the PGA Tour. The difference between the motivations of individuals affiliated with an amateur state golf association versus those affiliated with the PGA is easy to explain: The amateur associations are motivated to preserve tradition. The PGA and the PGA Tour are focused on the business of golf—earning money.

To sustain themselves, state golf associations usually rely upon handicapping accounts for more than 75% of their gross revenue, based on the following revenue model:

The Economics of Handicaps	Cost
Software providers' charge to state golf association	$3.05
State associations levy golf courses which provide service to their players	$12.00–$20.00
Golf course assessment/upcharge to player	$25.00–$65.00

The largest providers are the Golf Handicap and Information Network (GHIN), which is maintained by the USGA employees with an annual budget of $38 million. GHIN is provided through 71 state, regional or national golf associations to over 12,000 clubs and approximately 2.3 million golfers.[13] GHIN is maintained by the United States Golf Association®, and the staff is composed of USGA employees.

In 2016, the USGA is currently studying the economic model for State Golf Associations and changes are expected.

What Are the Implications for Golf Course Owners?

For golf course owners, it is imperative to realize that the brand of their facility can be impacted, both positively and negatively, by trade associations that are beyond their control. Associations and Equipment Manufacturers have mainly their economic interests at heart.

Therefore, the responsibility for profitability rests upon solely upon the golf course owner. Associations can create programs to grow the game, educate their membership to assist you, and sponsor governmental and research initiatives. But in the end, golf course owners control their own destiny.

13 http://www.ghin.com/content.aspx?id=77

Key Points to Remember

1) There are six trade associations that largely influence the policies of the industry and create brand recognition for the sport, heavily influencing the masses' perception of the game.
2) Remember that associations are business enterprises unto themselves. While they tell you, as any vendor would, that they care about you and have your interests at heart, their principal interest is in assuring their association's financial stability and keeping their jobs.
3) Many people do not trust the motivations of these organizations because they sometimes work at conflicting odds.
4) Cherry-pick your investments with associations, selecting educational programs and attending classes that have direct relevance to identified needs.
5) Golf courses should refrain from hosting any amateur tournaments at their course sponsored by golf associations unless the full value of green fees for the tee times used are received. Don't get sucked in by "it's good for the game." They are using your asset to benefit themselves, not you.
6) The PGA of America's educational programs leading to certification is properly balancing their members' affinity for the game of golf with the business of golf.
7) Equipment manufacturers limit the growth of the game with arcane descriptions of technology.
8) State golf associations have many opportunities to stimulate the growth of the game by leveraging their core constituency to create relevant social networks that provide services far beyond handicapping, including tee time reservations, Facebook, YouTube, and other social media functionality.

Concluding Thoughts

He is often in error, but never in doubt.

Unknown

Success is a lousy teacher. It teaches smart people into thinking they can't lose.

Bill Gates

Chapter 4

Ownership and Governance: A Privilege or Burden?

The mass of men never comes up to the standard of its best member, but on the contrary digress itself to a level with the lowest.

Henry David Thoreau

Chapter Highlights

This chapter discusses the forms of ownership of golf courses: municipal, military, daily fee, resort, and private, and the great divisions in structure, philosophies, and operating policies among these different types of ownership.

While these ownership groups all serve the golf industry, the divisions between them can be quite bitter, with daily fee operators often loathing their municipal brethren, citing significant cost advantages and crying for a level playing field in the land of capitalism. Should municipalities even be in the golf business? Finally, there is the evolving role of management companies. Whether or not management fees are justified by the increased profits they supposedly lead to, the intangible benefit of an owner not having to worry about day-to-day management may be fair compensation itself.

The Management Model

A golf course experience represents the intersection of farmers, short-order cooks, teachers, point-of-sale clerks and retail merchandisers, as golfers experience customer touch points on the assembly line of golf.

The services at these touch points are largely provided by low-paid, seasonal workers hired to fill a short-term need. Finding a team skilled in each of the seven disciplines (geographic local management analysis, playable days review, technology, financial modeling and benchmarking, the course [architecture, agronomy, operations], [golf, restaurant, merchandising], customer service) to provide an exemplary experience is a huge challenge.

A diversity of intellect, knowledge, and skills exists within the golf industry. Often assembled at a golf course are a few full-time and some seasonal workers rarely having an understanding of the course owner's vision, receiving scant training, and seduced to serve by thinking the fringe benefit of free or discounted golf offsets the low wages and long hours.

Thus the heart of the golf industry's woes lies within the *average* **golf course owner's inability to execute consistently.**

What then is the best management model?

Public or Private

The typical golfer thinks of golf courses in two ways: public and private.

Within those divisions are subcategories that include municipal, daily fee, semi-private, resort, private equity, private non-equity, and military golf facilities. No matter how we classify a golf course, the changing nature of supply within the golf industry has been dramatic, which is depicted in the graph on the next page.

Why does the type of ownership matter? It impacts every aspect of the operation, from course conditions to pricing and from rules about access to the depth and breadth of staffing. The type of ownership conveys a strong brand image in each golfer's mind before arrival at the course.

Municipal golf courses are often viewed as the entry door—the stereotype of inexpensive, affordable golf. Average course conditions, small clubhouses, and limited food service cater mainly to seniors, juniors, season pass holders, and new golfers. During the past decade, this stereotype has changed, as many municipal courses now offer high-quality experiences.

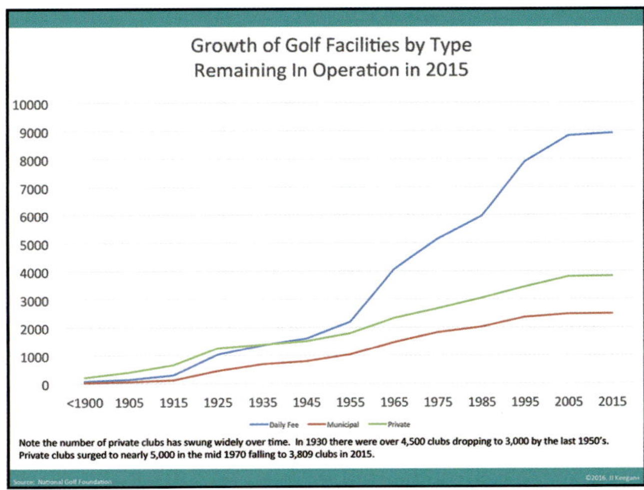

While looking to provide a recreational experience to its citizens, municipal golf encompasses the following goals and functions:

- Generating the largest possible return on investment to divert profits to support other nonrevenue-supporting park activities.
- Providing an appropriate return on investment with a value-based recreational activity for the citizens.
- Enhancing the lifestyle of constituents by catering to the perceived needs of niche groups—women, senior citizens, etc.
- Appealing to and facilitating the formation of core values among children, adolescents, and teens.

Regardless of the charter or operational framework of a municipal course, the pricing it sets becomes the "buoy" on which all prices in the market are set. As municipalities raise their prices, based on perceived increases in value, the prices at other courses in that market adjust accordingly.

In contrast to the varying mantra of a municipal golf course, the mission of the daily fee course owner is clear—maximize net income while providing a living for the proprietor and accumulating an investment return that secures the owner's future. That mission only becomes slightly tempered amongst a few golf course owners whose philanthropic interests result in their donating access to their facilities for charitable causes or to attract major golf championships.

For resorts, a golf course is an essential amenity offered. While it may be viewed as a profit center, its major contribution is to fill the hotel and restaurants, especially by attracting large corporate and social events.

Private clubs range in form and function. In small towns, they tend to serve the upper-middle class. Private clubs may be exclusive, and offer membership only to those for whom membership provides prestige, a designation far beyond the value of the experience offered by the club.

For example: Would you join a private club in a temperate southeastern U.S. climate with 18 regulation holes and a nine-hole par 3—a club that is closed all summer, and is virtually unplayable for several premium weeks in the spring? When described that way, the answer is probably "No." But that is a fair description of the Augusta National Golf Club, a private club that every serious golfer would jump at the chance to play let alone join.

Of the various clubs, none is under more attack from the changes in our society than the low- and mid-tier private clubs. In a race to remain relevant, they are quickly diversifying from country clubs into family entertainment centers.

Forms of Municipal Golf Course Management

Municipalities operate golf courses with organizational structures that include the following:

- Employees—city or county workers run the place just like the water department or the police force. Often these employees are budgeted through the Parks and Recreation Department.
- Leases with concessionaires, dispersing responsibility to one or many of a golf course's revenue centers. Of the main revenue centers of a municipal golf course (green fees, carts, merchandise, food and beverage, lessons, range, etc.), the most "leased out" center is food and beverage.
- Management companies such as Arcis Golf, Billy Casper, Kemper Sports Management, OB Sports, etc., that contract to run all or part of a golf operation.

As illustrated on the next page, municipalities have selected many different forms of operation.

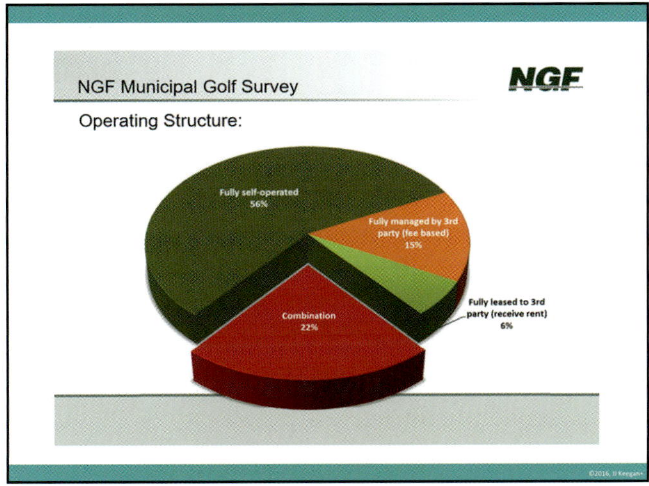

What is the best structure for the operation of a golf course? When using "employees," the swing of quality will hit both extremes, from outstanding, dedicated employees to those merely "punching the clock."

Leasing to individual concessionaires often produces less than desirable results. Concessionaires are for-profit entities, which create a natural conflict of interest between the scope of services and efficiency of operations.

Management companies provide a viable alternative in some circumstances. They often provide the expertise and the economies of scale that may be afforded by operating multiple properties.

The following is a summary of the financial implication of each alternative for the golf course owner:

Matrix of Decisions	Self-Manage	Management	Lease
Risk	Full Risk	Full Risk	No Risk
Capital Investment	Full Capital	Full Capital	No Capital, unless negotiated
Profits	Full Profits	Full Profits less a management fee	No Profits other than "rent."

Interestingly, municipalities divide the management of their facilities widely based on golf operations, maintenance, golf merchandise/shop and food and beverage, shown on the next page.

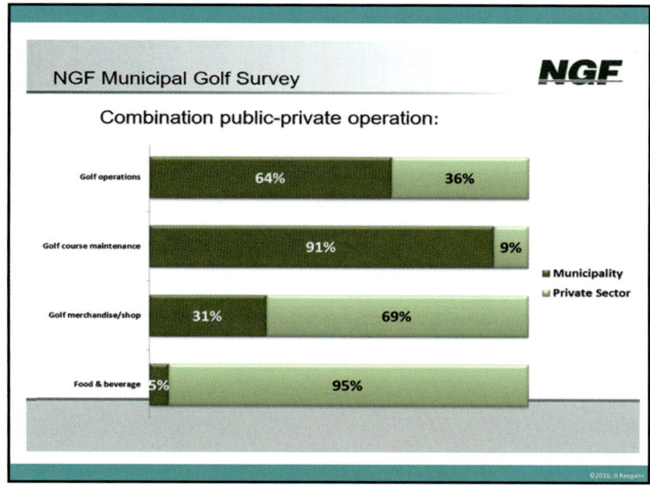

What is known is that food and beverage at all golf courses is an amenity, not a profit center.

Should Municipalities Even Be in the Golf Business?

The first municipal golf course, Van Cortlandt Golf Course, opened in New York City in 1895. It was built for the masses. The need to create golf courses for the masses became clear because the sport was dominated by private clubs during its early years. It wasn't until the mid-1930s that there was more public than private golf courses in the United States.

The opportunities to play golf, early on were limited to the well-to-do.

What is often lost in the debate on the viability of municipal golf courses is that golf is classified as a discretionary program. The allocation of resources for parks and recreation departments is determined by a matrix of core, important, and discretionary areas of importance by national standards, as shown in the diagram on the next page.

A priority of the Parks and Recreation Department is to ensure that the entire community has open park space at a minimum of 10 acres per 1,000 in population.

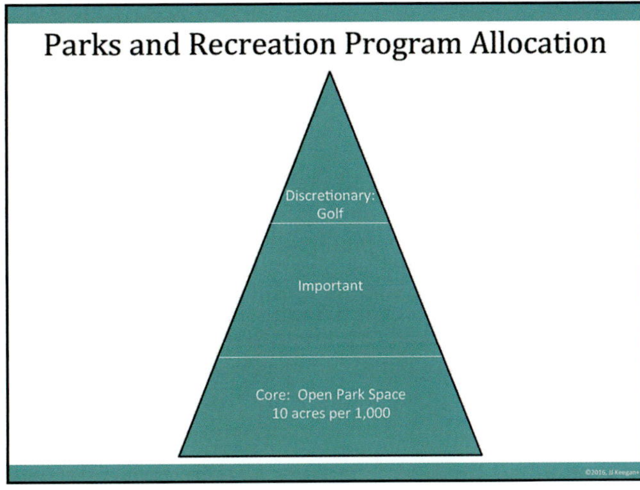

During the past few years, with the economic downturn, and specifically since 9/11, the decision for the allocation of municipal funds has been to provide police and fire with the highest priority, with other municipal services competing for the remaining resources.

A substantial number of municipal golfers believe a profit focus for golf is inappropriate, since other activities like libraries, parks, trails, and swimming pools, are supported by the taxpayers. Golfers feel that the real estate taxes they pay and their expenditure of disposable income in the community creates employment for all residents and justifies the financial support of a golf course by a municipality. To view and hear the philosophy of entitlement on full display, attend any city council meeting where golf course rate increases are being discussed. The golfers are often present in droves demanding that to which they believe they are entitled.

The evolution of golf in the United States might suggest that the need for municipalities to provide golf began to subside in 1970 with the surge in public golf opportunities at daily fee courses. The extent to which the number of daily fee courses exceeds the number of private clubs might be one benchmark that would ascertain the need for a municipal golf course within a defined market.

But if we acknowledge that there is a valid need for a golf course operated by a municipality, what niche of the golf market should it serve? Should it be an entry door to the game, like most "city park" golf courses, or should it be serve as a community center for many functions?

Qualitatively, it is fairly easy to justify a municipal golf course as a place for kids to learn, for First Tee chapters to be operated, for senior citizens living on social security to enjoy outdoor recreation, and for new entrants to the game to play with friends and family without the pressures of social decorum and etiquette that are so tightly observed at high-end daily fee courses and private clubs.

What is the answer? Should municipalities be in the golf business? The answer is clearly based on each person's value system, but the hope of most would be that the municipal golf course would be self-sustaining after reserves are established for the ongoing capital investment required. But are municipal courses achieving that benchmark?

Financial Performance Compared

Presented below is a comparison of the financial performance of municipal vs. daily fee courses:

Financial Performance
Municipal vs. Daily Fee Golf Courses

	Platinum Top 10%	Gold Top 25%	Silver Median	Steel - Bottom 25%
MUNICIPALITIES: 177 Courses Participating in Survey				
Rounds Played	51,782	40,000	29,500	22,584
Full-Time Employees	21	11	7	4
Total Revenues	$2,327,000	$1,675,000	1,068,865	720,941
EBITDA	1,631,493	814,558	100,000	40,520
DAILY FEE: 348 Courses Participating in Survey				
Rounds Played	44,432	35,000	25,000	18,000
Full-Time Employees	32	16	10	5
Total Revenues	$3,350,000	$2,087,484	$1,209,153	$659,768
EBITDA	$820,715	$454,558	$192,500	$41,000

Source: PGA Performance Trak, 2014 compiled in 2015

Often the big picture doesn't reveal weaknesses that may exist in the business model. In a presentation to the National Park and Recreation Congress in September 2015, the National Golf Foundation Consulting Division shed light on municipal finances, reporting:[1]

- 67% cover operating expense
- 39% have debt
- 40% cover debt service
- 73% are deferring capital improvements
- 39% are lowering maintenance standards

1 National Golf Foundation, "Improving the Profitability of Municipal Golf Courses," slide 22.

What is amazing is the poor financial performance reported when considering that the vast majority of municipal courses are located within the top 100-core based statistical areas where demand for golf is the strongest.

Who Has the Competitive Advantage?

The operation of municipal golf courses can be via a "general fund" or an "enterprise fund." In a general fund, the golf course operation is merely a component of the city's total budget. In an enterprise fund, the golf course operation is accounted for as a separate economic unit. The enterprise fund is structured as a separate, quasi-independent municipal economic entity in which profits and losses are separately measured and revenues not siphoned into the municipality's general operating budget.

Regardless of the form of business, municipal governments have a competitive advantage in the following ways:

1. Profit motivation is not as intense, since many Parks and Recreation activities, such as swimming pools, tennis courts, and soccer fields, are taxpayer supported without the expectation of profit. Many golf courses believe that if they are self-sustaining after depreciation, interest, municipal service charges, and amortization, everybody is happy.
2. They are better insulated from downturns in the business cycle, and they have the ability to reallocate funds, at least on an interim basis, which provides financial flexibility.
3. Many municipal golf courses are located near populated city centers, often because they were built decades ago.
4. Capital is usually easier to access because the government guarantee ensures its availability. Borrowing is also more economical—underwriting a capital expansion project via a revenue bond nets the municipal golf courses 2% to 4% lower borrowing costs.
5. The land on which the course is situated can be free to the golf course operation.
6. Governments are not obligated to pay property, income, and on occasion sales and alcohol taxes, and these courses benefit from the economies of scale when they purchase insurance coverage for fire, liability, and health.

7. Similarly, they can buy equipment under favorably negotiated municipal bid contracts. This advantage is minimized by those daily fee course owners who belong to the NGCOA, and its Smart Buy program, in which favorable pricing is negotiated for members.
8. Fees for water, sewer, electric, and gas may be discounted.
9. Navigating zoning changes and the permitting process may be easier to achieve.
10. Employees are attracted and retained with lucrative fringe benefits such as health and life insurance, annual mandated merit increases, and retirement compensation packages.

Certainly, these advantages realized by a municipal golf course operation are impressive. The $44,788 difference in operating costs ($968,865 for a municipality versus $1,016,653 for a daily fee course) is in part attributable to the cost advantages accorded a municipality.

That cost comparison might lead the casual observer to conclude that municipalities clearly have an advantage.

However, daily fee brethren have many incorrect perceptions about municipal courses, and operating a golf course in a municipal environment has many significant disadvantages.

First, the **incorrect** perceptions:

1. **Municipal courses intentionally underprice.** Because of their lower cost structure and because the underlying experience of most municipal golf courses is inferior to that of daily fee courses, lower pricing properly reflects the value of the product. For those municipal courses where greater value is accorded, such as Bethpage Black in New York, Torrey Pines South in California, Red Hawk Ridge in Colorado, and Brown Deer in Wisconsin, the rates are set at comparable levels to nearby daily fee courses for non-residents.
2. **Municipalities have the pleasure of responsibility without the accountability for showing a profit**. Many municipal managers may wish that were the case, but it is not.

   From the citizen-based golf advisory councils, to the director of parks and recreation, to the city manager, to the mayor and city council, to the taxpayers who have unlimited access to detailed data regarding the golf course under the Federal Freedom of Information Act, municipal golf courses operate under the full review and observation of everyone.

3. **Most courses do not recognize the cost of depreciation.** While the accounting systems of some municipalities are convoluted and use outdated technology, a detailed analysis will find nearly all golf courses being charged depreciation. While depreciation is booked, cash reserves are not segregated annually; hence, often there is a need to issue a revenue bond.

   Municipalities rarely calculate EBITDA and focus more on a "bottom-line" number.

4. **Municipalities are immune from the invisible hand of capitalism** that rewards those who manage well, and punishes those who underperform by forcing them to close.

   With the downturn in golf, many municipal golf courses are evaluating their options, including privatization, sale, or transitioning to open park space. You can expect to see the transformation of many golf courses to open park space when the cost to maintain open space is less than the cost to operate the golf course.

More alarming than the incorrect perceptions are the many significant and costly disadvantages of operating a municipal course.

First, a municipal golf course has to overcome the brand image of being a "muni." The heyday of municipal golf construction was the Eisenhower years, and many of the buildings and courses look their age. The cost to repair the infrastructure (and the image) nearly equals the cost of building a new golf course.

Other significant disadvantages of municipalities include:

1. **The payroll cost structure is higher than incurred by daily fee courses;** fringe benefits and retirement packages are mandated for all city employees consistently. With higher labor costs, municipalities are often forced to reduce drastically advertising and marketing.
2. **Labor issues are far stricter.** The process of hiring (job postings, interviews, testing, physical exams, etc.) is cumbersome. Just the negotiation of salary can be a long, tedious process. As for firing someone, it is nearly impossible. Except drug, alcohol, or theft issues, it would take at least six months to terminate an employee for mere non-performance or tardiness.

3. **Where labor unions are present, the problems are exponentially more complex.** Salaries are fixed, overtime rates are double, and work schedules are firm. Maintenance crews, for example, are often limited as to what trees they can trim. Many times other departments of a municipal complex must be scheduled for such work and charge the golf course fully absorbed rates that far exceed what private-sector firms would charge. Although daily fee owners may not see these as relevant issues, they truly are a huge challenge.

4. **Rate adjustments take at least 45 days.** Because they operate in a public forum ultimately accountability to the taxpayers, approval is required for all material decisions regarding fees and expenses that exceed a threshold ($15,000 in most cities).

5. **Because of the inflexibility on rates,** directors of golf are effectively precluded from engaging in proactively adjusting rates to keep up with changes in demand.

6. **Politics.** The influence of golfers on elected city officials, particularly commission or council members, should not be underestimated.

7. **Golfers are taxpayers who frequently demand low-priced season passes, improved conditions, and better service.** If councilmen or mayors balk, they might find themselves on the wrong end of an election with a vocal and passionate constituency (golfers) campaigning against them.

8. **As a municipality, the course is constantly expected to provide a wide range of services that are not profitable.** Golf camps, youth education programs, and donation of the course for community-sponsored events are frequent distractions.

9. **Procurement is cumbersome, requiring a lengthy bidding process,** and there is no assurance that the best vendor will be selected. A municipal bid takes from 60 days to 6 months. One city golf course lost its water pump, and it took nearly nine months to replace.. The superintendent was required to hand-deliver water in the interim because the cost of the item required a public bid.

10. **All of the financial information of a golf course is in the public domain.** One of the competitive advantages of a private business is the ability to mask your revenues and expenses from your customers. Municipalities don't have that luxury.

What is clear is that to the extent municipal golf courses provide a basic golf operation at an affordable price, daily fee owners are comfortable. When the municipality expands and provides an extensive array of mid- to high-tier golf, food and beverage, and catering and meeting functions, then the daily fee owner believes the line of fair competition has been crossed.

The Death Spiral

The financial and capital challenges that municipal golf courses are currently experiencing can be tracked through four distinct phases during the past several decades. These phases are as follow:

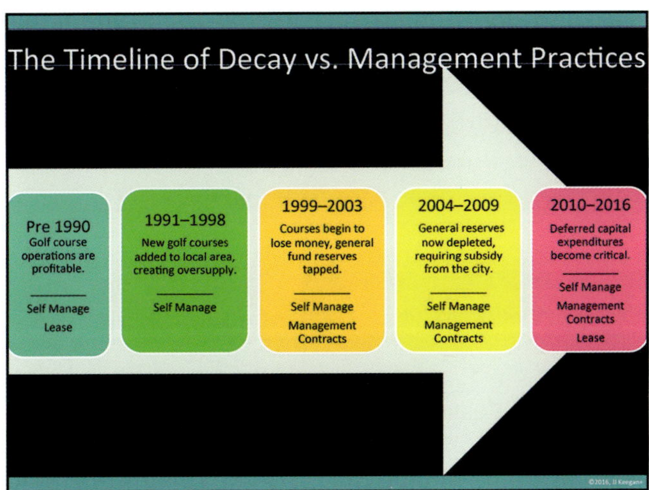

Up until the early 1980s, most municipal courses were managed 100% by municipalities. With the advent of management companies in the late 1980s, these firms were retained, they paid the cities a lease fee, and they benefited from the earnings with profits shared, in some cases, above certain thresholds.

With the boom in golf in the late 1990s, municipalities opted to either self-manage or to pay management companies a flat fee while retaining the profits for the cities' coffers. Gordon Gecko's greed became their mantra—let us make the money. It can't be that hard to manage a municipal golf course.

Unfortunately, many municipalities didn't fully comprehend the difficulty of creating a value-based golf experience while generating sufficient cash flow to offset the bond payments hidden within their often inefficient organizational structure.

The four factors that are driving municipalities out of the golf course business are (1) water, (2) labor cost, particularly where labor unions are present, (3) medical costs, and (4) pension benefits.

If Third Parties Are Better, Why Isn't Every Municipality Adopting That Form of Management?

The privatization of a municipal golf course meets with resistance from many sectors. Golfers are fearful rates will go up. Golf management and staff are afraid their jobs will be lost. Parks and Recreation Department managers are fearful capital improvements will not be made. The city council is fearful the benefits received will not offset the fees paid.

Billy Casper Golf Management, one of the leaders in the management of municipal courses, understands both the myths and the realities of this subject and presents the following reality check to municipalities during its presentations.[2]

Dispelling Management Company Myths

Myth	Reality
Rates will go up	Dictated by market/approved by owner
Residents will lose access	Locals are always #1 priority
Conditions will deteriorate	Improved conditions = more golfers
Employee house cleaning	Employers always seek good staff
Service will suffer	Professional staff delivers results

BILLY CASPER GOLF

Though golfers maintain that rates will go up, the city council usually determines the price. Management companies can increase rounds and revenue through tee time yield management, guest retention and acquisition programs, promotion and public relations, and cross-marketing opportunities.

The argument that residents will lose access is one of the "fear arguments" that golfers throw into the debate with little support. The reality is that 90% of rounds are played by golfers who reside within 10 miles of the course, programming is directed toward residents, and most courses are operating at less than 50% of capacity. Access to tee times is not a real issue unless the golfer is demanding a permanent prime time at 8:00 a.m. on the weekends.

2 Billy Casper Golf, "Management Alternatives," October 2011, slide 12.

It is truly a myth that course conditions will deteriorate under the care of a leading management company; these companies fully understand that improved conditions generate more golfers. By introducing agronomic plans and upgrading maintenance equipment and golf carts on a repair and replacement cycle, course improvements invariably improve.

Management and staff are fearful for their jobs. While the less competent maybe at risk, management companies don't have a bullpen full of talented help. They are constantly looking to hire locals; it's good business, provides golfers a consistent touch point, and allows the management company to introduce guest-oriented employee training.

As to the argument that service will suffer, management companies are usually on three-year contracts. While the municipal employee, in essence, has a guaranteed lifetime contract, the management company is at risk of being fired. Business plans, marketing plans, agronomic plans, employee training programs, and capital improvements are crafted and implemented to ensure a mutually beneficially long-term arrangement.

Thus, in deciding the optimum form of management for a municipal golf course, a private club, or resort, it is important to understand the pros and cons of that decision. The pros and cons of using a management company are summarized as follows:

Pros and Cons

Pros	Cons
Professional management skills are more diverse and better refined.	**Contract compliance.** Requires retention of contract administrator
Proven systems, policies, and procedures can be implemented faster, particularly in the areas of technology, marketing, and staffing.	**Financial stability.** The ability of a third party to meet its contract obligations is predicated on its having a firm financial position and the willingness to provide a superior product.
Efficient labor structure in number of personnel used and wages paid.	**Course Access.** Tournaments and more dynamic pricing.
Flexibility in contract negotiation and timeliness and cost efficiency of completing capital improvements.	
Stakeholders aligned more easily between city council, city management, course staff, golfers, and taxpayers.	

It is our feeling that the role of a management company should be to create a unique brand for the golf course and retain an outstanding management team. A management agreement should not be a lifetime annuity but rather a professional services contract where the fees are earned through generating a higher return on investment for the owner.

If the management is advocating that they will promote a golf course through marketing their brand, for me that is a disqualifier in selecting that company.

There are two other caveats regarding management companies. Because their fees range between $75,000 to over $200,000 per 18-hole complex, the clear economic benefit of retaining a third party needs to be demonstrated. Second, the ownership of the facility's customer database and website URL needs to reside solely with a golf course.

Are There Hidden Risks for a Course with a Third-Party Management Company?

The answer is "yes," but those risks can be by mitigated by agreement. There are several issues that need to be addressed.

A management agreement provides the least exposure. Merely ensuring that strategic plans are created and implemented with appropriate governance are the basics. Any rebates the management company is receiving from third parties engaged on behalf of the golf course should be disclosed. It should also specify that the management company will participate in all benchmarking available.

A lease places a golf course owner at far greater risk of having assets mismanaged, resulting in a large capital expenditure to restore upon default. Under a lease, capital improvements and their timetable must be defined. The ownership of intangible property also needs to be defined. For example, we have unfortunately observed several leasing companies that obtained the website URL for a golf course, then refused to transfer the URL and access to the website back to the golf course owners upon expiration of the agreement. Amazing but true.

Under a lease, there is also the question, "Who owns the customer database?" You might think that the question would be very simple to answer. Most golf course owners would quickly answer, "I own our customer database. Why would you think otherwise?"

If you use a third-party organization to operate your golf course or your food and beverage concession, depending on whether the contractual relationship is a management agreement or a lease, the ownership of the customer database and the associated transaction data are determined by the principles of the "law of agency."

Although the concept is simple, the ramifications to the "title holder" of the golf course are complex and may surprise you.

Who Owns the Economics?

Management companies believe that the individual who "owns the economics" of the course is rightly the owner of the customer database—not, by default, the golf course owner.

It is the belief of the management companies we polled that if the contractual agreement is a "management agreement," the golf course and the management company have a joint and equal interest in the customer database. If the contractual agreement is a "lease," the management companies believe that the customer database is the management company's sole intellectual property.

This has several negative ramifications for golf course owners. Upon the termination of a "management contract," does the management company have the right to use the golf course's customer information? To the extent that each party had a "joint and equal interest in the database," the answer would likely be "yes." In theory, the management company could then use its former client's customer database to compete against its former client if the management company represented another golf course in the local market. Unethical—yes; possible—yes; legally restricted—maybe not, especially if the rights to the intellectual property were undefined within the contract.

If the contract is a lease, even more dire consequences may result. The golf course owner is left with no information regarding its golfers' playing frequency and spending habits. The owner will lack any demographic information regarding the course's customers and be unable to contact them via e-mail. In essence, the golf course owner would be placed at a serious disadvantage in continuing to operate the golf course, whether through internal management or the retention of another firm.

In essence, if the ownership of the intellectual property is not defined in a lease agreement, the golf course owner, whether a daily fee golf course or a municipality, effectively becomes the indentured servant of the third-party company. The golf course owner is unlikely to be able to afford the economic loss from terminating the contract and having to create a customer database from scratch.

What About Private Clubs?

It is interesting to note that since 1950, the number of private clubs has shrunk from 62% to 25% of the golf courses in the United States.

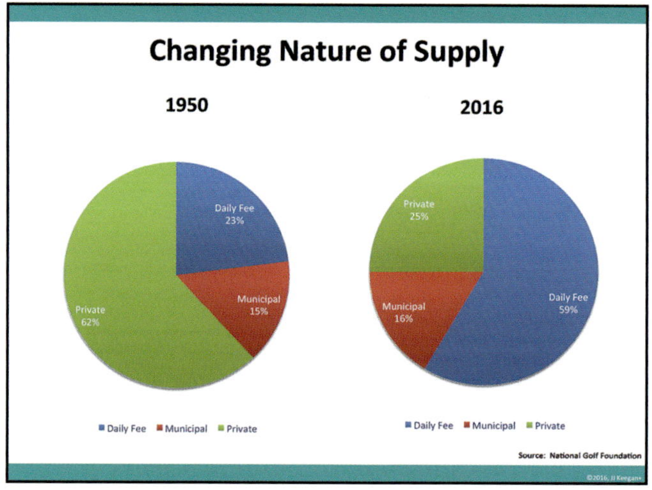

It is a surprising statistic, but there are fewer private golf clubs in 2016 than there were during the 1931 depression.

The change in these demographics makes one wonder, "Is the private club destined to become extinct with the changes in society's culture?" The answer is obviously no. Private clubs will always have their niche for social or practical reasons. The buzzwords surrounding a private club—exclusivity, culture, service, familiarity, tradition/history, quality, convenience, consistency—will always be applicable for a certain sector.

But there is a clear trend in 2016 on private clubs. Many are gravitating from golf-focused facilities to diverse family-oriented entertainment complexes to broaden their audience to a younger demographic.

Historically, private clubs were run by committees. Structured like businesses, the clubs had boards consisting of members from diverse backgrounds and skill sets. The typical organizational structure of a private club is reflected in the following chart:[3]

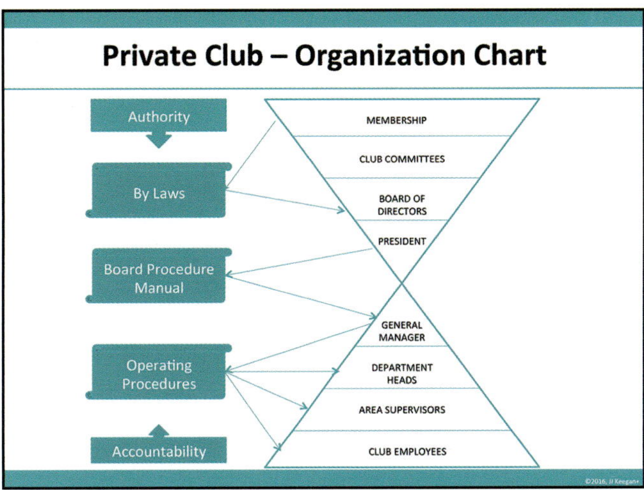

Private Club Governance

To operate a $6 million enterprise requires a lot of vision, talent, and patience.

Brad Klein, noted journalist and one of the leading professors of golf course architecture, wrote the following in *Golfweek* nearly a decade ago. It remains accurate today.

> "When it comes to running a private golf club these days, most boards are overwhelmed. If the politics don't get them, the business demands will."[3]

While each person on board may, individually, be a delight; collectively, the decision-making process in which they engage can be ineffective.

Klein echoed those sentiments, "The folks who gravitate toward power at a private club tend, in my experience, to be the kind who like to set the agenda.

3 Brad Klein, *Golfweek*, "Club politics in year of 'the deal,'" January 13, 2007, p. 9.

Rarely does the self-selection process of club governance produce decision-makers of moderate temperance and firm wisdom."[4]

Why does this behavior occur? Most people seek consensus rather than discord. Most individuals will compromise their personal positions to achieve group harmony—especially in a country club board setting where they aren't being paid and the meetings often run late. Thus, the aggressive individual can wear down the group, resulting in consistently poor decisions.

For group decisions to be effective, the group must possess three characteristics: they must be diverse, they must be decentralized, and each member must be independent.

What is the perfect board? First, the president of the board should be required to go through the rotation of chairs from secretary (to learn the bylaws), treasurer (to understand the finances), and vice president (to learn the management and operational issues) before becoming president (having developed the vision to lead from years of serving). Second, the board should possess the diverse educational background and have skills in the basic business disciplines: accounting, customer service, food and beverage, finance, human relations, and law.

The Cacophony of Chaos

Perfectly run clubs are "benign dictatorships." For a club to run properly, the general manager needs unilateral decision-making power, as long as it is consistent with the policies of the club.

As Klein believes, "Governing boards should do little more than set basic policy, with the details of implementation, operations and rules enforcement in the hands of professionally trained management."[5]

The following chart shows the ideal operational structure for a private club.

4 Ibid.

5 Ibid.

Private Club Management

Activity	Owner/Board	Management
Budget	Approves	Recommends & Provides Input
Capital Requests	Approves	Prepares Requests
Personnel Policy	Adopts	Recommends & Administers
Mission Statement	Adopts	Implements
Day-to-Day Operations	No Role	Makes All Management Decisions

Form Predicts Substance

So the question of ownership and governance begs the questions as to what business model is best. The quick answer depends on one's vision for the facility, the financial resources available, and the talent one can assemble to execute it.

For municipal golf courses, the role of municipal golf courses should be limited to providing playgrounds for kids to learn, places for First Tee Chapters to be operated, outdoor recreation venues for senior citizens living on Social Security, and courses where new entrants to the game can play with friends and family without the pressures of social decorum and etiquette so tightly observed at high-end daily fee courses and private clubs. We believe that for municipal golf courses to operate as high-end price point facilities and compete against daily fee courses is ill-advised in the vast majority of cases.

For municipalities, there are some key rules of thumb. If fringe benefits exceed 40%, a municipality should consider utilizing a third party to manage the golf course. If the value of the course is eroding and expenses are increasing, professional management is a viable option. If the course is incurring operating losses and lacks capital, leasing would be preferred. If a golf course is breaking even, covering debt and capital, self-management remains the preferred choice.

Private clubs that that are operated by a member-based committee system would be well-advised to abandon such form of governance and retain a professional golf management firm to operate the club, for very few committees make a meaningful, positive difference in the success of the club.

From a "business of golf" perspective, the daily fee ownership model seems most preferable. Owners make decisions that yield benefits to owners; this is the purest form of capitalism.

Regardless of the type of golf course, understanding the market, the customer base, and the facility's attributes are essential.

Key Points to Remember

1) Golf courses are considered either public or private. The forms of ownership include municipal, daily fee, semiprivate, resort, private-equity, private non-equity, and military.
2) The vast majority of the growth in golf courses has come from daily fee operations.
3) Municipal golf courses have four different and conflicting charters regarding the golf operation.
4) Municipal golf courses have three types of management systems: employees, independent leases, or management company contracts.
5) A municipality has cost advantage over its daily fee brethren.
6) Despite the cost advantage, many municipal golf courses are losing money.
7) Private clubs offer a haven of refuge to have and make friends.
8) If one opts to select a management company, the ownership of the intangible and intellectually property related to the course must be specified in the agreement.

Concluding Thought

You can only change your plan if you have one.

Randy Pausch, The Last Lecture

The test of a first-rate intelligence is the ability to hold two opposed ideas in the mind at the same time and still retain the ability to function. One should, for example, be able to see that things are hopeless and yet be determined to make them otherwise.

F. Scott Fitzgerald

Chapter 5

The Geographic Local Market Analysis and Weather Playable Days

Steps 1 and 2 of the JJ Keegan+ WIN™ Formula

You can tell whether a man is clever by his answers.
You can tell whether a man is wise by his questions.

Naguib Mafouz

Chapter Highlights

Global issues of the game are wonderful to know, but useless if they don't translate to your local market. The key rule is "Know thy market."

The demographics of your location is the most important piece of strategic information one can have. It is inconceivable to think of buying or owning a golf course without undertaking a geographic market analysis calculating whether your market is under- or oversupplied.

It is also inconceivable not to access advanced weather forecasting tools to efficiently schedule course events.

This chapter covers the importance of these two uncontrollable factors.

Playing the Hand Dealt Well

In creating a strategic plan, there are many uncontrollable factors. So far, we have ascertained the industry within which golf exists (entertainment and leisure), measured the impact of national supply versus demand, and considered the impact of other factors, including trade associations, equipment manufacturers, and service providers. We also examined which form of ownership provides the greatest competitive advantage.

Quantifying these uncontrollable factors is valuable because the data help us isolate and analyze the extent to which changes in rounds are attributable to uncontrollable influences versus controllable decisions made by boards of directors, owners, senior management, and staff.

In this process, we have progressed from those factors that have less direct impact on the golf course facility to those influences that more directly shape the strategic vision, the tactical plans, and the operation execution at a golf course.

Perhaps two of the most important uncontrollable factors are the local market supply versus demand and weather. These provide a first opportunity to calculate some benchmarks that will provide insights into the historical performance of the golf course and the likelihood of achieving future financial success. They represent the **first step in the JJ Keegan+ WIN™ process.**

The first step in the JJ Keegan+ WIN™ is getting a grip on our local market.

Demand—What Applies Nationally Doesn't Necessarily Represent Local Markets

The common notion is that the supply of golf courses far exceeds demand, and that the woes of golf courses to achieve positive financial results is largely attributable to this uncontrollable fact.

However, if one analyzes each state and the District of Columbia (51), core-based statistical areas (CBSA) (942), and zip codes (30,611) in the United States, some interesting insights are revealed. This analysis suggests that the demand for golf is very healthy, in relationship to the supply of golf courses in these states:

The top markets where demand is strong have some of the largest population centers in the United States. It is intuitive that land-locked locations such as Los Angeles, San Francisco, the New York metropolitan area, Chicago, and Washington D.C., where urban construction of golf courses is highly unlikely due to the value of real estate, would reflect strength. The sheer masses, though they may play less frequently than avid golfers, should bolster the average number of rounds per year.

Geography Name	Golfing Households Current Year	Golfers Current Year	Avid Golfers	Number of Facilities	Facilities Suggested Based on 464 Avid Golfers/18	Over Under Supplied (?)
California	1,572,435	2,384,565	639,063	910	1,377	467
Texas	1,187,239	1,583,135	424,280	773	914	141
Illinois	833,937	1,222,893	327,735	635	706	71
Utah	169,118	320,552	85,908	114	185	71
Washington	360,774	571,100	153,055	272	330	58
New Jersey	436,123	593,579	159,079	288	343	55
Arizona	415,063	616,560	165,238	315	356	41
New Mexico	98,150	183,389	49,148	81	106	25
Connecticut	230,214	330,235	88,503	174	191	17
District of Columbia	21,558	32,469	8,702	4	19	15

Source: National Golf Foundation Facility Database

These golf courses have a competitive edge over their peers because of the high number of golfers available per facility. They have the advantage of greater price flexibility, and they probably can get away with offering a less attractive experience than those in other areas of the country because demand is higher.

But what about where demand for golf is weak compared to supply? As shown here, golf courses located in the following states appear to present challenges to even the skilled golf course operator.

Geography Name	Golfing Households Current Year	Golfers Current Year	Avid Golfers	Rounds Demanded Local (Golfer Based)	Number of Facilities	Facilities Suggested Based on 464 Avid Golfers/ 18	Over Under Supplied (?)
Iowa	258,191	381,378	102,209	6,644,889	390	220	-170
Michigan	782,282	1,122,820	300,916	19,525,320	778	649	-129
Kansas	174,019	250,171	67,046	4,328,639	247	144	-103
Pennsylvania	704,091	976,730	261,764	18,319,174	661	564	-97
North Carolina	577,544	739,391	198,157	13,964,846	521	427	-94
Nebraska	149,477	220,442	59,078	3,758,920	217	127	-90
Arkansas	124,882	154,898	41,513	3,075,352	178	89	-89
Florida	1,198,046	1,628,051	436,318	31,641,348	1,027	940	-87
Maine	74,466	96,846	25,955	1,984,278	141	56	-85
South Carolina	329,419	439,909	117,896	8,368,482	339	254	-85

Source: National Golf Foundation Facility Database

Iowa leads the nation in 9-hole facilities. Michigan (778 courses), considering its limited playing season of less than 200 playable days, has long been branded as a summer tourist destination and regarded as an anomaly, with the fourth most golf courses in the country, after Florida (1,027), California (901), and New York (801).

Then why would so many courses have been built in Michigan? Interestingly, golf in the summer is viewed as an alternative to ice hockey in the winter.

These numbers serve as interesting fodder for thought and beg the question of whether the analysis can be extended to individual core-based statistical areas or counties.

In examining the demand for golf by core statistical area, the numbers do appear highly consistent, as reflected in the table shown here.

Area Name	Golfers Current Year	Rounds Demanded (Golfer Based)	Number of Facilities	Facilities Suggested Based on 1,732 Golfers/18	Under/Over Supplied
New York-Newark-Jersey City, NY-NJ-PA Metro SA	1,354,087	23,477,170	448	782	334
Los Angeles-Long Beach-Anaheim, CA Metro SA	764,789	11,486,055	159	442	283
Chicago-Naperville-Elgin, IL-IN-WI Metro SA	945,266	14,751,214	333	546	213
Houston-The Woodlands-Sugar Land, TX Metro SA	402,240	6,672,573	120	232	112
Dallas-Fort Worth-Arlington, TX Metro SA	449,544	7,491,689	159	260	101
Detroit-Warren-Dearborn, MI Metro SA	496,107	8,514,321	186	286	100
San Francisco-Oakland-Hayward, CA Metro SA	309,231	5,275,908	79	179	100
Seattle-Tacoma-Bellevue, WA Metro SA	316,285	4,777,551	85	183	98
Washington-Arlington-Alexandria, DC-VA-MD-WV Metro SA	421,248	6,975,607	150	243	93
Philadelphia-Camden-Wilmington, PA-NJ-DE-MD Metro SA	470,275	8,149,722	190	272	82

Source: National Golf Foundation Facility Database

©2016, JJ Keegan+

The top golf courses located with the CBSA achieve 51,111 rounds which far exceeds the national average of 30,636. Interestingly, there are 40.9 million rounds played on 2,207 golf courses averaging 18,529 rounds per facility that are not within core statistical-based areas in the United States.

Where demand for golf with the CBSA is weak is shown in the table here.

Area Name	Golfers Current Year	Rounds Demanded (Golfer Based)	Number of Facilities	Facilities Suggested Based on 1,732 Golfers/18	Under/Over Supplied
Myrtle Beach-Conway-North Myrtle Beach, SC-NC Metro SA	44,055	2,066,397	81	25	-56
Naples-Immokalee-Marco Island, FL Metro SA	34,178	1,153,368	70	20	-50
Cape Coral-Fort Myers, FL Metro SA	61,808	1,936,682	78	36	-42
Pittsburgh, PA Metro SA	182,256	3,838,714	143	105	-38
Hilton Head Island-Bluffton-Beaufort, SC Metro SA	26,934	964,272	52	16	-36
Port St. Lucie, FL Metro SA	39,465	1,085,220	57	23	-34
Syracuse, NY Metro SA	57,048	1,177,650	63	33	-30
North Port-Sarasota-Bradenton, FL Metro SA	71,278	2,108,201	67	41	-26
Rochester, NY Metro SA	85,979	1,772,813	75	50	-25
Utica-Rome, NY Metro SA	25,302	618,432	39	15	-24

Source: National Golf Foundation Facility Database

©2016, JJ Keegan+

Five of the first six markets (Myrtle Beach, Naples, Cape Coral, Hilton Head, and Port St. Lucie have one thing in common—they are popular tourist destinations in the United States that are dependent on the influx of golfers beyond their local area to ensure economically viability.

The real key is understanding within your local market the amount spent by residents on golfer per 18 holes and person. The following, based on the 918 core-based statistical areas, are the strongest markets for golf based on spending.

But even owning a golf course in a leading CBSA is insufficient to ensure financial success at your facility.

Area Name	Golfers	Number of Facilities	Golf Retail Spend	Green Fee Spend	Total Spending	Resident Spending Per 18	Per Person Spending on Golf
Vineland-Bridgeton, NJ Metro SA	7,907	1	1,649,760	7,051,703	8,701,463	8,701,463	1,100
Los Angeles-Long Beach-Anaheim, CA Metro SA	764,789	159	220,109,361	769,862,670	989,972,031	6,226,239	1,294
San Francisco-Oakland-Hayward, CA Metro SA	309,231	79	94,459,529	369,591,339	464,050,868	5,874,062	1,501
San Jose-Sunnyvale-Santa Clara, CA Metro SA	139,591	36	43,803,931	158,266,163	202,070,094	5,613,058	1,448
Washington-Arlington-Alexandria, DC-VA-MD-WV Metro SA	421,248	150	150,374,072	586,297,016	736,671,088	4,911,141	1,749
Anchorage, AK Metro SA	23,084	8	7,137,858	28,815,625	35,953,483	4,494,185	1,558
Seattle-Tacoma-Bellevue, WA Metro SA	316,285	85	92,664,040	305,069,937	397,733,977	4,679,223	1,258
Baltimore-Columbia-Towson, MD Metro SA	143,173	65	55,418,186	231,695,490	287,113,676	4,417,133	2,005
Vallejo-Fairfield, CA Metro SA	30,058	9	7,392,367	30,504,736	37,897,103	4,210,789	1,261

Source: National Golf Foundation Facility Database

To illustrate, Baltimore-Columbia-Towson area is ranked as the 8th best statistical area to own a golf course, reflected by the resident spending per 18 holes of $4,417,133 and the per person spending of $2,005. But is it a location where all golf courses prosper? Hardly. For The City of Baltimore's five golf courses, Pine Ridge generates more than $750,000 cash flow supporting the other four courses that lose significantly.

Pinpointing the Ideal Location

How then does one determine the ideal location for a golf course that has the opportunity to maximize its investment potential?

There are a series of seven hurdles that a facility must overcome to be financially successful shown on the next page.

If the MOSAIC profile is a negative number, the golf course will inevitably lose money. If a golf course is located in a diverse ethnic neighborhood, it will face economic challenges. If the population is very young or very old and the income is low, only an entry-level golf course has the possibility of breaking even.

For a golf course to be financially successful it should be located in an area where the MOSAIC profile index exceeds 20%; there is a concentration of middle-aged, well-to-do Caucasians where there are more than 2,200 golfers per 18 holes. Only then can a course anticipate being able to receive greater than $75 on a golf course than has a slope rating exceeding 130.

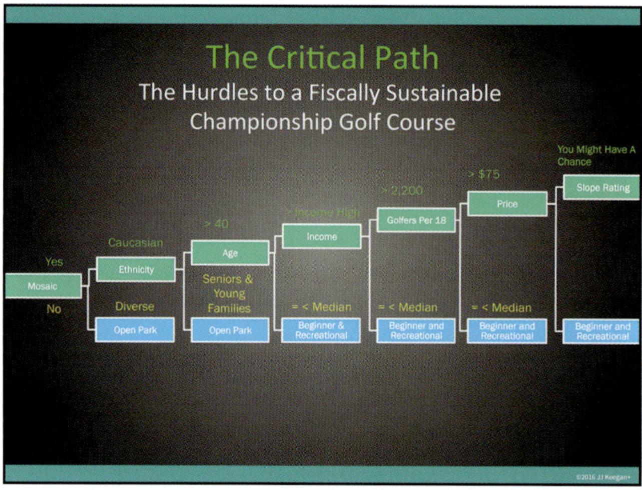

Sounds complicated, but this conclusion is based on extensive research we have conducted with leading golf managers confirming the theories presented.

Let's examine the hurdles.

What Do Starbucks and Golf Courses Have in Common? Far More Than You Think

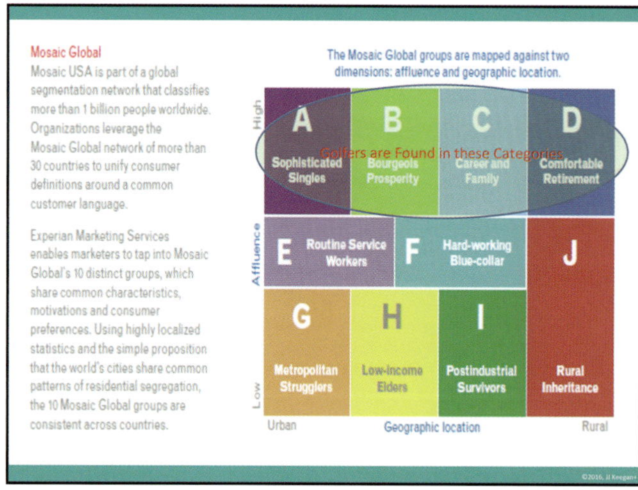

How do Nordstrom, Neiman Marcus, Outback, Starbucks, Four Seasons, Ritz Carlton, and every other department store, restaurant, and hotel chain determine the locations for their businesses? They evaluate demographics.

To determine the location of their retail locations, they use the MOSAIC™ lifestyle database, as illustrated by the table shown here.

The objective of this typology is:

- To classify neighborhoods in a way that provides the most powerful description of consumers' behavior, lifestyles, and attitudes.

- To identify lifestyle groups that are as recognizable and meaningful as possible to marketers.
- To ensure that each of the named groups contain sufficient numbers of households to be statistically reliable for most analysis.
- To ensure that each cluster is homogeneous regarding demographics and consumer behavior.
- To avoid an excessive concentration of individual U.S. MOSAIC types within particular geographic regions, except where appropriate."[1]

Golf courses that are located where there is a heavy concentration of lifestyle groups classified as "Sophisticated Single, Bourgeois Prosperity, Career and Family, and Comfortable Retirement" are likely to outperform those golf courses located in the areas classified as routine service workers, hard-working, blue-collar, metropolitan strugglers, low-income elders, or post-industrial survivors.

Every golf course is unique, and every market is local. Thus, to determine the financial potential of any golf course, it is essential that you understand the demand and supply details of the market starting with the MOSAIC profile. An example is shown here.

	Crystal Mountain Resort, MI	Don Vellmer, FSU	Oak Creek, Irvine, CA	Mussatto, Maccomb, IL	Pine Meadow, Mundelein, IL	Cedar Creek – San Antonio
	10 Miles	10 Miles	5 Miles	10 Miles	10 Miles	5 Miles
Top 4 Rating	−17.00%	−7.90%	40.30%	−22.10%	37.60%	31.90%
Sophisticated Singles	−2.90%	1.00%	12.90%	−2.60%	5.10%	3.20%
Bourgeois Prosperity	−6.50%	−1.30%	13.50%	−10.60%	21.50%	12.80%
Career and Family	−12.70%	−3.90%	19.80%	−9.50%	12.70%	21.30%
Comfortable Retirement	5.10%	−3.70%	−5.90%	0.60%	−1.70%	−5.40%
Routine Service Workers	−14.90%	−6.50%	−6.00%	−14.00%	0.10%	3.80%
Hard-Working Blue Collar	−3.80%	−5.40%	−10.40%	0.40%	−9.50%	−9.10%
Metropolitan Strugglers	−16.20%	26.10%	−9.70%	19.60%	−13.50%	−9.50%
Low-Income Elders	−1.40%	−1.80%	0.20%	1.50%	−0.90%	−3.00%
Post Industrial Survivors	17.50%	1.20%	−7.10%	3.60%	−6.50%	−6.70%
Rural Inheritance	35.70%	−5.80%	−7.40%	10.80%	−7.40%	−7.40%

Crystal Mountain, a fabulous resort course, 30 miles outside of Traverse City, MI is dependent upon the influx of tourists from Chicago and Detroit. Oak Creek, located at the Intersection of the 5 and the 405 in Irvine, California, is magnificently positioned to do well, as is Pine Meadow in Mundelein and Cedar Creek in San Antonio.

But the MOSAIC profile is only the first hurdle that one must overcome.

1 http://spatialinsights.com/catalog/product.aspx?product=80&content=1386

The Magic Brew

Blending the demographic factors within the competitive market defines the potential of a golf course. Shown here is this exercise from the Clemson University Strategic Planning pilot study that confirmed the potential (Irvine, CA) and the challenges that some (Chelan, WA, Macomb, IL) face from uncontrollable factors.

It is the mix of the MOSIAC profile, with the age, income, ethnicity, the demand measured by golfers per 18 holes and melded against the slope rating that forecasts that financial potential of 80% of the nation's golf courses.

Location	Miles	MOSAIC #	Age	Income	Hispanic	African American	Asian - American	Golfers Per 18	Slope Rating
Brooklyn Park, MN	10	0.90%	36	$63,595	5.50%	12.40%	7.30%	4,129	141
Charlotte, NC	5	-6.00%	34	$49,410	17.10%	32.30%	4.20%	3,843	120
Chelan, WA	10	-11.30%	41	$46,900	37.70%	3.40%	6.00%	398	119
Columbus, OH	5	-0.30%	33	$41,655	5.70%	30.00%	4.20%	8,584	125
Irvine, CA	5	40.30%	36	$90,186	14.30%	1.90%	32.70%	3,848	133
Irvine, CA	10	19.10%	36	$80,752	36.60%	1.60%	15.90%	3,680	133
Macomb, IL	10	-22.10%	28	$31,694	2.90%	6.20%	2.20%	742	133
Mundelin, IL	10	37.60%	40	$87,833	13.70%	2.90%	9.20%	1,524	138
San Antonio, TX	5	31.90%	31	$76,890	41.50%	6.50%	6.50%	2,298	131
Sarasota, FL	10	7.50%	49	$50,434	13.80%	7.30%	1.70%	2,350	117
Tallahassee, FL	10	-7.90%	29	$39,789	6.40%	35.00%	2.90%	3,261	131

It is our hypothesis, which is being tested under continuing research, that there is an ideal type of golf course for each community based on demographics. Preliminarily we believe the following correlation exists between the demographics within a 10-mile radius of the facility and the course's slope rating.

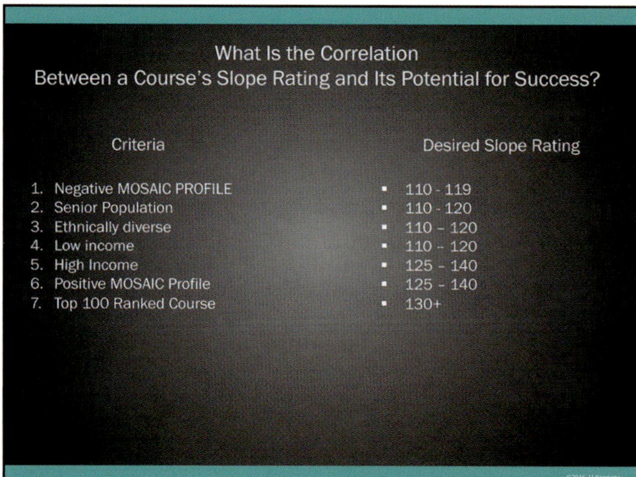

Understanding the unique market in which a golf course operates (the underlying demographics of its customers) is fundamental to maximizing its financial potential.

To guide golf courses to ensure that they can be financially successful, we at JJ Keegan+ developed in March 2016 the Predictive Score Index™, in which we made over 2 million calculations regarding the 15,204 golf courses considering the following criteria:

Facility	Demographics	Demand	Supply
Course ID	Population	Golfing Households	Total Facilities
Course Name	Total Population +18	Golfers (Reported)	Public Facilities
Address	Households	Rounds Played	Private Facilities
Zip	Age (Median)	Estimated Course Rounds - Market Supply	Premium >$71
State	Income (Med Hhld)	Golf Participation	Value $40-$70
Type	Income (Average Hhld)	Fee Spend (Facility Based)	Price <$40
Year Open	Ethnicity (% Cauc.)	Golf Retail Spend (Golfer Based)	Number of Holes - Total Facilities
Holes	Ethnicity (Hispanic)		Number of Holes - Public Facilities
Clubhouse Square Footage	Ethnicity (African American)		Number of Holes - Private Facilities
Fee – Weekend	Ethnicity (Asian American)		Number of Holes - Non Regulation (9 hole and Par 3s)
Fee - Weekday	Sophisticated Singles		
	Bourgeois Prosperity		
	Career and Family		
	Comfortable Retirement		
	Routine Service Workers		
	Hard Working Blue Collar		
	Metropolitan Strugglers		
	Low Income Elders		
	Post Industrial Survivors		
	Rural Inheritance		

This research facilitated our ability to rank order each golf course in the United States by their profit potential. Golf course managers can now immediately learn online at http://jjkeegan.golf the following:

1. **The Annual Potential Revenue at Your Golf Course**. Within 10 miles of each golf course, we evaluated the MOSAIC profile, age, ethnicity, income, the number of golfers per 18 holes in the competitive market, the prime time green fee rate, and the slope rating. With fused that data with the annual spending by golfers in the market.
2. **The Optimum Green Fee.** Understanding each customer's common characteristics, motivations, and consumer preferences, we interspersed that data amongst six yardsticks to calculate the correct rate in which the experience a facility offers exceeds or equals the tariff assessed. The slope rating, strategy, course conditions, types of grasses, facility's ambiance, and amenities provided are the six key ingredients.

Controlling the Uncontrollable

The last uncontrollable factor to be examined is the dramatic impact of weather on a golf operation. Mother Nature is fickle—she gives, and she takes. Hot, cold, snow, blizzards, avalanches, rain, sleet, thunderstorms, lightning, hurricanes, tornadoes, drought, wind—who knew weather came in so many flavors?

The analysis of the impact of weather is the **second step in the JJ Keegan+ WIN™ formula**.

How much would you pay to control the weather? If you only knew:

- How many employees will I need to schedule?
- How many golf playable days will my course have in the next 14 days?
- Will Mother Nature take care of my course watering needs?
- Will the weather be okay for the upcoming tournaments and outings?
- Do we need a back-up plan for the scheduled outdoor wedding next month?
- When should I choose to run promotions?

Trying to efficiently operate a business that is outdoors can be exasperating. Rain minimizes water costs, but sunny skies and warm days boost business. The weather has a material impact on the financial performance of a golf course. The power of just a one-degree difference in temperature or one inch of rain can significantly influence the golf course. Did you realize the following effects of weather change?

- 1° hotter = +1.3% beer or soft drink sales
- 1° hotter = +10% increase in sun care products sales
- 1° hotter = +24% increase in air conditioner sales
- 1° colder = +9% increase in women's outerwear sales
- 1° colder = 1.4% increase in coffee consumption

Fortune 100 companies in 23 countries believe in the power of weather changes and of forecasting those changes. They utilize Weather Trends International to help them generate a return on investments from $10 million to $230 million annually.

Weather Trends' clients include 3M, Ben & Jerry's, Black & Decker, Coca-Cola, Hershey's, J&J, Target, and Walmart. All of these companies utilize Weather Trends International's on-demand mapping, 20-year trend, custom alerts, sales and market planning, analytics, and forecasting to help them better understand how weather influences their sales. This information allows them to plan product manufacturing and shipment accordingly. Should snow blowers be available in Colorado in late September or early November? Should spring flowers be available for purchase in March, April, or May?

But, as you read this, if you are like most, you have grave doubts about the ability of any company to engage in accurate long-range weather forecasting.

So did the National Golf Foundation. In 2013, the National Golf Foundation put Weather Trends International to the test and had the company forecast eight months for the St. Louis. The results are as follows:

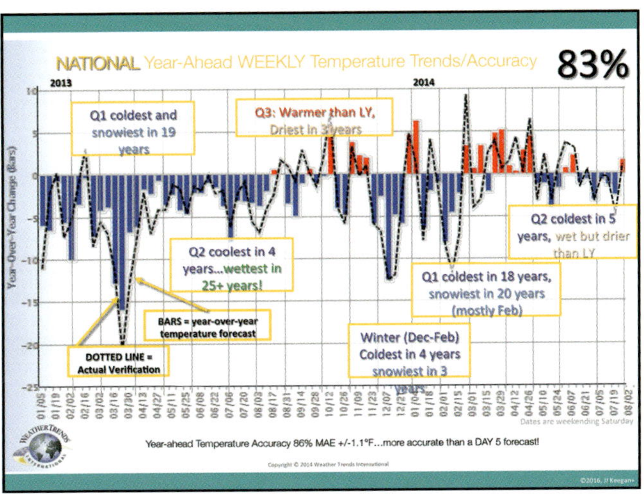

The blue and red lines represented their forecast. The jagged black lines represent actual. Amazingly accurate, especially considering that once the forecast was made, 11 months in advance, it was not changed.

How did they do it? Using proprietary algorithms and millions of lines of code to generate forecasts, Weather Trends provides 1- to 14-day and 3-, 6-, 9-, and 11-month global weather forecasts by Geo market or ZIP Code.

Because we live day-to-day, we develop an extremely short-term focus and lose sight of long-term trends. Weather varies by locale greatly each year as reflected here:

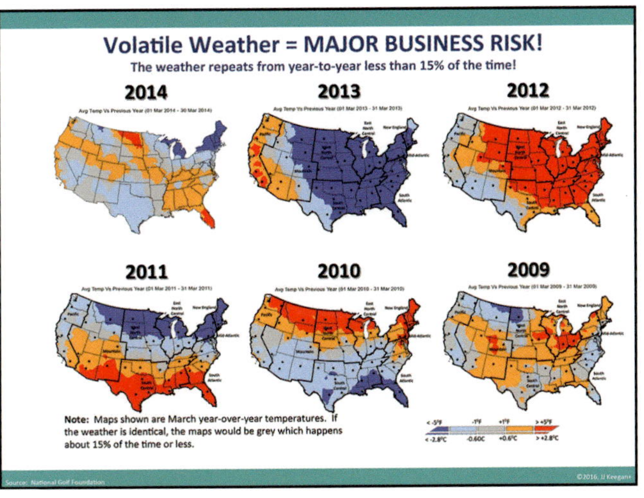

Weather repeats itself on an annual basis less than 15% of the time. What relevance does this information have for the golf course industry? Enormous.

Reports and Tools That Predict Future Operating Results

Weather Trends International has crafted a set of tools specifically for the golf industry that includes the historical reports shown in the following figure.

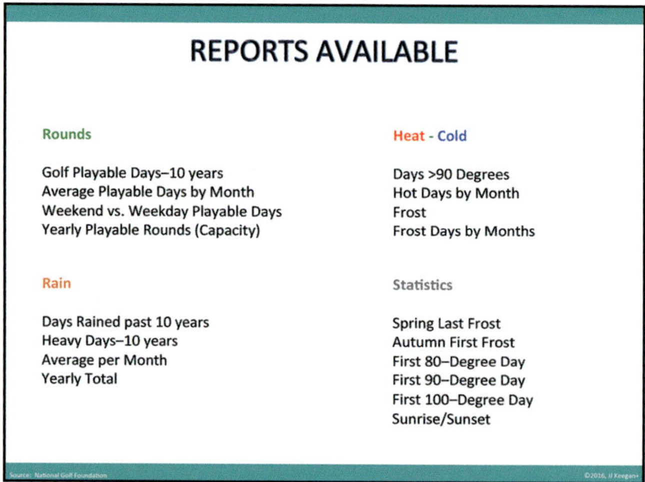

While historical data are always interesting, Weather Trends facilitates the ability to do the following:

1. Determine if management is under- or outperforming the weather.
2. Provide for efficient scheduling of events and staff.
3. Ensure optimum conservation of water resources.

Is Management Outperforming the Weather?

To ascertain management performance against the weather, a few data points are necessary.

First, determining the number of playable golf days at the facility throughout the past several years (preferably a decade).

- **A Golf Playable Days (GPD)** is defined as a day (sunrise to sunset) when the maximum heat index is above 45 degrees Fahrenheit and below 95 degrees, and there is less than 0.20 inches of rainfall.

- The **heat index** (HI) is an index that combines air temperature and relative humidity in an attempt to determine the human-perceived equivalent temperature—how hot it feels.

- **Total Possible Golf Playable Hours** is defined as the normal maximum number of possible golf playable hours between (sunrise to sunset) when the normal maximum heat index (a combination of temperature and humidity) is below 95 and above 45, and there are less than 0.20 inches of rainfall.

While one may debate the precision of these definitions, consistently applied, they are more appropriate than academic. With this information, the average revenue per playable day can be calculated and results measured over several years to evaluate management efficiency in managing weather.

We conducted at JJ Keegan+ a survey to determine how many golf courses tracked playable days. While 68% indicated that they did track playable days, how that day was measured varied widely. Answers ranged from "above 40 degrees," "above 50 degrees," and "above 60 degrees," to "any rounds played, April 1 to November 30, regardless of weather," "course is open," "weather permitting," "75% of tee sheet filled," "no frost or rain," and "no severe weather." It is some what amusing how unscientific were the criteria used by those courses that tracked playable days.

Examples of playable golf days, based on the more formal definition, are as follows:

Snapshot Across America

City	Days
Ann Arbor	183
Chicago	199
Denver	262
Flagstaff	258
Ocala	301
Sedona	313
St. Paul	184
Virginia Beach	236
Washington, D.C.	231
Winnipeg	167

Forecasting The Unknown

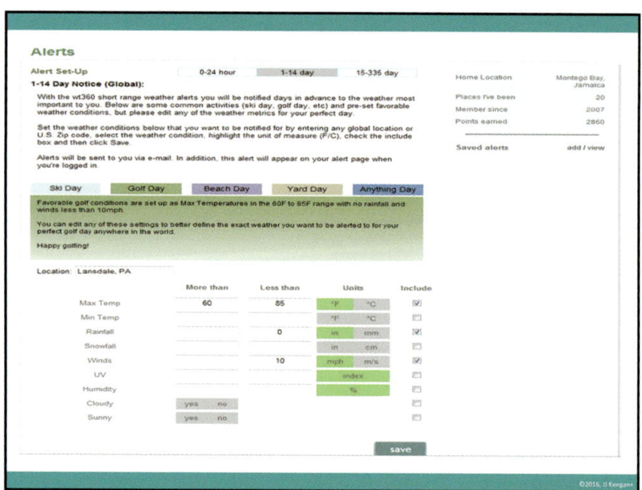

What makes the understanding of historical and weather forecasting essential is that the cost of these services can range from complimentary (for the basic weather alert service) to $2,500 annually per facility (for a comprehensive set of historical analysis and forecasting tools). This seems a nominal expense considering the potential of having some control over the effects of weather at your golf course.

The complimentary tool, shown here, allows you to set automatic alerts based on maximum and minimum temperatures, rainfall, snowfalls, winds, etc. You then choose the weather events desired and the notice time frame you want, save the template, and beginning saving money.

For those individuals seeking a more comprehensive weather forecast, Weather Trends International provides a custom forecast, encompassing from a week to an entire golf season, as illustrated here.

This forecast projects that Dallas and Denver are going to have far more rain during the summer of 2016 than the prior year. The winter in Chicago, Dallas, Denver, Miami, and New York will all arrive early and much colder than last year. Brr!

So if you had confidence that long-range weather forecasting was accurate, and you knew the forecast for 2017, how would you change your current plans? Here are a few ideas:

Key:
Dark Blue: much colder: <= 5 degrees colder
Light Blue: slightly colder: –1 to 5 degrees colder
Dark Green: <= 200% greater precipitation
Grey: similar as last year

1. Knowing season start timing on a by-city basis will improve revenue forecasting and enhance the strategic planning process.
2. Production profiles for clubs, balls, apparel, and other golf-related merchandise could be adjusted to better manage a possible overstock scenario and soften the need for dramatic markdowns.
3. Inventory allocation could be adjusted to place the most product in areas of the country with the most favorable weather.
4. Caution could be exercised in offering off-season rates in the spring, thinking that the revenue can be made up in the summer.
5. Outings and events could be scheduled for days on which the probability of rain is low.
6. Advertisements in local media could be placed for weekends during which weather is to be favorable.
7. If a superintendent knew that in 48 hours it was going to rain 1¼ inches, using 400,000 gallons of water on the golf course could be avoided, saving as much as $600 in water expenses.
8. A superintendent could defer a fertilizer application costing upwards of $10,000 with the knowledge that it would likely be washed away by heavy rains.

Arcis Golf and Century Golf, management companies, take weather forecasting seriously. They monitor budgeted playable rounds and the anticipated revenue per round. Based on the weather forecast thirty days in advance, they advise their clients as to the potential impact of forthcoming weather on the annual revenue goals. Very astute and very smart.

Key Points to Remember

1) Those in the industry maintain the golf industry is oversupplied and that their woes are principally related to this uncontrollable factor and the weather. As a general statement, the golf industry has more courses than needed. But the opportunity for each golf course is defined by the local market.
2) If a course is located in one of the Top 100 core-based statistical areas, demand may exceed supply, suggesting that holding firm on prices, if they match the experience, is appropriate.
3) It is vital to understand the following for your market: MOSAIC profile, age, income, ethnicity, and number of golfers per 18 holes with a 30-minute drive time. Those demographics define the price threshold that a course can achieve based on demand.
4) The slope rating of the golf course should be consistent with the demographics in the defined trade market.
5) While the weather is uncontrollable, it is absolutely manageable. By using the historical and forecasting services provided by Weather Trends International, an astute operator can make financial numbers dance by improving revenue through scheduling events wisely to reduce labor and water expenses. Go to www.w360.com and sign up for the complimentary basic weather alert service.

Concluding Thoughts

What gets us into trouble is not what we don't know; it's what we know for sure that just ain't so.

Mark Twain

We don't see the world as it is. We see it as we are.

Anaïs Nin

Chapter 6

Strategic Planning Summary

The Conclusion of Why

The greater danger for most of us lies not in setting our aim too high and falling short, but in setting our aim too low, and achieving our mark.

Michelangelo Buonarroti

Chapter Highlights

The first section of this book, concluding with this chapter, has focused on the uncontrollable factors that influence the business of golf. In essence, we have focused on the hand a golf course is dealt.

At its core, all golf is local, and all solutions are local. While each golf course has a unique personality, the business model to ensure a successful golf course is consistent. Thus, the vital need exists to create a strategic plan that precisely defines the vision, the opportunity, and the client base. The final step is creating vision and mission statements. Examples are provided from both municipal and private golf clubs.

This chapter highlights the fact that golfers are consumers who are attracted to and become loyal to facilities that create an emotional connection with them. It is not only about the golf but also about the experience enjoyed.

The Question of "Why?"

The beauty of the game of golf is that every golf course is unique. No two of the over 34,000 facilities are identical. Even if you play the same golf course hundreds of times, each round will offer different tee marker locations, pin positions, weather conditions, and playing companions. No two rounds of golf are identical.

What attracts a golfer to play one course versus another, particularly the same one multiple times? The simple answer is location. But that leads us down a false trail, for within most locales, particularly in the United States, you have many courses and clubs to choose from.

We believe, and have confirmed through multiple consumer surveys, that golfers or members subconsciously select where to play or join a club based on their value systems and self-image. Would a star professional athlete play on a regular basis a local municipal golf course where getting a tee time is difficult, and he or she would have to mingle with the masses while waiting to tee off? Not likely. His time is too precious, or her desire for privacy would prevail. Would a blue-collar worker, with no savings or financial resources, join an exclusive private club? Not likely. A probable lack of financial resources and the discomfort of not being in a familiar social network probably would make that golfer feel uncomfortable.

In essence, individuals buy what they can afford based on the experience they seek.

The golf course owner, the management team, and the board of directors craft that experience within the expressed vision, tradition, history, and governance of the facility. They define the brand promise, and that leads to who is likely to be attracted to and motivated to play that course or become a member of that club.

Successful facilities are exceptional at defining their vision and brand promise. As you walk into the Karsten Creek Golf Course in Stillwater, Oklahoma, the brand of that facility is clearly expressed. The plethora of trophies won by the Oklahoma State University golf team in NCAA competition adorns the walls. It is an impressive display of competitive success, and the golf course is consistent with that theme, as it is a true test of the game.

The brand promise at Cherry Hills Country Club, in Colorado, is also clearly communicated as you enter the clubhouse, as shown.

The history of the club, with its many national championships, is prominently displayed in a "museum" that the USGA helped construct.

It is that message that enables Cherry Hills to levy a significant non-refundable initiation fee while maintaining a long formal waiting list. That message has also facilitated the club's ability to undertake respectable capital assessments in the past several years.

Down the street from Cherry Hills is the Wellshire Golf Course, another 18-hole course. It is one of three Donald Ross golf courses within the state of Colorado (the famed Broadmoor resort and Lakewood Country Club are the other two). Ben Hogan won the Denver Open at the Wellshire in 1948. But that course is only able to eke out $42 per 18 holes of play.

Why such a large difference between the $150 guest fee at Cherry Hills and this municipal course operated by the city and county of Denver? Because the value offered is that significantly different.

At the Wellshire, the stately clubhouse is in disrepair. While a snack bar exists, the main dining areas are operated by a concessionaire, and only for catered events. The range is a lake with floating golf balls secured by a dam that leaks, necessitating the creation of a pond in the landing area on the 10th hole. And the course, despite its $700,000 budget, is poorly maintained. Dead trees and limbs abounded for years. The living trees encroach on the playing corridors. Where square greens and chocolate drops existed, round greens are now present. Double greens with centering bunkers joining the 4th and 13th holes appeared in 1926, but now there are two greens separated by rough. Although the course is profitable due to its prime location in Denver, it is substantially underperforming. The potential of the course is enormous if only city officials cared.

Though these two courses are only one mile apart, they are light-years away from presenting golfers or members the same experience. These examples demonstrate the importance of a well-developed strategic plan.

Without a defined strategic vision effective tactical plans cannot be developed. Without tactical plans, efficient operational execution cannot occur.

The result of this lack of strategic planning is highly predictable—policies, procedures, and practices become based on the ever-changing whims of the owner, management, staff, or upon the influences created by golfers. Management and staff, as best they might, will only respond to the latest self-imposed crisis or artificially defined priority.

As the saying goes, "Vision without action is a daydream. Action without vision is a nightmare." Either way, chaos ensues. Considering that 90% of golf courses operate without a strategic plan, perhaps the challenges the industry faces are self-imposed and emphasize why creating a strategic plan is so important.

Because we make decisions based on what we think we know the facts to be, the discipline of creating and writing a strategic plan, while tedious and often frustrating, produces riches regarding consistency and attainment of the goals established.

Vision and Mission Statements

The centerpieces of a strategic plan are the vision and mission statements that guide all decisions regarding the operation of the facility. Both of these serve different purposes for a company but are often confused with each other.

The Vision Statement focuses on the future; it is a source of inspiration and motivation. Often it describes not just the future of the organization but the future of the industry or society in which the organization hopes to effect change. An example of a vision statement for a municipal golf course is depicted on the next page.

The strength of the vision statement, which is about ideals and not the current environment, is that the golf course knows what it represents and, just as importantly, what it does not. By defining its vision, the club can align its infrastructure, facilities, and labor resources to match the service ideals envisioned.

Thus, in crafting a strategic plan, a broad vision of the bold initiatives that must first be established is emphasized; this gains the upper hand over a more chaotic management style involving an intense, meticulous focus on details that overwhelm and become difficult to execute consistently.

The Park District's Vision Statement

We will provide, in a responsible fiscal manner, as a recreational component of our leisure programs, golf consistent with the standards of the leading municipalities with respect to green fees, maintenance, and administrative operations in order that we maximize revenue, increase operational efficiency, and ensure optimum customer service as prudent stewards of a government-owned asset.

Many golfers have unreal expectations. There is always a challenge of meeting a customer's needs with champagne tastes and a beer budget. We have participated in many meetings with golfers, who left to their druthers would create a vision statement like the following:

The Golfer's Vision Statement
This Is A Joke ☺

Living in a very wealthy, well-to-so suburb of Chicago, we are accustom to enjoying the finest life offers. Therefore, we expect to be provided superior municipal golf courses with spectacular clubhouses providing excellent food/ beverage/banquet facilities and a diverse array of merchandise at highly discounted rates as compensation for the taxes we pay. Our courses will be perceived as the best among neighboring districts. The losses incurred should merely be considered part of our tax dollars, as the libraries, pools, and other parks activities are supported comparably.

The connection between vision and operation is captured with the facility's mission statement that includes not only the facility's vision and purpose but also the basic services that the club provides. The Mission Statement concentrates on the present; it defines the customers, critical processes and it informs you about the desired level of performance.

Once created, the club's mission statement should be used everywhere to communicate and reinforce the vision and to remind the golf course community—owners, management, staff, members or golfers, and vendors—why the facility exists. The vision and mission statements might be viewed as the "Why" as defined by Simon Sinek that motivates and binds the customer's loyalty.

One of the most efficient ways is to communicate the mission statement is on the website as shown here.

This statement has many compelling adjectives to attract a golfer: "serenity," "moments from the tranquil Atlantic Ocean," and a "haven from the daily grind of life."

The Private Club Mission Statement

Blending the rich history of Chinese culture, (Name Withheld) Golf Club will embrace international operating philosophies and provide members and their guests an exclusive haven to participate in an experience comparable to the most prestigious clubs in the world. Members are responsible to support the club and respect the staff, while five-star diamond service will be the cornerstone of the club operation.

This "WHY" statement transcends cultures and nations. Thus, an appropriate mission statement for an Asian private club is shown here.

From this statement, the facility clearly focuses on:

- Exclusive
- Finest array of recreation and leisure centered on golf
- Respectful, unparalleled service
- Focused differentiation

This statement defines for the member the experience to be expected and received.

While the purist academician might debate that the mission statement and its brand are different, such is idle fodder. It is essential to realize that every golf course is unique and conveying its differences are vital.

How then do you differentiate one's facility from the competitive set in the local market?

Defining the Unique Vision

The reasons that people play golf are incredibly varied.

The young are excited to discover a new sport, learn discipline, and respect the core values of a game. For family and friends, golf provides a way to deepen relationships and experience leisure in a time-fractured world. As to sportsmanship, golf provides a forum for competition and athletic prowess, and for some, it brings great riches and international fame. For business people and women, golf gives an opportunity (beyond webinars, e-mails, and teleconferences) to pierce the formal rigors and the impersonal nature that are business and connect with co-workers and customers, demonstrating that each cares about the other beyond what may be perceived in the work environment. For the senior citizen, a golf course represents the office where a seasoned golfer can regale his or her buddies with tales of days gone by and his or her many accomplishments. For the golf course residential homeowner, the course is a beautiful backyard. For the wealthy, it is a place to celebrate their lineage and their fortunes, as well as the fact that they have escaped, either through inheritance or hard work, the financial bullets of life.

Each group has a different set of needs, wants, and desires. Thus, how a golf course creates and consistently delivers an emotionally compelling experience to match those needs, wants, and desires will determine its financial results.

Creating the Compelling Emotional Experience

How is that emotional experience delineated and conveyed to attract customers? What is clear is that every facility has its unique personality.

Golf is about enjoying nature and people in a leisurely environment.

Golf courses are successful not only by what they offer but by how they make people feel about themselves; golf meets the psychological and physical needs of many.

For the golfer, the ability to hit the risk-reward shot to get on the 16th hole at Bandon Dunes or to attempt to reach the par 5, 18th hole at Pebble Beach is all about the experience. You seek to play St. Andrews not because of the fabulous quality of the golf course but because of its history. Who doesn't want to pause on the Swilcan Bridge where so many great golfers have stood? For those who reach that pinnacle, it is not about the game but life's journey and escape from the rigors of the daily world.

The personality of a golf course is shown in many ways. One of the clearest ways to define the emotional experience is via the clubhouse, as illustrated in the picture shown here.

At the private Midland Country Club, Michigan, this 90,000-square foot facility supported largely by Dow Chemical is perhaps the clubhouse of the future—not defined by its size but its functionality. It features corporate conference rooms; offers golf, recreational, or social membership; and offers a fitness area and spa, aquatics, child care, and several dining alternatives including a sports bar.

Measuring the Gap Between Hope and Reality

A golf course's ability to create an appropriate emotional experience is a function of its cash flow plus the investment either in equity or debt. That is the trap for most golf courses and clubs. Very few can carry and amortize more than $1 million in debt. With the golf course being a living organism requiring an annual capital investment of more than $130,000 in funds allocated to reserves, and with a median earnings before interest, taxes, depreciation and amortization at golf courses in the United States of $223,138, the margin for error in operating a golf course is very slight. Hence the essential requirement that a facility knows its vision, its why for existing, and what it is not.

The value in golf derives from two basic components that all golf courses share: the physical infrastructure—property, plant, and equipment (the course, the clubhouse, and maintenance equipment) and the human element—the personnel. How these resources are applied determines the experience created.

How can the gap be measured between the vision and the actual performance? The investment return that the golf course generates from its assets can be measured and compared to industry peers as summarized in the chart shown here.

All Facility Types: What's Possible

958 Courses Participating	Platinum Top 10%	Gold Top 25%	Silver Median	Steel Bottom 25%
Rounds Played	42,171	31,200	22,000	15,342
Full Time Employees	52	25	11	6
Total Revenues	5,463,032	3,000,000	1,650,000	819,809
Member Fees and Dues	2,850,000	1,250,000	235,000	70,000
Green Fees	1,161,194	596,313	275,000	137,000
Cart Fees	390,798	277,068	177,308	100,884
Merchandise	410,000	252,000	145,000	74,252
Golf Shop Salaries	500,000	341,317	216,312	130,000
Maintenance Salaries	805,000	500,000	300,000	200,000
Maintenance Expenses	581,000	388,000	226,551	126,500
EBITDA	1,500,000	650,000	223,138	55,979

Source: 2014 PGA Performance Trak Annual Operating Survey Conducted in 2015.

We often forget that the ability of a golf course to create a customer experience is predicated on the assets available. While some personnel may be more creative or efficient, or better able to invest surplus time, on balance, the availability of capital to invest in assets or personnel largely influences the experience delivered.

Thus, to the extent the customers have the expectation of experiencing a "gold-level" course at one that generates only "steel-level" revenues, this gap will be problematic as operating losses are likely from providing superior value more than the price charged.

These guideposts are the foundation for the creation of a strategic plan. By providing a written document that defines the golf course's future direction, it becomes a beacon on which ownership, the golfers, and management and staff can align what the value proposition is for the facility.

When your staff is imbued with a vision, as are those who work at Bandon Dunes, Black Wolf Run, Pelican Hills, Robert Trent Jones Trail, and many other fine facilities, a superior experience consistent with the price charged results. And that experience doesn't have to be at a high-end private country club. It can be created at a municipal or daily fee golf course.

Where that vision is missing and where the passion of employees is at a low ebb or is completely absent, as is so often the case at municipal golf courses, the financial potential will not be reached.

The Formula

There is one formula that defines the success of every commercial enterprise.

Why would you pay $4 for a cup of coffee, whether at Starbucks or for my favorite scrumptious Mint Condition Mocha at Caribou? Certainly you wouldn't pay that for 16 ounces of flavored water.

You buy at Starbucks or Caribou for the ambiance. Starbucks today is like the bar on the old *Cheers* television series. It's the place to go, to be recognized by the barista who calls out, "Good morning, Skinny Vanilla Grande Cappuccino coming right up," before you even order. Starbucks is about asking the manager, Judy, about her two cats, two dogs, and four teenage girls or how Julie's last cardio session went as she prepares for the 10K Bolder Boulder in between the times she prepares coffees and fetches pastries.

People pay what they pay because the experience received, regarding its value, equals or exceeds the price paid. The formula is:

$$\text{Value} = \text{Experience} - \text{Price}$$

Where the experience exceeds or equals the price, the value is created and customer loyalty developed. Conversely, to the extent that the price exceeds the experience created, the value is squandered, and customer attrition occurs.

History, tradition, and culture are difficult to create. None of them can be created with capital investment alone. They must develop over time with the use of a meticulous set of standards that remain consistently implemented and often are very elusive. The best experience can only be created in the long-term through positive cash flow.

Thus, the importance of strategic planning.

Key Points to Remember

1) People don't buy WHAT you do; they buy WHY you do it. Do you know why you do what you do? When that is known, the route to achievement will be clear.
2) A golf course is a sanctuary that provides serenity and leisure in a world in which we are over-stimulated and bombarded with messages that seem meaningful but are meaningless. A golf course provides a respite for a brief moment of time, a respite that we sorely need to balance life's forces. Hence, whether it is played on a nine-hole chip-and-putt course or on a rigorous championship course, golf represents an oasis for those seeking an emotional experience.
3) Expectations of the customer must be measured against the assets available to create the experience desired.
4) Without a written plan that precisely states the vision, the resources to be allocated, and the operational execution that is to occur, the results achieved will be more by accident and luck than because of expertise.
5) Understand that all golf is local and that every solution is unique. Ascertaining the uniqueness that a facility possesses is perhaps the most difficult exercise it will undertake for the answer is intangible and very ethereal.

Concluding Thought

A wise man recognizes the convenience of a general statement, but he bows to the authority of a particular fact.

Ralph Waldo Emerson

I've missed more than 9000 shots in my career. I've lost almost 300 games. 26 times, I've been trusted to take the game winning shot and missed. I've failed over and over and over again in my life. And that is why I succeed.

Michael Jordan

SECTION 2

Tactical Planning Chapters 7 through 11

Tactical planning is considered the process of creating actionable goals, which will be accomplished from today up to three years into the future, that are aligned with the strategic vision. Thus, in Section 2, we are going to cover the following:

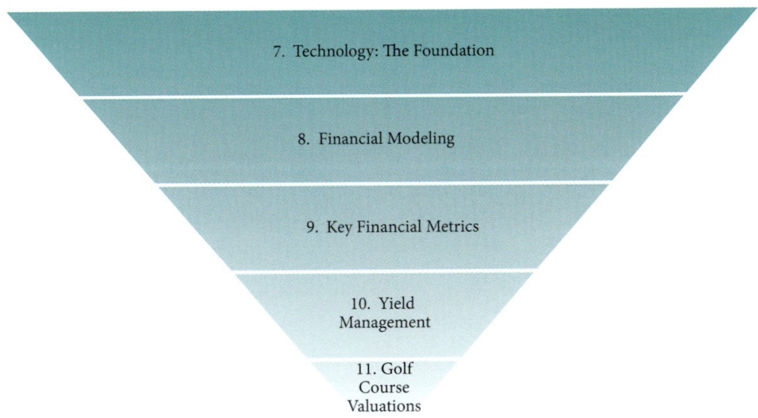

This entails an understanding of the components beyond daily golf operations that determine success: technology, key metrics, financial modeling, yield management principles, and proper golf course valuation. Embracing these concepts is essential for the investment return of a golf course to be realized.

Perfect markets do not exist in the world. Capitalism is simply the smart understanding of dislocations and taking advantage of the lazy who are unable or unwilling to search for the competitive advantages.

Unknown

Chapter 7

Technology—The Foundation

Step 3 of JJ Keegan+ WIN™ Formula

All that is gold does not glitter; not all those who wander are lost.

J.R.R. Tolkien

Chapter Highlights

Technology is the foundation for meaningful proactive management, and it is the first chapter on tactical planning.

The foundation of every successful golf course is a technology platform that seamlessly integrates the elements of all profit centers into a streamlined information and reporting system. It is ironic that one of the tools designed to create simplification, to provide meaningful insights, and to facilitate the ability to effectively manage a golf course becomes one of the most frustrating aspects. Such need not be the case.

This chapter presents a model of how to select technology. Interestingly, vendors often lack the willingness to foster the best business interests of their clients by refusing to integrate with other software applications.

Understanding the role of technology is important because software systems produce the numbers by which an adept manager can increase revenue and control expenses.

Core Fundamentals

How would a football, hockey, soccer, or basketball game be played if there were no goalposts or nets? Without goals, there is no game. The same applies for business; without a goal, there is no way to measure how effectively you are managing the business.

The financial statements of business are the instruments by which business is managed. As a plane is not flown without instruments, a business shall not be operated without precise guidelines as to financial goals. The technology implemented serves as the foundation for the creation of accurate financial statements and is the **third step in the JJ Keegan+ WIN™ process.**

The easiest way to create meaningful financial information is through the acquisition, implementation, annual training, and constant upgrade of a fully integrated golf management system.

Golf course owners can generate value from computers in many ways, including:

Objective	Result
Better Control	Uniform policies consistently applied. If the choice is to improve decision making at a staff level, a computer is a good answer.
Security	Monitor theft and control price changes.
Better Data Collection	From information comes the power to manage.
Accessibility	Access to data when you need it and wherever you are.
Customer Demographics	Increase customer market share.
Open to Buy	Optimize inventory turnover while minimizing cash investment.
Yield Management	Optimize revenue per tee time.

It is important to understand that technology is merely a tool whose investment return should be measured.

The Challenges Are Many

Geoffrey Moore, in his book *Crossing the Chasm*, classifies buyers and the pace at which they adopt new technology into five distinct groups:[1]

1 Geoffrey A. Moore, *"Crossing the Chasm"* (New York, Harper Business, 1999), p. 17.

Innovators, representing 2.5% of the population, are the first people to adopt any new technology, and are the first to appreciate the technology for its sake. Being technology enthusiasts, they want access to the most technically knowledgeable person; they want to get the new stuff first, in spite of the known inconveniences they are likely to suffer.

Early Adopters, representing 13.5% of the population, are the rare breed of people who have the insight to match an emerging technology to a strategic opportunity. The core of their dream is a business goal, not a technology goal. Visionaries are not just looking for improvement; they are looking for a fundamental breakthrough.

The Early Majority, representing 34% of the population, are the pragmatists seeking productivity improvements for their existing operations. They are change agents seeking to get a jump on the competition, whether from lower product costs, faster time to market, a complete customer service, or some other comparable business advantage.

The Late Majority, representing 34% of the population, are conservatives who are against discontinuous innovation. They seek tradition more than progress. Having a slight fear of high tech, the late majority tends to invest only at the end of a technology life cycle, when products are extremely mature, market-share competition has driven prices low, and the products themselves can be treated as commodities.

Laggards, representing 16% of the population, find committing to a new system is a much greater act of faith than they imagined. For a vendor, selling to this segment is a shaky venture at best.

It might be brutal but unfortunately accurate to reflect that within the golf course industry, these categories are more likely to be represented by 1% innovators, 5% early adopters, 20% early majority, 35% late majority, and 39% laggards. Golf course owners are slow to accept and adapt to change, particularly technology.

The complexity of business rules compounds this confusion. No two golf course facilities operate with the same set of procedures. Rate structures, access policies, and operating formats vary at each facility. Therefore, they each desire the software vendor to tailor the solution to conform to their existing business rules. Trying to develop and support all of the required software changes often proves too complex and expensive.

It is always amazing to me how a single golf course manager can dictate to a software vendor the necessity for extensive customization of a software package to conform to the business practices at that course, even though the vendor's software product has been successfully installed on more than 500 golf courses. Rather than using the best practices of their peers, managers in many cases refuse to change their habits, policies, and procedures when adopting an integrated system.

However, despite the benefits, which far outweigh the cost of an integrated system, the installation of the integrated system is always met with understandable resistance from the staff. Understanding social psychology can lessen the frustration knowing:

1. Individuals are already "at capacity" in a zero-sum game.
2. The volume of information available is paralyzing.
3. Humans value routine.
4. Despite the merit of innovation, most people will not readily adopt it if they have to change habits.
5. Staff who are intimidated by their lack of technical knowledge become aggressive and claim the software is flawed or lacks support.

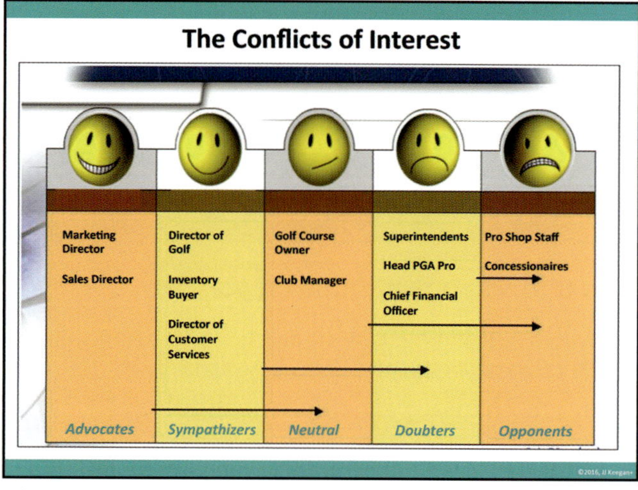

Within a golf course hierarchy, the advocates and opponents for implementing the system can usually be categorized according to their level of responsibility, depicted as follows:

As a result of this internal dissension as to what functionality is required and what vendor should be selected, many purchase decisions are made on the recommendations of friends, brand image of the vendor, or price.

It is my observed opinion, from watching the selection of software by golf courses for nearly three decades, that over 25% of the golf courses select the wrong vendor, despite what may appear to be extensive due diligence and investigation through the typical Request for Proposal process.

Rarely is the actual functionality of the software the real deciding factor. Often the decision makers can't accurately differentiate one software product from another. The look and feel seem to have a far greater weight in the decision than the actual capability of the product.

Why? Having multiple proposals by multiple presenters to multiple decision makers creates a process that often leads to wrong choices when golf courses choose software vendors.

Impeding Yourself While Being Impaled

Golf courses succumb to too many faulty practices. Because of their previous investment in legacy hardware and software, many golf course operators try to make the existing system work when the optimal solution is to start over.

Other challenges are frequently seen include:

1. A golf course has disparate technology from different vendors that aren't integrated. It could even be stated that of all of the golf facilities in the United States, perhaps as few as 15% have one vendor handling all of the information-processing requirements. From third-party tee time reservations, to tournament management, to handicapping, to food and beverage, to the banquet and catering, to property management systems, to e-mail marketing, to the creation and maintenance of a website, many vendors dominate a particular market segment.
2. Some management companies use multiple vendors for a diverse array of their courses.
3. A golf course uses only certain components of a comprehensive solution in an attempt to save money.
4. A golf course selects an integrated golf management system that does not uniquely and automatically create a customer access unique number. This is a fundamental requirement to tie a tee time reservation to a point of sale transaction for a specific customer. Lacking this integration, all transactions are dumped into a single omnibus account.

5. Golf course staff are not required to or don't capture salient customer information.

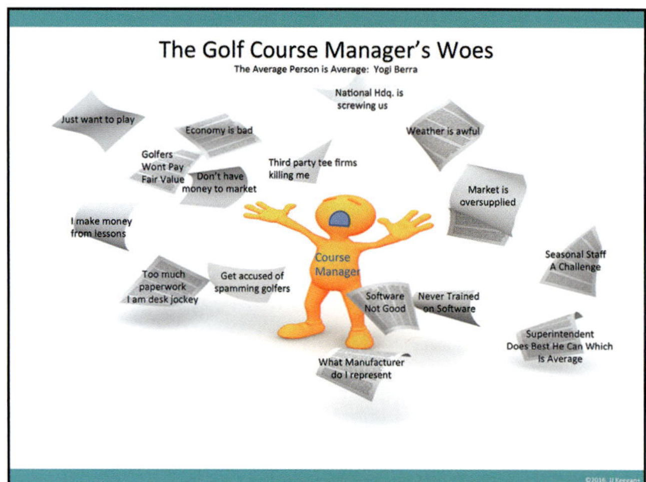

It is not unfair to describe the use of technology at a golf course as shown here.

The role of software vendors is to create the technology to provide information on which a golf course can operate efficiently to optimize the financial return on its capital investment.

Creating all the software tools that a golf course needs is a daunting task and isn't effectively achieved by any firm. Golf course owners are left with little options to license point of sale and tee time reservations, a food and beverage module, email marketing tools, website development and yield management from multiple vendors.

Some of the challenges facing golf courses are increased by their software vendor. Software companies, save for Golf Channel and Jonas, are small businesses with the net income providing a standard of living for the owner. Thus, self-preservation at the expense of a golf course owner's interest can be a dominant theme.

Many vendors lack the ability, and in some cases are outright unwilling, to work with other service providers to create the integration tools necessary to serve their client, especially if a competing third-party vendor has comparable software modules.

The territorial nature of software firms seems to be prevalent for several understandable but unsustainable reasons:

1. Many of the providers sell competitive products and want to encourage end-to-end solutions of their products.
2. Integration to a third-party vendor requires work for which direct compensation is rare.

3. An inherent belief that their software creates all of the information required for meaningful analysis.

The vision of integrated technology in the golf industry is not a question of "if"; it's a matter of "when." This movement will be accelerated when golf courses demand that software vendors make it happen and require, as part of their software license agreements, that vendors integrate the course owners' required solutions. It may even require a few facilities switching POS providers from the inflexible to the more flexible.

Without full integration of the essential components, golf course management is at a disadvantage in engaging in meaningful customer relationship management. When integration occurs, the sophistication and affordability of the tools will erase one of the historical advantages that large management companies had possessed over daily fee operators in having superior financial and customer information by which to manage effectively.

The Ideal Data Flow

The contents of five modules are needed to create an effective customer relationship program. For golf, the ideal system will have the following components: (1) website, (2) electronic tee sheet, (3) customer database, (4) a customer relationship management system, and (5) a broadcast e-mail and text messaging system linked together as depicted in the chart on the next page.

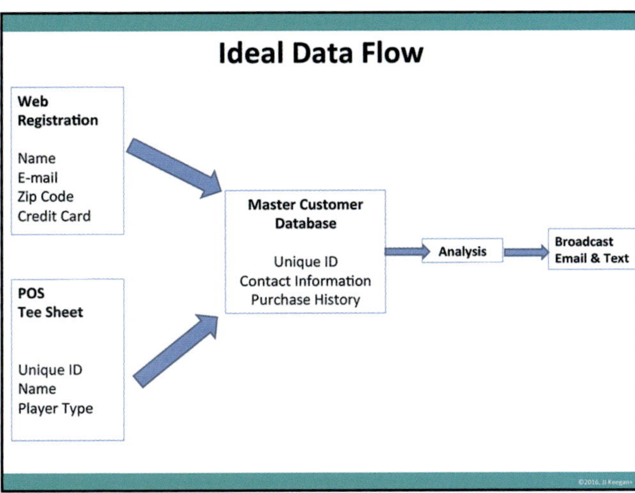

A truly useful software system will provide golfers with the ability to either self-register on the Web, or be registered by staff personnel.

Because there are many customers who may be one-time visitors, many golf course managers don't have a compelling desire to register all customers. However, it can and should be done. We have observed that the best golf courses may capture up to 95% of customer names and e-mail addresses but capture only 60% of the transactions by linking the customer's name to the transaction. Merely gathering the e-mail address allows you to know who your customers are. Tracking the transaction data provides insight as to how much revenue each customer generates.

The electronic tee sheet is the basic building block of a well-designed customer relationship management system. Each golfer should be registered by the day of play and time of day. When the golfer or the employee clicks to process the transaction, the POS system automatically calculates the correct green fee for that golfer by category, day of the week, and time of day. Most people don't realize that a golf course may have more than 75 different rates. The POS system that processes the cart, merchandise, and other items creates a unified customer record.

Without the integration of these systems, a repository of meaningful customer information (i.e., customer spending, accurate round statistics by golfer type, or the ability to ascertain statistical course utilization as measured by revenue per round or revenue per available tee time) is not created. Thus a potential resource for future management is lost.

By amassing a customer database of meaningful information, customer loyalty can be created. The by-product is that the golf course derives the following benefits:

- Maximized Revenue
    - Web-based marketing presence for national exposure
    - Reservation cards sold for premium access
    - Dynamic yield management
- Increased Operational Efficiency
    - Better internal control
    - Improved reporting
    - Elimination of repetitive tasks by staff
- Enhanced Customer Service
    - 24-hour access to tee-time reservations
    - E-mail and text communication of promotions, tournaments, updates
    - Prepaid gift cards sold online

If It Were Only that Easy

There is a caution: the expectation to achieve the benefits of a fully integrated golf management system will take longer than you hope. The chart shown here highlights the normal rate of adoption and acceptance of a new system.

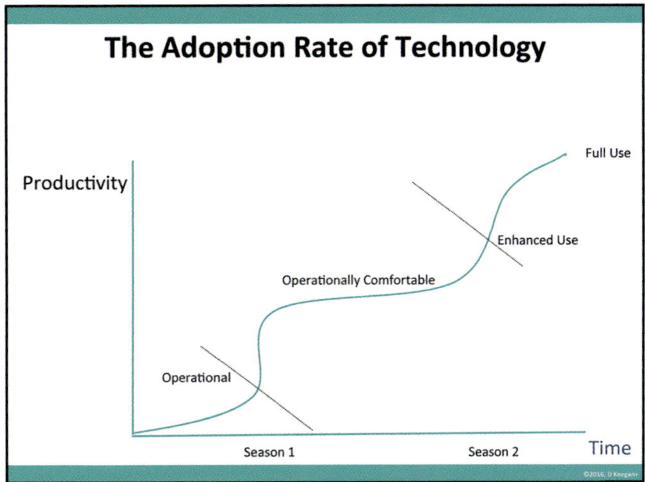

Golf course personnel tend to go through four phases as they learn new software:

1. Unconsciously incompetent—don't know what they don't know. (35%)
2. Consciously incompetent—frustration, anger, and finger pointing during which the individual blames others for their failure to accept accountability or responsibility for their plight. (40%)
3. Consciously competent—basic skills are learned and used. (20%)
4. Unconsciously competent—use of the product is second nature, and all features are used. (5%)

These percentages reflect the competency of staff at any point in time in using a golf management system.

Unlike the general business application software to which we all have become so accustomed (Word, Excel, PowerPoint, and Outlook), the user interface from one vendor software to another is dramatically different. Some use an icon-based approach while others use a hierarchical system reflective of a very dated DOS-based application.

I would wager that no matter the depth of your technical expertise and computer familiarity, there are very few who would be able to use any vendor's software without additional assistance and training. The proper configuration of a golf management software system, with its numerous templates, fee tables, SKU charts, report preferences, and security-level permissions reflecting the unique policies and procedures of that facility, is a daunting task to organize fully.

And if they acquire a system that meets their basic needs and are satisfied, every set of annual upgrades introduces a whole new round of frustrations for golf course personnel as they grapple with the changes. It is not uncommon for a customized feature designed for a client to break when the generic upgrade is installed.

Who's at fault? What we are confident of is that the executives at the golf course management companies are customer-centered and committed to serving golf course owners. While one or two firms may love the courtship and hate the marriage, at their core, they are unified in ensuring that their firms' software is properly and fully utilized.

In defense of the software firms, what is demanded of them regarding functionality and support far exceed the amount of money paid by most golf course owners who pay cash.

Buying What You Need to Buy and No More

Could any golf management software system be used at any golf course? Not a chance!

The information system needs of a municipal golf course, daily fee, private club, and resort are vastly different. For instance, the customer database and the reports desired at a nine-hole municipal golf course like the Tony Butler Municipal Golf Course in Harlingen, Texas, differ significantly from the requirements of the five-course complex operated by the State of New York at the famed Bethpage State Park.

So what does a golf course need? To clarify the fundamental requirements, the following chart highlights the **principal priorities** at each of the varied types of golf courses.

Module	Component	Daily Fee	Municipal	Private Club	Resort
Accounting		X		X	
Food and Beverage				X	X
Marketing	E-mail & Text	X	X		
	Customer Relationship Management	X	X	X	X
	Social Media	X	X	X	X
Hotel Interface					X
Membership				X	
Merchandising					X
POS	Computer	X	X	X	X
	Tablet	X	X	X	X
	Wireless	X	X	X	X
Reporting	Pre-Formatted Report	X	X		
	Open Database Query System	X	X	X	X
Tee Time Reservations	Call Center				X
	Electronic Tee Sheet	X	X		
	Online Reservations			X	
	Yield Management	X	X		X
Application Interface to 3rd Tee Time Networks		X			

While this chart is designed for the golf course looking to define its needs precisely, it is woefully inadequate.

To illustrate, the talented Jim Roschek, PGA, who oversees the Alamo Golf Trail in San Antonio, says one of his highest priorities is an open database query system that consolidates the customer transaction information from the eight golf courses so that he can effectively engage in customer relationship management. It is his goal that when a golfer who is a loyalty card member approaches the first tee, the course host's (starter) iPad tablet, with the RFID technology embedded in the golfer's loyalty card, will immediately display the customer's name to allow for the personal recognition of that valued customer, just as guests at the Ritz-Carlton might experience.

Need a Scorecard to Tell the Players? Picking the Right Horse to Ride

Who then will help you manage your business more efficiently?

Vendor	Niche	Strength – 1	Strength – 2	Strength - 3
Chelsea Information Systems	Municipal, Residential Communities	Web Based/leased system	Lottery and First Come/ First Served Format	Support IVR phone system via VOIP
Club Prophet	Daily Fee, Municipal, & Private	Monthly fee – no contract & multi site locations	Reporting system	Custom development focus
EZ Links - Core	Daily Fee & Municipal	Call center with dynamic yield management through multiple distribution points.	Client list	Offer Barter
EZ Links - IBS	Daily Fee and Private Club	Breadth of product line for private & city clubs	Historical brand reputation	Monthly payment model
GolfNow Open Course	Resorts	Integrates into hospitality solutions	Robust customer relationship management	Multi-course open architecture
GolfNow Reservations (Formerly Fore!)	Single course municipal and daily fee	Value based	Core functionality	Installed customer base > 2,000
Jonas Club Management	Private	Depth and Breadth of Modules for Private Clubs	Corporate resources	Management team
Teesnap	Daily Fee & Municipal	Tablet based software	Graphical user interface	Enterprise Reporting
Vermont System	Municipal & Military Golf Course	Very stable, well run company with 1,100 clients	Integrated system for Parks and Recreation	Handle all branches of military currently

Presented in the figure shown here is a list of vendors, along with our summary of what we believe to be their special niches and their corporate strengths. As impartial spectators in the golf software game, we believe that this chart will enable you to make the first cut in determining which of these might be the best vendor for you (see chart here).

There are many other software firms serving the golf course management sector. 1-2-1 Marketing, Course Trends, Cybergolf, J2 Golf Marketing, and Legendary Marketing are leaders in building websites for golf courses and providing e-mail marketing communication systems. ClubSoft and Northstar Technologies are emerging companies in the private club market. Clubessential and VCT focus on creating online communities for private clubs. Blue Golf, Boxgroove, Golf Pipeline, Golf Box, Golf Genius, GolfNet, Handicomp, and iWanamaker also provide software to the golf industry with various niche applications.

There Is Nothing More Controversial Than Barter

Because of constrained cash flow strain among golf courses, many operators have opted for the barter model.

There are a growing number of software firms accepting "bartered" tee times in exchange for their software and services. Course Trends, EZLinks, GolfNow/ Golf Channel, and Quick18 are among those firms.

It should be highlighted that these firms also offer a "cash model" for their technology.

The barter concept is straightforward. With golf courses operating at 52% of capacity nationally, the golf course is asked to provide the software vendor one or two tee times which the vendor can sell through its sales network to regain the funds it would have received for the preferred up-front cash payment.

These firms have been able to create websites on which they offer local market tee times for multiple golf courses on a single Web page. The customer now has a choice of many. Many golf course owners believe that these third-party sites are encouraging their customers to play elsewhere and that the software companies are offering the tee times at a lower price than what is available at each golf course. Golfers are being trained, they say, to purchase golf based on price. Some worry that each member of a foursome made up of individuals who have never previously played together could have paid a different green fee.

The issue as to whether third-party intermediaries and bartered tee times are beneficial for the golf course owner generates constant debate. In November 2015, The PGA of America and the National Golf Course Owners Association (NGCOA) announced a partnership to form Golf USA Tee Time Coalition, designed to provide education for golf course owners, operators, and PGA members and serve as an industry monitor for compliance of third-party online tee time providers. The goal of the alliance is to **create a more competitive and balanced marketplace in public golf**.

Throughout the debate, we pondered, from our quantitative analysis perspective, whether this issue is mostly emotional and reflective of the subconscious or a silent admission by golf course owners of their inability to properly manage a golf course.

As spectators listening to the divergent views of an extremely heated argument, we offer in the figure shown here our synthesized analysis of this debate.

It is estimated that more than 60% of America's facilities work in some fashion with third-party resellers.

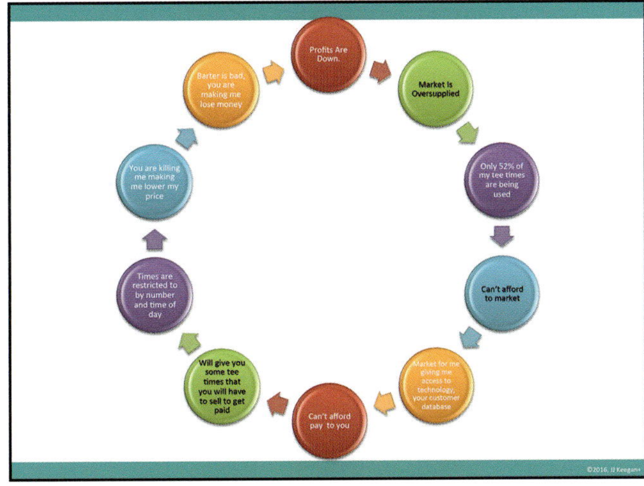

Calculating the Impact of Barter

Number of Courses Participating in Barter	6,000
Estimated Annual Revenue Per Course from Bartered Tee Times Sold	$30,000
Gross Revenue from Barter	180,000,000
National Golf Industry Revenue	21,000,000,000
Revenue Paid to Third Parties?	0.85%

Here are some quick numbers—approximately 15% of the 465 million rounds played in 2015 were booked online, based on the NGF Demand Model. Less than 1% of all tee time inventory that is made available to consumers via the Web is bartered. Putting aside the debate and running the numbers, the impact of providing third parties bartered tee times is estimated here.

Third parties can hardly be the cause of the woes of the industry.

That is the positive spin, now to the other side of the coin.

Pariah of the Industry?

Last-minute tee time providers are viewed as the pariahs of the golf industry by the PGA, the NGCOA, and course owners. To properly frame the issue, you must understand certain fundamentals:

1. **Are last-minute tee time services going away? Never.** They are here to stay. At the end of the day, customers select the distribution channel for purchasing goods and services that provide them the greatest value.

2. **Are last-minute tee time services financially beneficial for the golf course owner? More often than not - no.** While they can create incremental revenue, the customer loyalty to a specific course is compromised by a last-minute service.

3. **Is it likely that a national reservation system for golf will ever be created? Not in the foreseeable future.** Golf is a local game. Ninety percent of all rounds are played within 10 miles of the golfer's residence.

4. **Will golfers be willing to pay a booking fee to reserve a tee time?** Not likely, unless the discount provided and the booking fee is less than they

can purchase directly from the golf course. Further, golfers are not willing to prepay when they have no economic incentive to do so.

5. **Are golfers willing to accept non-refundable policies?** No, not unless they can book a specific day at a specific time that they would otherwise not be able to reserve through the normal reservation practices. For the customer, golf is a discretionary hobby, not a business. Golfers are rarely emotionally tied to a specific date and time.

The fact is golf courses are losing control of their ability to set prices. Thus the ability of a course or industry to rectify the current dilemma is nettlesome.

A Marketing Tool or Is One a Fool?

In deciding the value of barter, you might ask if third-party tee time providers are detrimental to the financial interests of golf course owners, how have they been able to achieve such market penetration?

The pitch used by these third-party profiteers is quite convincing:

- Our services are FREE. Just give us one tee time per day you will not otherwise sell. Our service costs you nothing.
- As marketing experts, we will bring new customers to your course and help you create incremental revenue. We will provide your course exposure to our database of more than 30,000 local golfers.
- We will sell those hard-to-liquidate times on Monday–Thursday afternoons that you will otherwise not sell.
- Provide us a copy of your e-mail files and we will do a special custom announcement to your core customers.
- We will provide you with a website and/or electronic tee sheet to post tee times to your URL.

Sounds impressive, and if you know how to use the tools it is a great deal for the golf course owner. But "using the tools" is a great big "if " that too many owners fail to comprehend.

Implications for the Golf Course Owner

The proliferation of technology companies poses a threat to golf course owners' relationships with their customers. The risks include:

- The erosion of green fees from net rates, standby bookings, and auctions
- Redirection of play away from their properties
- Siphoning of ancillary revenues associated with traditional merchandise
- Leveraging relationships to sell customers non–golf-related goods and services

However, if the golf course operator isn't smart enough to get off the heroin of giving away as many as two tee times per day, the beneficiary will be the third-party operator and the discount-seeking golfer.

From an entrepreneurial and capitalist perspective, third-party firms should be saluted for identifying an opportunity and providing the consumer a better alternative.

Discounting has become so pervasive that it is going to be difficult to eradicate. Turning higher-paying customers into low-paying customers isn't a winning formula.

What then is the best solution in the current environment?

For the golf course owner, the formula is the Southwest Airlines model—your best price can only be available on your website. This will allow you to capture (via the reservation system) the golfers' contact information and create an e-mail or text messaging marketing campaign.

Golf course owners should proceed with caution and utilize the services of a third party tee time distributor only when they can:

- Avoid exclusive agreements.
- Require that the best price can be obtained only through the golf course's website.
- Ensure that the golf course's database is protected from resale.

- Receive the name, phone number and e-mail address of all tee times booked by the third party at their golf course.
- Ascertain the cash value of the services/equipment received in the partnership.
- Determine how many rounds sold through barter came to the course solely on account of that third party (true incremental business).
- Quantify how many third party rounds came to the course, which would have come even without the third party (revenue sacrificed), such as loyal customers who happen to switch channels to save on hot deals or get reward points.
- Measure the difference between rounds sold for the benefit of the golf course vs. trade (barter) rounds sold. The idea ratio is 10 to 1.

Ultimately consumers will dictate what they are willing to pay. From the perspective of the 24 million golfers, technology has brought efficiency, creating data providing them the upper hand, and allowing the principles of capitalism and free markets to reign supreme.

Key Points to Remember

1) The role of technology is to improve your customers' experiences, making it easier and faster for them to do business with you while satisfying their preferences.
2) Golf course personnel are laggards on the adoption of technology.
3) There is much fear, uncertainty, and doubt when selecting a software vendor. Once selected, golf course staff are loath to change systems.
4) The attitude and aptitude challenges of the staff are compounded by the reticence of software vendors to cooperate in creating effective integrated solutions.
5) The process of selecting a golf management system comprises issuing a brief RFP, conducting Web-based demonstrations, and on-site presentations.
6) Having fully integrated golf management systems is a prerequisite for maximizing the investment return of a golf course. These systems facilitate the creation of a customer database with meaningful data in which the relationship can be cost-effectively managed.
7) The Sinek motto is "People don't buy what you do. They buy why you do it." As a golf course operator, your WHY is your passion for creating a superior entertainment and leisure experience for your customers. Passion is contagious. Technology allows you the freedom to become passionate.

Concluding Thought

The great pleasure in life is doing what people say you cannot do.

Walter Bagehot

The biggest risk is not taking any risk... In a world that's changing quickly, the only strategy that is guaranteed to fail is not taking risks.

Mark Zuckerberg

Chapter 8

Financial Modeling
Step 4 of JJ Keegan+ WIN™ Formula (continued)

If I have the belief that I can do it, I shall surely acquire the capacity to do it.

Mahatma Gandhi

Chapter Highlights

There are many factors that influence the net income of a golf course. Key management reports are available to guide decision-making.

The development of financial models facilitates the accounts that need to be monitored, the probable revenue mix, and how to minimize controllable expenses, including what constitutes reliable labor standards.

If you can understand the insights provided by the financial statements (balance sheet, income statement, and cash flow statement) you have already gleaned 75% of the information needed to manage a golf course effectively.

The result of financial modeling is a comprehensive financial projection that offers key benchmarks. These metrics can be monitored through a daily flash report to ensure revenue is maximized and that the operations are efficiently managed.

The Generally Accepted Goalposts

Financial statements are the measuring stick of a business's financial performance. For a golf course, the financial information that each course requires comprises:

1. Historical Financial Statements
2. Budget
3. Revenue Plan
4. Capital Expense Plan
5. Utilization Profiles
6. Key Performance Indicators

Examining the financial statements against related industry benchmarks is the **fourth step in the JJ Keegan+ WIN™ process.**

Historical financial statements include the balance sheet, the income statement, and the cash flow statement. The balance sheet reflects the financial strength of the golf course. The income statement mirrors the health of operations. The cash flow statement provides analysis of the operating, investing, and financing activities and is a useful tool in determining the short-term viability of a company.

A golf course's financial statements are comparable to a doctor reviewing a patient's x-rays. A tumor or broken bone is easy to spot. Is the business properly capitalized? Is liquidity sufficient? Are the receivables at risk? Are the payables tardy, or the deferred liabilities extensive? More information can be learned about an operation from reviewing financial statements than from any other source.

Because of the myriad numbers available, being able to rely on a few financial statistics is beneficial.

Financial ratios can be used to quantify the many indices of business, providing an indication of financial health. For example, profitability ratios measure the firm's use of its assets and the control of expenses necessary to generate an acceptable rate of return. Liquidity ratios measure the availability of cash to pay the debt. Activity ratios measure how quickly the firm converts non-cash assets to cash assets. Debt ratios measure the firm's ability to repay long-term debt. Market ratios measure investor response to owning a company's stock and also the cost of issuing stock.

While there seems to be a limitless number of financial ratios, the key ones include:

- Profitability Ratios
    - Profit margin = Net Income/Revenue
    - Operating profit margin or Return on sales = Earnings before interest and taxes/Sales
    - Return on equity = Net profits after taxes/Stockholders' equity or tangible net worth
    - Return on investment = Net income/Total assets
    - Asset turnover = Sales/Assets
    - Return on assets (ROA) = Net income/Total assets
- Liquidity ratios
    - Current ratio = Current assets/Current liabilities
    - Acid-test ratio (quick ratio) = [Current assets – (Inventories + Prepayments)]/Current liabilities
    - Receivables turnover ratio = Net credit sales/Average net receivables
    - Inventory turnover ratio = Cost of goods sold/Average inventory
- Activity ratios
    - Average collection period = Accounts receivable/(Annual credit sales/365 days)
    - Average payment period = Accounts payable/(Annual credit purchases/365 days)
    - Inventory turnover ratio = Cost of goods sold/Average inventory
- Debt ratios
    - Debt ratio = Total liabilities/Total assets

- Debt to equity ratio = (Long-term debt + Value of leases)/Stockholders' equity
- Long-term debt/Total asset (LD/TA) ratio = Long-term debt/Total assets
- Times interest-earned ratio = Earnings before interest and taxes EBIT/ Annual interest expense
- Debt service coverage ratio = Net operating income/Total debt service

With this list of ratios you should be able to determine the financial stability of a golf course.

There is a catch. Financial statements and their various derivatives present a dilemma to the golf course owner. So many numbers are available—from general ledger accounts to budgets, to labor-hour reporting, to daily operations, to monthly and annual financial statements—that it is easy to become overwhelmed. There is also a certain resignation that the numbers viewed are historical and not accurate predictors of the future.

While "assets," "liabilities," and "equity" are common financial terms, there have been, in the golf business, varying opinions as to the definition of certain terms. In March 2002, the NGCOA and other associations adopted a set of standards to ensure that growth indicators are measured consistently from year to year.

The most important definitions included in this industry list follow.[1]

Rounds

> Regulation Round: A *regulation round* of golf is defined by one person who tees off in an authorized "start" on a regulation golf course. The round is not defined by the number of holes played or the fees paid.

Participation

> Participant: A *participant* is a person five years of age or older who played at least one regulation round of golf or utilized an alternative facility or golf range at least once in the past 12 months. The total

1 NGCOA, "Golf Industry Definitions," http://www.ngcoa.org/pageview.asp?doc-511.

number of participants is determined by adding the number of golfers, alternative golfers, junior participants, and range users.

Golfer: A *golfer* is a person age 18 or older who has played at least one regulation round of golf in the past 12 months.

Occasional Golfer: An *occasional golfer* is a golfer who plays less than eight regulation rounds in a year.

Core Golfer: A *core golfer* is one who plays 8 to 24 regulation rounds in a year.

Avid Golfer: An *avid golfer* is one who plays 25 regulation rounds or more in a year.

Types of Facilities and Courses

Regulation Golf Facility: A *regulation golf facility* is defined as a golf complex where there is at least one regulation golf course.

Regulation Golf Course: A *regulation golf course* is defined as any 9- or 18-hole golf course that includes a variety of par 3, par 4, and par 5 holes, and is of traditional length and par; a 9-hole facility must be at least 2,600 yards in length and at least par 33; an 18-hole facility must be at least 5,200 yards in length and at least par 66.

Alternative Golf Course: *Alternative golf courses* include the following:

Par 3 Courses: *Par 3 courses* are courses consisting exclusively of par 3 holes that average at least 100 yards in length.

Executive Courses: *Executive courses* are short courses with a variety of par 3, par 4, and par 5 holes. Eighteen-hole executive courses are 5,200 yards in length or less, with a par of 65 or less.

Pitch & Putt Courses: *Pitch & putt courses* are short par 3 courses where the holes average less than 100 yards in length.

Courses: Structure

Public Access Golf Course: A *public access golf course* is a facility that provides the least limited access and which may or may not offer memberships.

Public access courses include:

Municipal Golf Course: A *municipal golf course* is one that is owned by a tax-supported entity such as a city, county, or state and which is open to the general public at all times.

Daily Fee Golf Course: A *daily fee golf course* is a privately owned course that is open to the public without restriction.

Semiprivate Golf Course: A *semiprivate golf course* is a public course that also offers memberships.

Military Golf Course: A *military golf course* is one affiliated with a military base where members of the military and their families receive preferred rates.

Private Golf Course: A *private golf course* is a facility where the play is restricted to members and their guests. A private golf course can be either equity (owned by the membership) or non-equity (corporately-owned).

Resort Golf Course: A *resort golf course* is a golf facility usually affiliated with a lodging component.

These definitions are important because they serve as the foundation for the accepted accounting principles for the golf industry. By ensuring that the financial statements are consistent with industry definitions, meaningful comparisons can be made.

Lost in the Details

It often seems that hundreds of everyday events influence the net income of a golf course. However, in focusing on those details, most golf course managers lose the perspective necessary to bolster the net income and investment return from their golf course.

Simply stated, an income statement has three components: revenue, expenses, and the resultant net income. A manager should focus on a few key items.

Golf course owners have significant influence over only the following areas highlighted with black boxes as on the next page.

Rounds as measured by green fees, member dues, and season passes account for about 60% of gross revenue and materially impact all other revenue departments. The revenue derived from carts, food and beverage, merchandise, and lessons is directly correlated to the number of rounds. It takes a lot of additional work to increase incrementally the revenue in those departments.

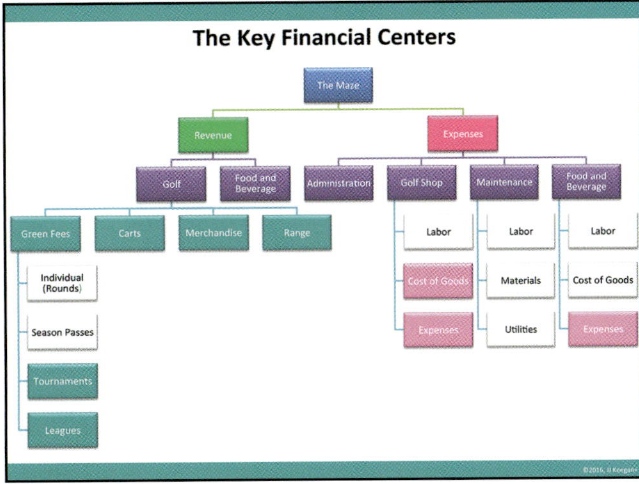

With the average golf course operating at slightly over 50% of capacity, in theory, a course should be able to double its revenue and increase its net income at least tenfold.

For a golf course operator today, revenues are challenged. This leads one to think that increased profits are available from the effective control of expenses. If it were only that easy.

Expenses are a continuing and nettlesome concern for the golf industry, especially as operating margins get squeezed. It would be hard to identify an aspect of course development and operations that has not been negatively impacted by inflated costs, from construction materials to fuel to food and beverage supplies to maintenance products and equipment to labor. Water, fuel, fertilizer, and labor costs all are extremely volatile and seem to increase exponentially in price.

While there is the temptation to cut costs, or, as the expression goes, "suck the paint off of the walls," such a strategy is a short-term accommodation and a long-term strategic mistake. It is difficult to shrink your way to greatness.

Comprehensive financial analysis is one of the few medicines available to manage the current ills and prevent long-term financial woes

Tying It All Together

Creating a proper financial model has two benefits: (1) Historical data can be compared to industry benchmarks to detect and evaluate operational efficiencies;

and (2) financial projections can be created in which the rates and expenses can be experimentally adjusted to calculate the likely impact on the golf course's financial statements.

The process we use involves the following steps:

1. The general ledger trial balance by account is examined.
2. The data by general ledger category is exported into Excel worksheets.
3. The general ledger accounts are allocated into appropriate golf course industry standard financial reporting models.
4. Three-year historical income statements are created consistent with generally accepted accounting principles for golf courses.
5. The historical financial statements are analyzed for trends and compared to industry benchmarks for reporting variances and operational deficiencies.
6. Five-year financial projections are developed using different estimates for rates, labor, and other expenses.

You might love to spend all day pounding the keyboard and watching the Excel spreadsheet update with numbers that would numb your mind, but what purpose would that serve? The race is won by those who are efficient, not by those who invest the most hours. Why not use a set of templates to accurately assess current operations and predict future performance?

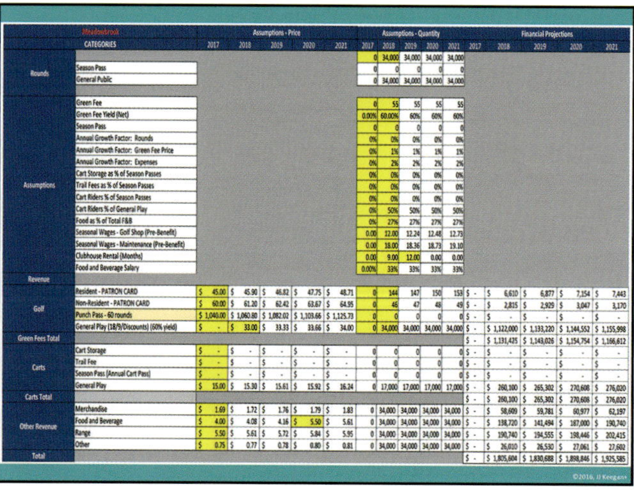

	Meadowbrook	Assumptions - Price					Assumptions - Quantity					Financial Projections				
	CATEGORIES	2017	2018	2019	2020	2021	2017	2018	2019	2020	2021	2017	2018	2019	2020	2021
Rounds							0	34,000	34,000	34,000	34,000					
	Season Pass						0	0	0	0	0					
	General Public						0	34,000	34,000	34,000	34,000					
Assumptions	Green Fee						0	55	55	55	55					
	Green Fee Yield (Net)						0.00%	60.00%	60%	60%	60%					
	Season Pass						0	0	0	0	0					
	Annual Growth Factor: Rounds						0%	0%	0%	0%	0%					
	Annual Growth Factor: Green Fee Price						0%	1%	1%	1%	1%					
	Annual Growth Factor: Expenses						0%	2%	2%	2%	2%					
	Cart Storage as % of Season Passes						0%	0%	0%	0%	0%					
	Trail Fees as % of Season Passes						0%	0%	0%	0%	0%					
	Cart Riders % of Season Passes						0%	0%	0%	0%	0%					
	Cart Riders % of General Play						0%	50%	50%	50%	50%					
	Food as % of Total F&B						0%	27%	27%	27%	27%					
	Seasonal Wages - Golf Shop (Pre-Benefit)						0.00	12.00	12.24	12.48	12.73					
	Seasonal Wages - Maintenance (Pre-Benefit)						0.00	18.00	18.36	18.73	19.10					
	Clubhouse Rental (Months)						0.00	9.00	12.00	0.00	0.00					
	Food and Beverage Salary						0.00%	33%	33%	33%	33%					
Revenue																
Golf	Resident - PATRON CARD	$ 45.00	$ 45.90	$ 46.82	$ 47.75	$ 48.71	0	144	147	150	153	$ -	$ 6,610	$ 6,877	$ 7,154	$ 7,443
	Non-Resident - PATRON CARD	$ 60.00	$ 61.20	$ 62.42	$ 63.67	$ 64.95	0	46	47	48	49	$ -	$ 2,815	$ 2,929	$ 3,047	$ 3,170
	Punch Pass - 60 rounds	$ 1,040.00	$ 1,060.80	$ 1,082.02	$ 1,103.66	$ 1,125.73	0	0	0	0	0	$ -	$ -	$ -	$ -	$ -
	General Play (18/9/Discounts) (60% yield)	$ -	$ 33.00	$ 33.33	$ 33.66	$ 34.00	0	34,000	34,000	34,000	34,000	$ -	$ 1,122,000	$ 1,133,220	$ 1,144,552	$ 1,155,998
Green Fees Total												$ -	$ 1,131,425	$ 1,143,026	$ 1,154,754	$ 1,166,612
Carts	Cart Storage	$ -	$ -	$ -	$ -	$ -	0	0	0	0	0	$ -	$ -	$ -	$ -	$ -
	Trail Fee	$ -	$ -	$ -	$ -	$ -	0	0	0	0	0	$ -	$ -	$ -	$ -	$ -
	Season Pass (Annual Cart Pass)	$ -	$ -	$ -	$ -	$ -	0	0	0	0	0	$ -	$ -	$ -	$ -	$ -
	General Play	$ 15.00	$ 15.30	$ 15.61	$ 15.92	$ 16.24	0	17,000	17,000	17,000	17,000	$ -	$ 260,100	$ 265,302	$ 270,608	$ 276,020
Carts Total												$ -	$ 260,100	$ 265,302	$ 270,608	$ 276,020
Other Revenue	Merchandise	$ 1.69	$ 1.72	$ 1.76	$ 1.79	$ 1.83	0	34,000	34,000	34,000	34,000	$ -	$ 58,609	$ 59,781	$ 60,977	$ 62,197
	Food and Beverage	$ 4.00	$ 4.08	$ 4.16	$ 5.50	$ 5.61	0	34,000	34,000	34,000	34,000	$ -	$ 138,720	$ 141,494	$ 187,000	$ 190,740
	Range	$ 5.50	$ 5.61	$ 5.72	$ 5.84	$ 5.95	0	34,000	34,000	34,000	34,000	$ -	$ 190,740	$ 194,555	$ 198,446	$ 202,415
	Other	$ 0.75	$ 0.77	$ 0.78	$ 0.80	$ 0.81	0	34,000	34,000	34,000	34,000	$ -	$ 26,010	$ 26,530	$ 27,061	$ 27,602
Total												$ -	$ 1,805,604	$ 1,830,688	$ 1,898,846	$ 1,925,585

©2016, JJ Keegan

To illustrate, the table shown here shows a five-year cash flow forecast that required less than 15 minutes to prepare.

The model shown here determined the break-even point for a $10 million golf course renovation closed in 2015 by a flood. This template also includes the variables regarding operating expenses and capital budgets.

Is it perfect? Probably not. But for the time invested, is it a valuable tool to determine the revenue of a golf course? Absolutely.

With a firm understanding of a golf course's historical performance in comparison to industry standards, there exists a great opportunity to create financial projections that emphasize a golf course's existing strengths and to correct its weaknesses.

The Key Numbers

It is essential that a golf course owner grasps a few fundamental financial relationships to guide the operation. The financial analysis does not have to be exhaustive or all-consuming. As in any business, a lot of numbers are generated. In golf, there are only several that matter as shown here.

The Key Reports

Customer Analysis

1. Customer Distribution: stratifies golfers into 10 segments by number and spending
2. Customer Demographics: age, income, and ethnicity of your customers
3. Customer Retention: core, new, and lost customers
4. Customer Spending by Class: SKU generates highest yield per transaction
5. Customer Spending by Individual: the best customers by frequency and spending
6. Zip Code Analysis: residential and business location of customers

Facility Analysis

7. Merchandise Sales by Vendor: rank vendors orders by inventory, sales, and turnover
8. Reservations by Booking Method: customer preferences, .i.e., phone, website, etc.
9. Reservations by Day of Week: highlights demand by day to facilitate proper pricing
10. Revenue Benchmarks: benchmarks (green fees, carts, etc.) compared to norms
11. Revenue Per Available Tee Time: established net rate per round by time slot
12. Revenue by Department: focuses on revenue centers
13. Revenue Per Hour: identifies which hours generate the most revenue
14. Rounds per Revenue Margins: customer frequency versus yield per customer
15. Course Utilization: demand vs. supply by time slot

The following sections include an explanation of each report and its vital role in golf course management.

Customer Analysis

Report 1: Customer Distribution

Customer relationship management is focused on identifying a facility's best customers to ensure that they are accorded service commensurate with their loyalty to that facility. At a golf course, 15% of the customers typically generate about 60% of the revenue.

The chart shown here highlights the importance of identifying customers and further segmenting them as acquired, core, or defectors to ensure their continued loyalty. The chart represents the month of April at a Florida municipal golf course.

Customer Revenue Distribution Report

Distribution	# of Player	% of Players	Total Rounds	Rounds /Player	% of Total Rounds	Revenue /Player	Total Rev/Round
1	7	0.14 %	166	23.71	3.68 %	$1,900.61	$80.15
2	60	1.20 %	222	3.70	4.92 %	$214.56	$57.99
3	131	2.62 %	276	2.11	6.12 %	$98.18	$46.60
4	191	3.81 %	289	1.51	6.41 %	$67.38	$44.53
5	247	4.93 %	405	1.64	8.98 %	$52.11	$31.78
6	332	6.63 %	426	1.28	9.44 %	$38.71	$30.17
7	374	7.47 %	400	1.07	8.87 %	$34.39	$32.15
8	499	9.96 %	598	1.20	13.25 %	$25.77	$21.51
9	706	14.10 %	862	1.22	19.10 %	$18.21	$14.91
10	2,461	49.14 %	868	0.35	19.24 %	$5.00	$14.18
Total	5,008	100.00 %	4,512	0.90	100.00 %	$25.66	$28.48

Look at the revenue per player per round generated from just seven customers: $1,900.61. Do you think this course can afford to lose one of these customers? Not likely.

Without undertaking this analysis of a golf course's database, a typical general manager might report revenue was up slightly over the prior year and fail to realize that the course had a 33% customer turnover. In analytical work performed for clients, the amount of revenue from acquired customers, approximating 20% of gross revenue, approximates the revenue lost from defectors.

This report is designed to provide an index by which you can compare customer usage at your facility to industry standards and provides, in 10% incremental brackets, the number of golfers it took to generate the 10% of the course's gross revenue.

Report 2: Customer Demographics

Who is your customer? The ability to effectively market your facility is highly dependent on knowing the detailed demographics of your customers—their name, zip code, cell phone number, e-mail address, etc. From direct mail to targeted e-mails to text messages to zip code analysis for print or other media ads, it is critical for your club to collect this data. This report will give you a quick look at statistics that are vital for effective marketing.

Report 3: Customer Retention

The purpose of this report is to identify the core customers, those customers who played the course for the first time during the defined interval, and those defectors who previously played your golf course but have not frequented it recently. When unique marketing messages are created for each of these targeted segments, the response rate contributes materially to building revenue.

Fifty percent of the customers that play a golf course in a specific year will not return in the following year. Those "defectors" are often offset by newly acquired customers. This turnover velocity within a customer database is often not realized because of the time horizon, 12 months, in which the changes occur. If a golfer has not played a golf course within 90 days, there is a high probability that the customer has been lost.

The Customer Retention report is designed to compare two time periods. It can compare days, weeks, months, years, etc. The report will show you the names of the players and compare "This Period" vs. "Last Period" for revenue, visits, yield, and rounds.

An example of this report is shown here.

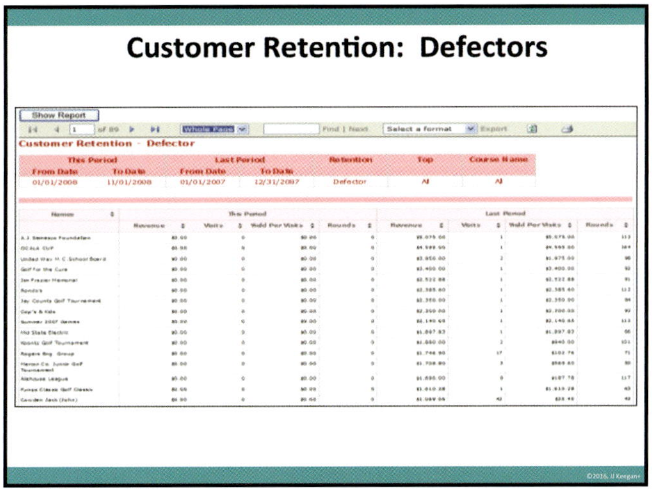

Customer Retention: Defectors

Customer Retention - Defector

This Period		Last Period		Retention	Top	Course Name
From Date	To Date	From Date	To Date			
01/01/2008	11/01/2008	01/01/2007	12/31/2007	Defector	All	All

This report shows numerous golfers who were frequent customers in the prior year but didn't return. Surveying these customers would be a source of insightful information and help course managers reconsider a facility's operational practices to enhance retention.

Tournaments are one of the largest revenue sources. Filtering this report to highlight tournaments indicates that there were 18 groups generating more than $4,000 in one year that did not return to the course the next year. With the average earnings before taxes, interest, depreciation, and amortization over $200,000, these lost customers represent 36% of the course's annual earnings.

Report 4: Customer Spending by Class

By customer class, we mean which group generates the highest gross revenue and the most revenue per round?

This report allows you to identify which group is producing the most revenue. It also helps you affirm the importance of that group by enabling you to create a targeted e-mail message to the segment you identify.

Report 5: Customer Spending by Individual

This report measures gross revenue by the individual customer so that you can identify which customer generates the most revenue for the facility.

It also reveals the importance of tournament and outing playing to gross revenue. Often, 20 tournaments on 20 days will contribute 20% of the gross revenue of that facility for the entire year.

This report highlights a facility's best customers and allows you to understand when customer recognition is appropriate.

Report 6: Zip Code Analysis

How, when, and where should a golf course advertise? Are national, regional, or local publications appropriate? This report helps answers that question by displaying the residential location of your customers.

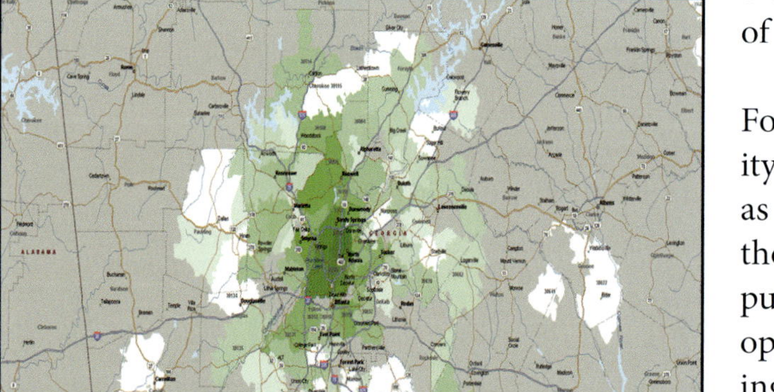

For most courses, the vast majority of revenue is generated within as few as four zip codes. Knowing those zip codes determines which publications are best selected for optimum utilization of advertising expenditures.

Facility Analysis

Report 7: Merchandise Sales by Vendor

This report analyzes the merchandise inventory and rank orders vendors by revenue and by net income. The report will display which vendors generated the most revenue at the highest gross margin. Conversely, it will identify vendors that are underperforming and should be deleted from the inventory.

The typical golf course should have about 15 to 20 vendors. If this report extends to several pages, there is a great opportunity to reduce the number of lines carried, which will simplify purchasing and reduce inventory on hand that has low margin and low likelihood of selling.

Report 8: Reservations by Booking Method

The first contact a golfer often has with the facility is in booking tee time reservations. There are many ways to make tee time reservations: by an individual in the golf shop, via call center, via a kiosk, third-party broker, or via the facility's website.

This report shows you how golfers are reserving tee times at your facility. It is important that each booking method is quick and easy. As the most cost-effective method for booking a tee time for a golf course, the online reservation system merits special attention.

Report 9: Reservations by Day of Week

The goal of any golf course is to maximize its revenue. It is assumed that weekends, when most customers are not working, are the busiest days of the week and therefore prices are set higher, often as much as 25% higher, than on weekdays. This assumption often proves incorrect, however.

This report will display which days of the week are busiest and will facilitate your determining should Friday be set at weekend rates or should the same rate apply to every day of the week. Ultimately, the decision on setting rates is a subjective science, but having quantitative information available reduces the error rate significantly. This report is to guide you in setting the correct green fee.

Report 10: Revenue Benchmarks

This report will provide key benchmarks on a revenue per round basis for the five departments according to generally accepted financial reporting for golf courses: green fees, carts, merchandise, food and beverage, and other.

These benchmarks can be compared to industry averages created by Golf Datatech, Club Benchmarking, and ORCA.

This report also shows the interrelationship between the departments. Green fees drive the volume of revenue for each of the segment categories.

Report 11: Revenue per Available Tee Time

Optimizing gross revenue is finding the proper balance between the number of rounds and the price per round. A key statistic is a net rate per round.

Each golf course, depending on the market niche it serves has a revenue target. At a minimum, that target represents total expenses divided by projected rounds. That number represents the break-even point of the golf course.

This report is designed to help a golf course manager ascertain to what extent his facility is achieving its revenue per round goal and whether the prices per hour are appropriately balanced. Best practices suggest that well-run golf facilities will attain a net rate per round of 70% to 75% of the posted green fees rate.

Therefore, daily tracking of rounds and anticipation of slack time within each day is key to administering yield management.

In what I like to call, "The Good, The Bad, and The Ugly," the purpose of this report is to quickly identify timeslots where you are hemorrhaging money versus those that are performing well. Use of marketing tools and pricing strategies can help you improve your bottom line.

Report 12: Revenue by Department

This report represents gross revenue in the aggregate by the five key departments at the golf course. It allows a golf course manager to ascertain whether the departments will meet their budget for the month and, if not, which of the revenue centers underperformed. When contrasted to the benchmark revenue reports that reflect revenue on a per-round basis, this report aggregates total dollars generated by each department.

Gross Revenue By Department

Gross Revenue by Month Detailing Five Profit Centers

Months	Rounds	AVG Rounds /Day	Total Revenue	AVG Revenue/ Day	AVG Revenue/Round	Green Fees	Green Fees/Round	Merchandise	Merchandise/ Round	F&B	F&B/Round	Other	Other/Round
Jan	2,829	91.26	84,568.89	2,728.03	29.89	42,447.62	15.00	5,936.88	2.10	4,694.09	1.66	31,490.30	11.13
Feb	5,696	203.43	167,747.30	5,990.98	29.45	92,947.96	16.32	12,176.30	2.14	10,587.27	1.86	52,035.77	9.14
March	6,882	222.00	195,868.47	6,318.34	28.46	109,374.74	15.89	15,463.28	2.25	13,832.23	2.01	57,198.22	8.31
April	5,984	199.47	182,708.77	6,090.29	30.53	84,103.35	14.05	24,494.60	4.09	16,880.57	2.82	57,230.25	9.56
May	6,309	203.52	180,960.02	5,837.42	28.68	84,150.79	13.34	17,792.40	2.82	19,349.11	3.07	59,667.72	9.46
June	6,111	203.70	179,759.79	5,991.99	29.42	80,349.09	13.15	19,785.27	3.24	21,441.96	3.51	58,183.47	9.52
July	5,826	187.94	159,813.97	5,155.29	27.43	75,612.75	12.98	15,542.36	2.67	18,977.05	3.26	49,681.81	8.53
Aug	5,664	182.71	172,134.28	5,552.72	30.39	68,875.58	12.16	21,188.72	3.74	19,519.87	3.45	62,550.11	11.04
Sep	4,665	155.50	146,266.09	4,875.54	31.35	53,270.06	11.42	11,750.27	2.52	12,799.85	2.74	68,445.91	14.67
Oct	5,348	172.50	173,906.58	5,609.89	32.52	57,578.85	10.77	20,298.35	3.80	13,018.06	2.43	83,011.32	15.52
Nov	6,168	205.61	177,213.81	5,907.13	28.73	67,025.55	10.87	13,944.58	2.26	13,018.08	2.11	83,225.61	13.49
Dec	6,966	224.71	208,277.00	6,718.61	29.90	80,519.07	11.56	25,265.81	3.63	18,070.34	2.59	84,421.78	12.12
Total	68,448	187.53	2,029,224.97	5,559.52		896,255.41		203,638.82		182,188.48		747,142.27	
Course Average				100.00%	29.65	44.17%	13.09	10.04%	2.98	8.98%	2.66	36.82%	10.92
Industry Benchmarks				100.00%	38.12	61.62%	21.67	8.28%	2.56	19.28%	4.17	10.82%	9.72
Variances					(8.47)	-17.45%	(8.58)	1.76%	0.42	-10.30%	(1.51)	26.00%	1.20

Report 13: Revenue per Hour

The goal of a golf course is to generate revenue. It is widely felt that "prime time" is from 8 a.m. to 10 a.m. This report reflects in which hour most of the revenue is generated. Surprisingly, it is often not during prime time but rather in the early afternoon when revenue per hour is maximized. That fact is contrary to the popular wisdom that Monday–Thursday noon to 3 p.m. are the slowest times at the golf course. This report is designed to facilitate identification of which hours of the day generate the most revenue. Although the largest revenue per hour may be in the early afternoon, that doesn't necessarily mean that rates should be raised to the highest level during that time interval. Again, it is a question of balancing rounds versus the rate per round to achieve the desired goal.

Report 14: Rounds per Revenue Margin

Each golf course sets rates based on customer type, day of the week, and time of day. This report focuses on the differential between the resources consumed (the number of tee times used by a customer type) versus the revenue generated by that customer type. For example, volunteers and season pass holders often use the golf course to a far greater extent than they generate comparable revenue. On the reverse side, non-residents at a municipal golf course often contribute far more to the gross revenue than the percentage of rounds they play.

Measuring Effective Rates

Detractors

Green Fees	Yield Margin
Golf Course Employee	-4.13%
Season: Staff/Faculty	-3.67%
Comp Round	-3.49%
Season: Alumni	-1.94%
University: Twilight	-1.86%
University and Public: Evening	-1.85%
Season: Retired Staff	-1.53%
League Rate	-1.35%
Public: Twilight	-1.32%
Season: Student	-0.77%
Raincheck Redemption	-0.43%
University: Monday	-0.24%
ICA	-0.09%

Supporters

Green Fees	Yield Margin
PGA Card: Monday - Thursday	0.26%
PGA Card: Friday - Sunday	0.40%
University: Tuesday - Thursday	0.50%
Senior Special	1.31%
Public: Weekday	2.78%
Special	2.85%
University: Friday - Sunday	3.36%
Public: Friday - Sunday	11.45%

This report provides managers insight on which groups are generating the greatest "margin" to their facility. Are you seeking to raise revenue? The answer is often simple—provide the group that yields the highest revenue per round the greater access to the tee times and the course. On the left is an extract of such a report for a public golf course.

In this case, all those with negative numbers are using the facility to a greater extent than they are paying for. It would suggest the rates in these categories could be increased.

This report will also illustrate why season passes, offered by 71% of municipal and many daily fee golf courses, are usually a very bad deal. On the left is a chart highlighting a California golf course that eliminated its unlimited play annual pass program.

Here Is Why Annual Passes Are a Bad Deal

Year	Revenue Contribution	Rounds Consumed	Unfavorable Variance
2XX1	16.02%	42.35%	-26.33%
2XX2	16.90%	38.33%	-21.43%
2XX3	14.37%	35.74%	-21.37%
2XX4	7.91%	30.32%	-22.41%
2XX5	6.61%	24.36%	-17.75%
2XX6	16.57%	24.02%	-7.45%
2XX7	19.88%	29.32%	-9.43%

Note the significant improvement in the revenue contribution margin starting when the modified rate structure was implemented. Still not good, but progress is being made.

Report 15: Course Utilization

In 2015, the average golf utilization—the number of rounds divided by the capacity—was slightly higher than 50%. This report provides a benchmark against that national average.

This report, presented below, also shows which hours within a month are near capacity, suggesting that an increase in green fees within those time slots might be appropriate, and alternatively, showing the slack periods in which, if dynamic pricing were in place, the green fee rates might be lowered:

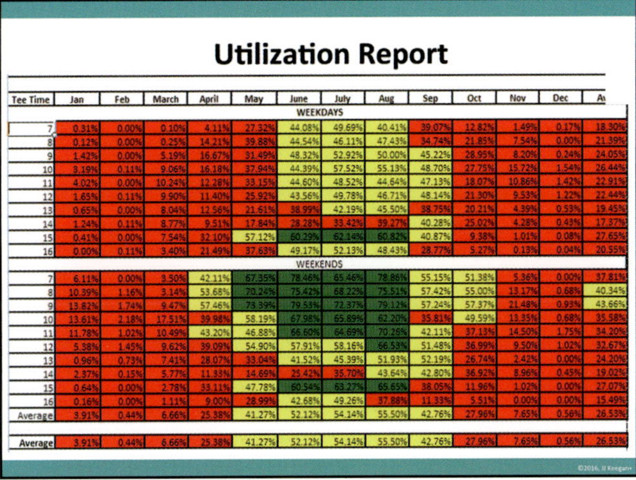

Utilization Report

Tee Time	Jan	Feb	March	April	May	June	July	Aug	Sep	Oct	Nov	Dec	Av
WEEKDAYS													
7	0.31%	0.00%	0.10%	4.11%	27.32%	44.08%	49.69%	40.41%	39.07%	12.82%	1.49%	0.17%	18.30%
8	0.12%	0.00%	0.25%	14.21%	39.88%	44.54%	46.11%	47.43%	34.74%	21.85%	7.54%	0.00%	21.39%
9	1.42%	0.00%	5.19%	16.67%	31.49%	48.32%	52.92%	50.00%	45.22%	28.95%	8.20%	0.24%	24.05%
10	3.19%	0.11%	9.06%	16.18%	37.94%	44.39%	57.52%	55.13%	48.70%	27.75%	15.72%	1.54%	26.44%
11	4.02%	0.00%	10.24%	12.28%	33.15%	44.60%	48.52%	44.64%	47.13%	18.07%	10.86%	1.42%	22.91%
12	1.65%	0.11%	9.90%	11.40%	25.92%	43.56%	49.78%	46.71%	48.14%	21.30%	9.53%	1.22%	22.44%
13	0.65%	0.00%	8.04%	12.56%	21.61%	38.99%	42.19%	45.50%	38.75%	20.21%	4.39%	0.53%	19.45%
14	1.24%	0.11%	8.77%	9.51%	17.84%	28.28%	33.42%	39.27%	40.28%	25.02%	4.28%	0.43%	17.37%
15	0.41%	0.00%	7.54%	32.10%	57.12%	60.29%	62.14%	60.82%	40.87%	9.38%	1.01%	0.08%	27.65%
16	0.00%	0.11%	3.40%	21.49%	37.63%	49.17%	52.13%	48.43%	28.77%	5.27%	0.13%	0.04%	20.55%
WEEKENDS													
7	6.11%	0.00%	3.50%	42.11%	67.35%	78.46%	65.46%	78.86%	55.15%	51.38%	5.36%	0.00%	37.81%
8	10.39%	1.16%	3.14%	53.68%	70.24%	75.42%	68.22%	75.51%	57.42%	55.00%	13.17%	0.68%	40.34%
9	13.82%	1.74%	9.47%	57.46%	73.39%	79.53%	72.37%	79.12%	57.24%	57.37%	21.48%	0.93%	43.66%
10	13.61%	2.18%	17.51%	39.98%	58.19%	67.98%	65.89%	62.20%	35.81%	49.59%	13.35%	0.68%	35.58%
11	11.78%	1.02%	10.49%	43.20%	46.88%	66.60%	64.69%	70.26%	42.11%	37.13%	14.50%	1.75%	34.20%
12	5.38%	1.45%	9.62%	39.09%	54.90%	57.91%	58.16%	66.53%	51.48%	36.99%	9.50%	1.02%	32.67%
13	0.96%	0.73%	7.41%	28.07%	33.04%	41.52%	45.39%	51.93%	52.19%	26.74%	2.42%	0.00%	24.20%
14	2.37%	0.15%	5.77%	11.33%	14.69%	25.42%	35.70%	43.64%	42.80%	36.92%	8.96%	0.45%	19.02%
15	0.64%	0.00%	2.78%	33.11%	47.78%	60.54%	63.27%	65.65%	38.05%	11.96%	1.02%	0.00%	27.07%
16	0.16%	0.00%	1.11%	9.00%	28.99%	42.68%	49.26%	37.88%	11.33%	5.51%	0.00%	0.00%	15.49%
Average	3.91%	0.44%	6.66%	25.38%	41.27%	52.12%	54.14%	55.50%	42.76%	27.96%	7.65%	0.56%	26.53%
Average	3.91%	0.44%	6.66%	25.38%	41.27%	52.12%	54.14%	55.50%	42.76%	27.96%	7.65%	0.56%	26.53%

Key: Blocks in red indicate that the course has less than 40% utilization for the month. Yellow indicates utilization between 40% and 60% and green reflects utilization of over 60%.

Another purpose of this report is that it will often reflect whether the tee time prices within the day are properly set. For example, if the afternoon rates are discounted too significantly, one might notice a significant drop off in play the hour before the afternoon rates become effective. Such a scenario would suggest that three- or four-tier pricing might be more appropriate than a dual-pricing schedule.

A tee time is a perishable commodity. There exists a theory that if the green fees were accurately priced by day, hour, and month the course would operate at 100% of capacity. In comparison to the 50% utilization of a golf course, in 2015 hotels were operating at 80% utilization, while the airline industry was operating at near 70% capacity.

These reports, while important, provide little benefit if the insights created are not implemented. With this information, however, course operators find it easier to make informed decisions that will lead to an increase in the investment return of the facility.

Flash Cards

JJ Keegan+ conducted a "flash poll" of 500 industry leaders, asking one question, "What are the five key benchmarks (key performance indicators) that you rely on to manage operations?" On the next page are the consensus responses.

Key Performance Indicator from Golf Industry Leaders

Daily Fee - Municipal	Private Club	Resort
Labor as a % of Gross Revenue	Rounds played by members	RevPar = Revenue per Available Round
Merchandise Sales and Cost of Goods Sold	Guest Fees	Utilization percentage based on available rounds
Total Starts	Member Retention	Labor dollars per round
Revenue per round: green fee + cart fee	New Members + Waiting List	Costs per hole & per round
Net income	Change in Initiation Fee	Conversion ratio of resort golf rounds to resort room nights
Loyalty Rating from Customer Survey	Cash Requirements	Retail sales per round & per room night

These serve as a good starting point for the efficient management of a golf course monitoring these key performance indicators daily.

Key Points to Remember

1) Financial statements are the goalposts of business.
2) In all of the sports, there is only one number that matters—the final score. In business, there's the only number that matters—net income, as it is the long-term measure of customer satisfaction.
3) There are four kinds of key ratios that measure the strength of business: profitability, liquidity, activity, and debt. A fifth standard ratio, market activity, is not applicable for golf courses.
4) Financial modeling is at the foundation of the success of a golf course. Rather than a punitive tool to hold management and staff hostages to meeting artificially derived targets, operational templates provide quick insights into the interrelationships of the various revenues and expenses at a golf course.
5) A golfer has played a regulation round if he or she teed off in an authorized start on a regulation golf course, regardless of the number of holes played or the fees paid.
6) A golfer is a person age 18 or older who has played at least one regulation round of golf in the past 12 months. Occasional golfers are defined as those who play less than eight regulation rounds; core golfers play between 8 and 24 regulation rounds, and avid golfers play 25 or more regulation rounds per year.
7) There are key performance metrics for the golf industry. Among the most important are gross revenue by department per round, course utilization, revenue per available tee time, revenue by golf type, customer quintiles, acquire/core/defectors, zip code analysis, and net income break-even analysis.
8) Select five key performance indicators that measure 75% of your revenue and emphasize them on a "leaderboard" in the staff area of the facility.

By understanding the financial statements of a golf course, facility managers can undertake tactical planning designed to enhance the strengths, address the weaknesses, exploit the opportunities, and deal with the threats that the facility faces.

Concluding Thought

Most people see what is and never see what can be.

Albert Einstein

He who wants the rose must respect the thorn.

Persian Proverb

Chapter 9

Benchmarking the Key Financial Metrics

Step 4 of JJ Keegan+ WIN™ Formula (continued)

The degree of one's emotions varies inversely with one's knowledge of the facts.

Bertrand Russell

Chapter Highlights

Would you consider driving a car without the speedometer or cooking a prime rib dinner without a meat thermometer?

If you've answered "no" to these, why would you manage a golf course without comparing your operating performance to the national, state, and local benchmarks available by Club Benchmarking, Golf Datatech, ORCA Reports and many other reliable firms that reveal the operating performance of golf courses? Golf course owners, through these services, are afforded the opportunity to highlight strengths and weakness against their competitors.

This chapter covers the importance of utilizing these reports and information on how to become an active participant in submitting your information on a confidential and highly secure basis to these national research efforts.

That Is Too Much Work

For those just wanting to cut to the chase and get a snapshot of a golf course's financial picture, there are only a few questions you need to ask:

1. What is your rack rate?
2. How many rounds of golf (starts) did you have during the past 12 months?

If you multiply the rack rate times the number of rounds times 60%, you have a close approximation of the course's green fee and cart revenue. Based on your intuition as to the location of the golf course and the neighborhood you observed driving to the course, you can reasonably adjust your estimate of the golf course's financial potential.

The question of how many rounds a course plays is not deemed to be too intrusive—merely casual conversation at the course. From knowing that answer alone and looking at the size and condition of the clubhouse, examining the quality of the turf at the driving range, walking onto the practice putting green, and counting how many employees you see, you can reasonably estimate the profitability of the golf course.

A secondary set of numbers that will fine-tune your revenue projections are:

1. How many season passes or memberships do you sell and at what rate? The less, the better.
2. What is your revenue per round? If it is less than 50% of the rack rate, too many discounts are being offered.
3. How large is the pro shop? A small pro shop with little inventory is unlikely to generate over $100,000.
4. Is your food and beverage principally used by golfers, or do you have extensive outside dining guests for lunch and dinner? If the facility has only a snack bar or small restaurant, the facility is unlikely to generate over $100,000 in sales.
5. Does the facility have a large banquet and wedding facility? If so, revenues for those activities can exceed $1 million.
6. How many leagues, tournaments, or outings do you conduct? Most golf courses average about 33% of total play.

Regarding expenses, there are several numbers that provide the big picture:

1. What are the cost of your water and utilities? If water is over $100,000, there is a real concern.
2. Are maintenance expenses between 31% and 36% of total revenue? If maintenance expenses exceed 50% of revenue, issues abound.
3. What percentage are fringe benefits of total payroll? If the number exceeds 40%, privatization of the golf course through a third-party management company is advised where 22% to 26% is usually achieved.
4. How many labor hours are invested in maintaining your golf course? If you are in the northern climate, budgets exceeding 17,000 generate an alarm. In a southern climate, hourly budgets exceeding 28,000 are a concern.
5. Does the outstanding debt exceed $1 million at a public facility and $3 million at a private club? If so, there should be a concern about the ability to service debt.
6. What is your deferred capital expenditures (CapEx) in comparison to your capital reserves? If your deferred CapEx is greater than $3 million more than capital reserves, congratulations, you have entered the death spiral of declining revenues from providing a deteriorating golf experience.

It is surprising that so few numbers can tell such a large story about the probably financial of success for a club. This methodology is called heuristics. Heuristics is a science founded on experience-based techniques for problem-solving, learning, and discovery that finds a solution which is not guaranteed to be optimal, but good enough for a given set of goals. Where the exhaustive search is impractical, heuristic methods are used to speed up the process of finding a satisfactory solution via mental shortcuts to ease the cognitive load of making a decision.

For the golf industry, which largely lacks a detailed financial or operational orientation, these "rules of thumb" provide quick guidelines to monitor the performance of a golf course.

Three Blind Mice?

The ability to obtain precise financial information regarding industry benchmarks is a challenge.

One of the industry trends that shows the decreasing lack of cooperation to create national benchmarks is observed by the number of courses participating in the Annual Operations Survey conducted as part of PGA PerformanceTrak. This service compiled over 50 reports, presenting information by type of facility and ranking by quartile, and with the ability through advanced search criteria to monitor results nationally, by state, or by PGA Section for the number of holes desired. Reports available included:

- Total Rounds Played
- Peak-Season Combined Golf and Cart Fee
- Number of Full-Time Employees Facility-Wide
- Total Facility Revenues
- Total Green Fees and Guest Fees
- Total Cart Fees
- Golf Merchandise Revenue
- Range Revenue
- Food and Beverage Revenue
- Cost of Goods Sold
- Combined Food and Beverage Cost of Sales
- Golf Operations Payroll, Employee Benefits
- Golf Course Maintenance Payroll, Employee Benefits, Contractor and Temporary Staffing Costs
- Total Facility-Wide Net Operation Income

The number of respondents have fallen as follows: 2,350, 1,959, 1,695, and 957 in 2011, 2012, 2013, and 2014, respectively. As a result, in January 2016, the PGA of America announced the discontinuation of this valuable service. It is disappointing, but not unanticipated, how few golf courses participate in the varying benchmarking services available.

Why are the participation rates of the golf course so low? Sadly, the cause is a lack of sophistication on the part of many golf course owners as small business entrepreneurs. Because their livelihood is dependent upon the cash flow generated by the course, they hold a false belief that protecting their "trade secrets" is beneficial. Because golf is often a cash business, golf course owners are also sometime finicky and resist. Management companies are also very hesitant to participate in national benchmarking studies. To provide a platform on which their performance might be reviewed by their owners causes great angst. In contrast, throughout the hospitality industry, vital operational benchmarks are shared for the collective welfare of the industry.

Implementing such a system is like a term paper; it is a very iterative process. While many golf course owners and managers would like to have comprehensive comparative data on a local basis, the innovators and the early adopters quickly become frustrated with the results as they produce sample sizes too small to be meaningful. So do you publish the survey data that would indicate general national trends, hoping that those who review the report will be motivated to participate in future surveys, or do you just give up?

The solution to creating meaningful data depositories is readily available and would be simple to implement, but because of parochial boundaries and defined territories, it is not likely to occur in the short- or intermediate-term.

The good news is that if you are using benchmarks, you will be outperforming the financial returns of your direct competitors, increasing your customer loyalty, and ultimately gaining a significant market share advantage.

Valuable Benchmarking Options

For those owners looking for more in-depth financial information four alternatives are available:

1. Complimentary monthly reporting by Golf Datatech
2. Complimentary service provided by the R&A
3. Subscription service by Club Benchmarking and ORCA Reports
4. Licensed national surveys by Club Managers Association of America, Golf Course Superintendents Association of America, National Golf Course Owners Association, and the National Golf Foundation

Successful operators must understand, manage, and anticipate certain key operating statistics and industry benchmarks to maximize the bottom line.

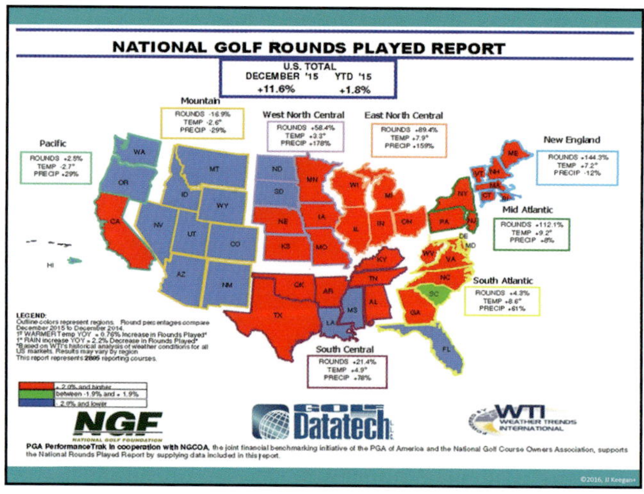

Golf Datatech creates a monthly national rounds report illustrated to the left. This report highlights changes in rounds from prior periods, temperature, and precipitation. Over 3,000, golf courses participate in this monthly service.

Golf Datatech also provides specialized market research covering retail sales, inventory, pricing, and distribution. With the plethora of FREE standard reports that Golf Datatech publishes monthly, a golf course can easily determine which brands they are carrying in each line of merchandise carried.

The Golf Datatech Retail Market Reports provide timely and accurate data on market share, unit sales, dollar sales, average pricing, inventories and distribution for golf balls, golf clubs (woods, irons, putters, and wedges), footwear, bags, and gloves. Also, Golf Apparel Reports are available covering the categories of men's and women's shirts, tops, bottoms, and outerwear. These reports provide meaningful insights and are invaluable, as illustrated here:

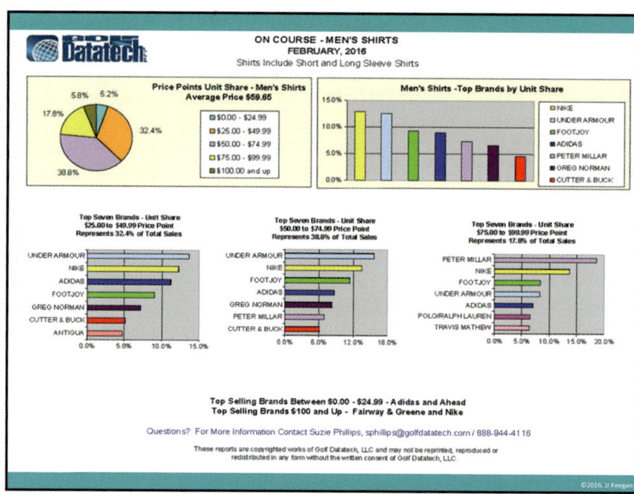

Would you go to Walmart to buy a Zegna Italian suit or a Robert Graham shirt? For an entry-level golf course with green fees under $25, would you carry Peter Millar or Fairway & Greene? Nope. There is an unofficial rule of thumb. The price of a golf shirt sold at a facility should be comparable to its green fee.

The process used by Golf Datatech is very comprehensive:

> "Sales data for all Retail Reports is accumulated monthly from hundreds of retail outlets and projected to the total market based upon proprietary models created by Golf Datatech.

> Sales and inventory data is transmitted to Golf Datatech through each shop's point-of-sale software system and includes units sold, actual selling price, and inventory remaining. Individual shop data is collapsed into totals within the database to insure confidentiality.
>
> Golf Datatech reports are currently produced monthly for the United States, the United Kingdom, Germany, and Sweden."[1]

In February 2013, a benchmarking tool shown below was introduced by the R&A. Titled "Course Tracker," its goal is to accomplish the following:[2]

1. Monitor, analyze, and evaluate your course's progress.
2. Identify where your business can make and save money.
3. Track income and expenditures and plan for the future.
4. Generate illustrated reports to help you make informed decisions.
5. Anonymously benchmark with other similar courses.

This service is being used by the members of numerous golf associations around the world, including Australia, England, Ireland, New Zealand, Portugal, Scotland, and Wales.

Within the United States, Club Benchmarking offers business intelligence tools with strong ties to the Why? How? What? model. It has also built a platform that is used in Australia and New Zealand. It provides the most comprehensive financial analysis for private clubs, with nearly 1,000 participating in the subscription-based service. The company offers online access 24/7 to accurate apples-to-apples club industry data, key performance indicators and reports for every area of the club, and powerful filtering tools that let subscribing courses control their comparison sets by many criteria (including, but not limited to, revenue, geography, and dues).

1 http://www.golfdatatech.com/research-products/retail-market-reports/overview/

2 https://www.coursetracker.org

Developed in cooperation with club general managers, board members, committee members, and audit firms, the platform has been adopted by the Club Managers Association of America (CMAA) as the industry's central database of standardized data. For the CMAA, Club Benchmarking now powers all of the CMAA's annual Club Industry Reports (Finance and Operations, Policies and Procedures, Compensation and Benefits, and Economic Impact).

Club Benchmarking's philosophy, which is on point, is that while every golf course is unique, the industry is governed by a common business model, clear key performance indicators matter, and food and beverage is not a profit center. A key component of its model is an executive dashboard view applying standard business measures such as gross margin, fixed expenses, labor, dues, and debt ratios, etc., acting as a benchmarked alignment point for boards and managers.

A list of its comprehensive solution is shown below.

Club Benchmarking's research has provided some remarkable insights from its financial insight model. At the middle of the industry (median), private clubs generate gross margins of 56% to 62% throughout the United States. Interestingly, The median private club has just under $7M in revenue.

Private club data points as a percent of total operating revenue include:

- Member dues – 50%
- Payroll – 54%
- Maintenance costs – 31% in most of the United States up to 36% on the west coast where water costs are higher.
- General and administrative costs – 23%
- Buildings and maintenance – 18%
- Fixed charges (RE tax, liability insurance, interest) – 11%

- Golf operations labor – 10%
- Food and beverage net loss – 3%

A comparison of a golf course's financial numbers to these industry benchmarks serves as a good reference point to measure both strengths and weaknesses in a golf operation. It is about understanding the facts vs. opinion and changing "I think" to "I know."

Benchmarking is more about learning about your operations, not others, for it represents fact-based leadership using factors to discharge your fiduciary duty by using ratios and indexes.

Club Benchmarking reports are very easy to generate and export into PowerPoint, Word, and Excel, producing graphs and charts as illustrated here.

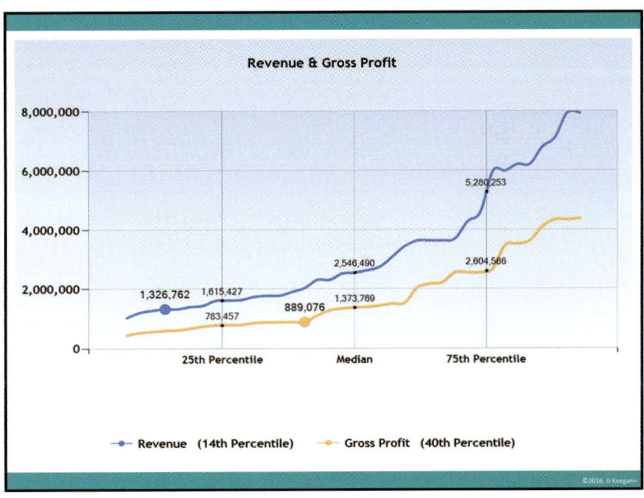

In 2015, Club Benchmarking formed an extension, Links Insight, to focus on daily fee, municipal, and military golf facility markets with an initial emphasis of aggregating the financial data for the leading resorts in the United States.

Its website, shown here, states, "While all non-private facilities may be termed public, there are major differences in the business models of each of the verticals above. We intentionally tailored Links Insight to address those individual differences while maintaining a single interface, data gathering mechanism, reporting, and analysis tool that allows all public facilities to use and access the same system."[3]

My Food Operation is Eating Me – Any Benchmarks?

Profitable Food Facilities (PFF) is a food and beverage consulting group that is frequently asked, "What should our food costs and labor costs be at a private country club?"

To answer that, one must differentiate between a snack bar and a full-service restaurant. There are two distinct businesses at a club: a la carte dining and banquets and special events.

A typical full-service restaurant not associated with a golf course targets overall food costs at 30%, labor costs at 30%, and other costs at 30%, for a profit of 10%. Some operations are more profitable than others, and these numbers vary slightly depending on the concept.

As Michael Holtzman, president of PFF, highlights so adroitly, "A club has a unique set of challenges:

- Open on slow days
- Big pours at the bar
- Free items are given away (coffee in the morning, ice cream at dinner, etc.)
- Member privileges (I belong to a club, so the food should be less)"

As a result, the average private club loses $250,000 annually in F&B which is truly staggering, as these losses are ultimately assumed by the members as part of their dues or assessments.

Some solutions proffered by Michael Holtzman include:

- Manage payroll on a daily basis.
- Stagger the "start" and "end" times.
- Eliminate overtime.

---

3 http://www.linksinsight.com/about-us/company-overview

- Banquet servers should not make more than $15–$20 per hour.
- Service charges for banquets should be added to the facility's revenue, with the server being compensated based on the prevailing wage.
- Cost out every menu and catering item. Target 20%–25% banquet cost and 30%–33% a la carte dining cost. If anything is over 40% food cost, change the portion, the ingredients, or the price. If it is still over 40%, don't sell the item.

The End Game

Is it harder to increase revenue or to decrease expenses?

A story is told about Henry Ford, the founder of the long-standing U.S. automobile company. The company was struggling during its infancy, and expenses were exceeding revenue. Everyone at a meeting of company executives was offering ideas as to what could be cut. Finally, in exasperation and frustration, Henry Ford said, "I got the answer. We can cut all the expenses and just shut this place down. Obviously, that won't work. So let's determine where we need to make an investment that will achieve our goals."

Who knows whether that story is true. But it illustrates a great point.

Increasing revenue is dependent upon making assumptions with no certainty as to their realization. Because it is easier to address that which is known, expenses become the focus.

Managing a golf course can seem daunting, often like trying to solve a Rubik's club. It is vital that like activities at a golf course be grouped into comparable general ledger accounts with department and sub-department reporting. Individual green fees, season passes, maintenance labor equipment and materials, capital expenses, food and beverage labor, and food and beverage expenses lend themselves to modeling aided by the use of benchmarks to set the foundation for the analysis.

Hence, start by gathering the industry benchmark data as a foundation for your analysis. Implementing the changes indicated then will begin the process of turning a struggling club into a profitable one.

Key Points to Remember

1) Golf Datatech and Club Benchmarking provide valuable data repositories in which the financial performance for golf courses can be compared.
2) Rounds as measured by green fees, member dues, and season passes account for about 60% of gross revenue and materially affect all the other revenue departments.
3) With the preparation of historical financial statements, variances with industry data can be examined closely to determine abnormal operating patterns at the facility.
4) With a firm understanding of a golf course's historical performance in comparison to industry standards, there exists a great opportunity to create financial projections that emphasize a golf course's existing strengths and correct its weaknesses.
5) The course's retail buyer should compare and contrast merchandise product lines to the median household income within 10 miles of your golf course to determine if the most optimum products lines for the golf course's customers are being stocked.

Concluding Thought

If a thing is done wrong often enough, it becomes right.

Leahy's Law

People who do not break things first will never learn to create anything.

Philippine (Tagalog) Proverb

Chapter 10

Pricing and Yield Management Step 4 of the JJ Keegan+ WIN™ Formula (continued)

"The best way of learning about anything is by doing."

—Richard Branson

Chapter Highlights

Since the advent of public golf in the late 1800s, yield management, by design or by accident, has been an integral part of pricing at golf courses. Prices that change by time of the day, the day of the week, player type, season, and year are examples of the use of basic yield management theory.

While historical attempts at adjusting rates to influence demand were unscientific, more accurate adjustments are now possible due to the evolution of technology and the ability to construct a database that accurately portrays the utilization of the golf course for multiple years. Those who operate a golf course can now appropriately balance the capacity of the golf course at the highest net revenue per reservation.

Opponents of a dynamic pricing structure seem to believe that customer dissonance from strangers who meet on the first tee and discuss the varied prices they have paid will create customer service issues. But it is known, understood, and accepted that the rate structure for airfares, hotels, and even car rentals is the standard way efficient managers price commodities today.

This chapter provides insights on how today's golf manager can implement powerful and profitable pricing.

The Core Components

Yield management is a term everyone says they understand, but few have the knowledge to comprehend its intricacies.

Revenue management consists of thoroughly grasping the fair market value for each tee time sold. Components comprise the demand available, appropriately pricing by customer segment and adroitly managing the numerous distribution channels (phone reservations to the golf course or via central reservations, and online booking via website, mobile applications, e-mail or text messages, etc.) undertaken directly by the customer, a travel agency, or a wholesale third-party distribution company.

The implementation of revenue management (also known as yield management or dynamic pricing) is one of the greatest opportunities for a golf course management to increase its revenue.

To do so, the path begins by recognizing that the golf industry prices its tee time inventory based on a flawed model and being willing to embrace a new paradigm. That starts with understanding the fair market value for a tee time.

What Is Fair?

Fair market value is defined as "the price for which property can be sold in an 'arm's length' transaction; that is, between informed, unrelated, and willing parties, each of whom is acting rationally and in its best interest."[1]

Realizing that most golf courses have more than 75 different rates that vary by day of the week, time of day, day of the year, and age of the golfer, there is no more subjective area than green fees.

Some golf course owners, particularly those at newer facilities, establish the green fees based on cost plus desired return on investment. The expenses are estimated, the required debt service coverage calculated, and the desired investment return projected; then the green fees are set based on the aggregate total

1 Cisco Systems Capital, "Financial Glossary," http://www.cisco.com/warp/public/csc/about_financing/glossary.html

divided by the projected rounds. This sort of pricing might pacify the banker, but it does nothing to assure that value is provided to the golfer.

Others set the green fees based on market value. This is the "feels right" method. Either the fees from the prior year are adjusted for inflation, or perhaps a sampling is taken of comparable facilities, and a rate is chosen that feels competitive.

Still others base their fees on some subjective perception of the value of the golf experience. How else could one justify the difference between a golf course charging over $500 per round and one that charges less than $30? Both courses are between 6,000 and 7,400 yards, have 18 holes, and take roughly 4½ hours to play.

That substantial difference would have to be justified based on the location of the course, conditioning, strategic shot values, time of the year, surrounding scenery, the architect, or championships held at the facility. Pebble Beach does a good job of filling the golf course at a premium rate. But there is only one Monterey Peninsula.

There is a formula, often invisible to the owner, for what golfers are willing to pay.

The Value Gap

Golfers are very astute and value-driven. Golfers measure their experience based 90% on the course and 10% on the service standards encountered.

By examining all of the components of a golf experience, a golf course manager can calculate the value of the experience, compare that to the rate charged, build a marketing campaign based on its unique value, and stimulate revenue.

For purposes of stimulating creative thought on alternative methods, a potential model for establishing green fees would comprise six variables: slope rating (difficulty and shot values), strategy, conditioning, playing texture variety, ambiance, and customer amenities.

Each of these components and their effect on the proper price for the green fee is discussed next.

1. **Slope Rating:** The greater the slope rating, the greater the challenge, and the greater the diversity of golf shots provided the higher the green fees should be. To play a flat municipal golf course short in length with nominal hazards is a completely different experience than a championship bunker-strewn, lake-filled, tree-lined golf course.

   While a debate on shot values is subjective, a quantitative way to measure shot values might be on the course's slope. Thus the premium charged by difficult courses like the Stadium Course at TPC would be justified.

The green fees could be set based on the following:

Slope from Middle Tee	Base Green Fee
Under 113	$20
114 –120	35
121–130	50
131–140	75
Over 140	$100

2. **Strategy:** What is better—the 120-yard par 3 strewn with bunkers, the island green, the dual fairway hole that provides both a safe and a hazardous route, or the well-designed dogleg left that places the hazards on the left? The answer is all of the above. Hit the precise shot, and you are rewarded.

   Take the first safe route, and the second shot becomes more of a challenge. Risk for reward—this is the essence of the game. You might consider adjusting your green fees for the following:

Strategy	Adjustment to Green Fee
The vast majority of holes are straight; the course is flat; few trees, bunkers, dunes, and water hazards; and options to play hole are well-defined, providing few options. No requirement to position shots. No risk/reward options.	−10
A few doglegs with modest bunkering and trees, some rolling terrain, green complexes are uniform throughout the course. One or two risk/reward options.	−5
Terrain, bunkers, water hazards, trees, and green complexes provide typical golf experience.	0
One-third of golf holes provide a unique golf experience requiring thought to navigate risk/reward successfully.	+5

Strategy	Adjustment to Green Fee
Up to two-thirds of golf holes provide a challenging experience where the placement of the drive and the second shot has a significant impact on the ability to score well.	+10
The par 3, 4, and 5 holes have varying length, i.e., par 3s of 120, 150, 180, and 210 yards. Course may have dual fairways, bunkering that pinches the fairway, streams crossing the fairway and the green, narrow green openings, green side bunkers of varying depth, and heavily contoured putting surfaces.	+20

3. **Conditioning:** Well-manicured golf courses should charge a premium. The investment made in maintaining a course ranges from $200,000 to over $2 million, and the conditioning is rated by golfers as one of the two most important criteria.

   The following chart suggests adjustments that could be made to the green fees based on the current course condition:

Condition	Adjustment to Green Fee
Poor, requiring winter rules to be played	–10
Greens aerated during past two weeks	–10
Standard, greens stimped at 8 to 9	0
Good, one cut of rough, single mowing pairing on fairway and greens	+10
Excellent, two cuts of rough, cross cut fairway, green stimped at 9 to 10	+20
Tour quality, greens stimped at over 11	+30

4. **Playing Texture Variety:** For the golf devotee, nothing is prettier than a golf course that has well-manicured bentgrass tees, fairways, greens that have been cross cut, Kentucky blue grass rough with two cuts, and bunkers lined with rye for stability and fescue and Scottish broom for appearance. Conversely, a course that is poa annua or Bermuda grass looks less defined.

Grasses	Adjustment to Green Fee
One strain	–10
Two strains	0
Three to four strains	+10
Four or more strains in which bent, blue, fescue, and Scottish broom are used	+20

5. **Ambiance:** In the mountains, along a river, by an ocean, spectacular vistas, a well-known architect, a fabulous clubhouse, an extensive practice facility—all would command a premium that should be added to the green fee.

Ambience	Adjustment to Green Fee
Unique tee markers	+5
Flower garden at entrance	+5
Flower garden at three or multiple locations on course	+10
Extensive practice facility with unlimited practice privileges for registered golfer	+20
Top 10 architect	+25
11th–50th ranked architect	+10
River or ocean comes into play	+10
The theme of the course: Tour 18, Cowboy's Club, etc.	+10
Conducted LPGA or Senior PGA event	+10
Conducted PGA Tour event	+20
Conducted USGA national championship	+20

6. **Customer Service Amenities:** While every golfer is looking for "something free," amenities provided could be packaged into the basic green fees. We have observed over 100 different amenities disbursed at golf courses, starting at the bag drop area, locker room, first tee, the cart, pro shop, on the course, and in the cart return area. These range from engraved bag tags, to bottled water and suntan lotion, to certificates of accomplishment for besting par on a signature hole. The creativity of golf course managers in making the customer's experience special has been noteworthy. We have even witnessed free food on the course, for example, fish tacos at Cabo del Sol or chocolate chip cookies at Hualalai. The green fee could be increased based on the number of amenities provided the golfer based on the following chart:

Amenities Provided	Adjustment to Green Fee
0–2	+0
3–5	+2
6–10	+5
11–20	+10
21–40	+20
Over 40	+50
Note: 0–2 would likely represent tees and ball markers in the pro shop.	

If you take this model and apply it, it provides an approximate estimate of the correct price. Following are two examples:

Category	City Park— Denver Colorado	Cowboys Club— Dallas, Texas
Slope	$39	$100
Strategy	0	10
Conditioning	–5	0
Playing Texture	–5	0
Ambience	0	20
Customer Service	0	10
Estimate Value-Based Green Fee	$29	$140
Notes: The weekday green fee at City Park is $27. Cowboys Golf Club green fee on Master's weekend was $129.95.		

Looking for another alternative pricing model? Consider charging by the hour, which might be based as shown on the following chart:

Type of Course	Hourly Rate
Steel, i.e., entry-level municipal	$ 6.00
Bronze, i.e., average daily fee	12.00
Silver, i.e., above-average daily fee or mid-tier private club or resort	25.00
Gold, i.e., top-end daily fee, above average private club or resort	50.00
Platinum, i.e., top-end golf facility.	75.00

For those seeking to use a cart, one could add $4 per hour for the cart per golfer at the entry level and slightly tier the pricing as the quality of the facility improves. The permutations are limitless, but the concept of a single hourly rate is simple.

Yes, there are many logistical hurdles to implementing such a concept (collecting at the end of the round for golf secured in advance by credit card; a fast group gets stuck behind a slow group and demands the lower rate; individuals wanting to play only for one or two hours and returning to the clubhouse via fairways being used by other golfers). Notwithstanding the challenges, this novel approach could create a marketing buzz that might attract golfers.

Thus, each facility should ask—"What would be the perfect round at our facility?" "How do we consistently deliver that experience?" "How can we exceed expectations that justify the fees assessed?"

Training Wheels

Because the golf course has a perishable inventory, fixed capacity, predictable time-related demand, and high fixed and low variable costs, it is an industry that is ideal for revenue management, whether by offering an all-inclusive one-price fee or by unbundling the various components at a golf course (green fee, cart, range balls, etc.) like the airlines do for checking bags, sitting in a row with extra room, and other such services.

Tee times are like airline seats. Once the airliner takes off, the empty seat is worthless, and once the 9:45 a.m. tee time comes and goes, it's gone forever. The goal is revenue optimization.

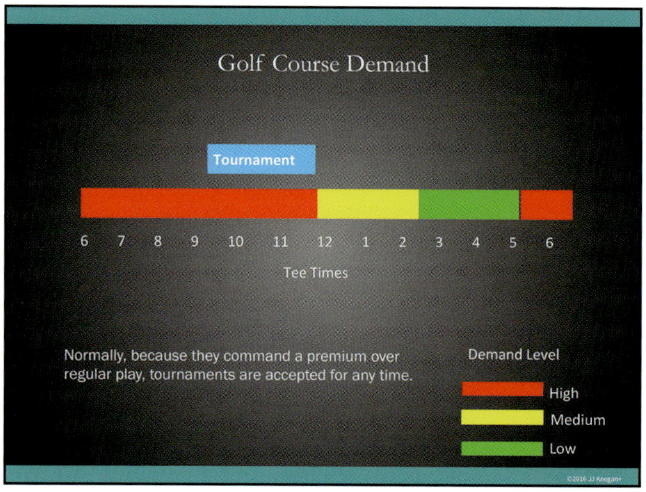

Often, it is thought that the objective of revenue management is to raise rates to maximize utilization. This is wrong!

The real objective is to maximize revenues and profits through the effective management of product availability. For a golf course, typical demand is reflected as shown in the figure here.

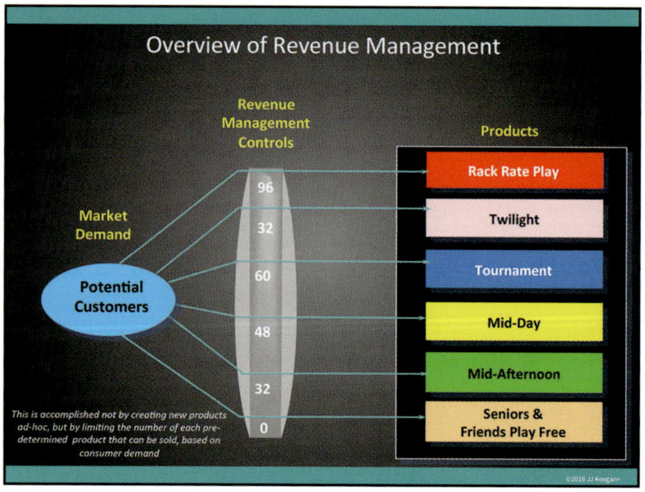

Revenue management is the discipline that allows companies to create many, many products that attract market demand, and then manage that demand in a manner that maximizes revenues, as illustrated in the figure shown here.

The figure might be applicable for a weekend when demand would be higher, and the desire to let seniors or coupon-holders have access to the course would be small.

To maximize revenues, the revenue manager must determine the quantity of each product to make available for sale, at each course, for all days in the future.

Assuming products are controlled on an hourly basis from 6 a.m. to 4 p.m., a revenue manager with five golf courses and an average of only five products must actively manage the availability of 1,500 products per day. If the product availability is managed for only the next seven days, 10,500 controls must be checked and set each day.

While it sounds precise, without an appropriately constructed software optimization module that accurately captures the historical demand at the facility, revenue management is very subjective and requires a lot of guesswork— at least initially.

While the basic theory is simple, it gets complicated very quickly. To illustrate, on what date do you base your demand forecast on, for example, the 1st of June, the 152nd day of the year or the 1st Friday in June? Forecasting rounds played on the 4th of July, a national U.S. holiday, demonstrates the challenge as well. The rounds played will vary significantly if July 4th is on a weekend rather than on a Tuesday or Wednesday. And if the 4th of July is on a Friday, the demand on the following Sunday will be far less than if the 4th of July occurs during the middle of the week.

Since the various possibilities boggle the mind, it is little wonder that demand pricing has gotten very little attention in the golf industry. It is way too complex to attempt to figure out manually. If one were to develop the software to implement dynamic pricing, the investment exceeds seven figures. And that may be why demand pricing is only now coming into vogue as more and more yield management software programs become available.

Why the Golf Industry Model for Tee Times Is Flawed

As the industry moves to demand pricing, an examination of golf's historical pricing practices provides insights in comparison to other industries. For example, the airline yield management model is shown in the figure shown here.

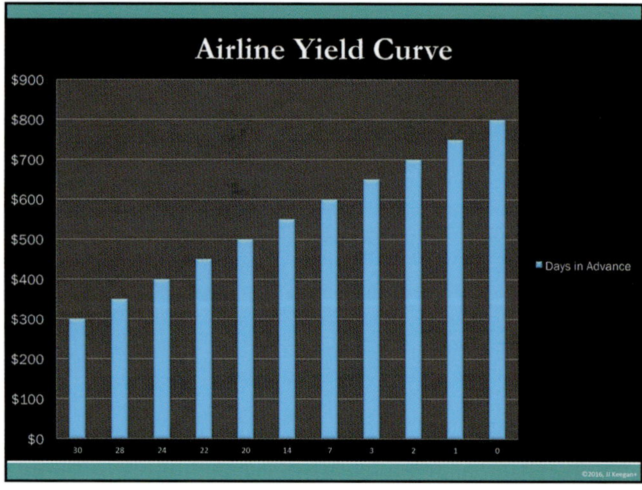

Everyone knows that the best values for airlines are obtained 14 or more days in advance on a non-refundable basis. The theory is that recreational travelers are motivated by the lower fares, and because of the certainty of their vacation, they are willing to purchase on a nonrefundable basis. Conversely, business travelers, because of less certainty as to when or where they need to be and from their increased ability to pay, are charged a higher fare for booking in the days just before departure.

In contrast, the majority of golf courses use a static pricing model with a tendency to discount tee times late in the booking cycle. While few facilities use software that enable dynamic pricing, psychologically, many operators panic as the day of play approaches, and some engage in flexible pricing that results in the yield illustrated in the figure shown here.

What is ironic is that the greatest demand to book a tee time occurs when tee times first become available (30%) and within 48 hours of the tee time requested (40%). What most operators fail to grasp is that the odds are better for raising prices close to the day of play, not lowering them.

The Odds Are in the House's Favor

Who is better off—the course that plays 24,000 rounds at $40 per tee time or a facility that plays 40,000 rounds at $24 per tee time? Trick question.

For a gross revenue perspective, both facilities generate the same gross revenue. The highest revenue is achieved by selling 32,000 rounds at $32 each, as shown in the figure shown here.

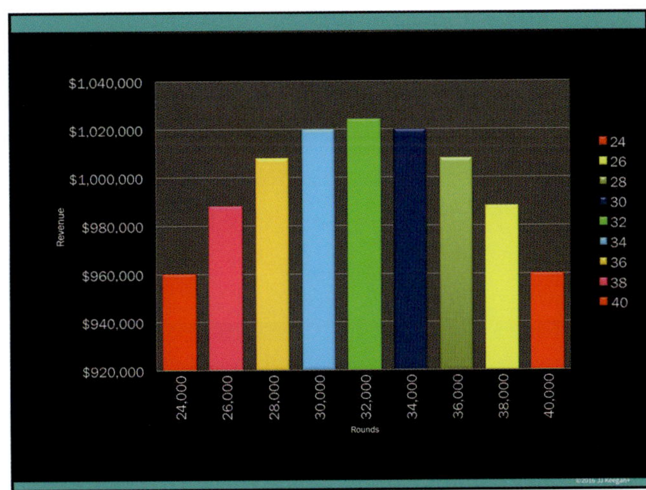

While the wear and tear on the course is higher on the course that played 40,000 rounds, that cost is often negligible. The object is simple—maximize revenue.

In Las Vegas, the odds favor the house. Over the long run, more money is lost by customers than won. It is not a zero-sum game. The casinos win. The same favorable odds are available to golf courses if they understand the dynamics of discounting versus raising rates.

Many golf course managers are lulled into the economic trap of believing that more rounds, even at a slight discount, are financially advantageous. Discounting is a slippery slope. Looking at this chart proves why it is sheer folly to participate in coupon books offering two-for-one green fees.

Decrease in Price	Number of Additional Rounds Required to Offset Discount
5%	5.26%
10%	11.11%
15%	17.65%
20%	25.00%
25%	33.33%
30%	42.86%
35%	53.85%
40%	66.67%
45%	81.82%
50%	100.00%

A golf course offering a 50% discount would need a 100% increase in rounds to recover the revenue lost. How can any facility offer such a discount?

The logic is that if the lower rates attract a golfer to the course for the first time, he or she will be so enamored with the experience that return trips will produce a profit many times the discount was given. JJ Keegan+ research has shown that these discount-oriented golfers spend little money on the course, bring few additional customers during their visits, and return infrequently and only when they again can play at a reduced price.

Someone who has taken the opportunity to purchase a product for $20 will seldom feel good about purchasing the product again for $40.

Raising prices annually is a practice most golf courses have gotten out of the habit of doing. Citing the economy, the competition, and the growing influence of third-party tee time purveyors, they have been locked into a mindset of paralysis. Shown here is the positive impact on gross revenue when prices are increased.

If For No Other Reason,
Here Is Why You Should Increase Your Prices

Price Movement	Amount	Impact	To Break Even
Decrease Price	50%	100%	Need to Double Rounds
Increase Price	50%	33%	Can lose 1/3 of rounds
House Odds are In Your Favor		67%	

Interpreted, if a golf course increased its prices by 50%, it could lose 33% of the rounds played yet still generate the same gross revenue, with far less work, far better course conditions, and the same bottom line.

The odds are in the favor of the golf course, as shown in the chart. While this chart exaggerates the extreme of discounting versus price increases, it does support the theory that golf courses make a mistake discounting, believing additional rounds are the path to profitability.

Creating a Winning Hand

Winning poker is not just about maximizing the pot on a good hand, for many players will generate some return with strong cards, but it's also about playing a bad hand well. As has been said about the game of golf, "It's not how many great shots you hit but how many really bad shots you don't." If the goal is to increase net income, it is only logical that dynamic pricing is implemented.

Shown here is an easy-to-understand pricing model that would benefit all public facilities, and it would be accepted by customers based on the values they would receive.

Golfers looking to secure a prime tee time, be it on a Saturday morning or a holiday weekend, are willing to pay a premium to secure that preferred time, if for no other reason than it allows them to plan effectively the balance of their day with family and friends. And charging a premium secured by credit card would increase revenue and enhance the value to the customer. Or if a tourist is traveling to a resort over a holiday weekend, paying a premium to secure a preferred time is a win-win situation.

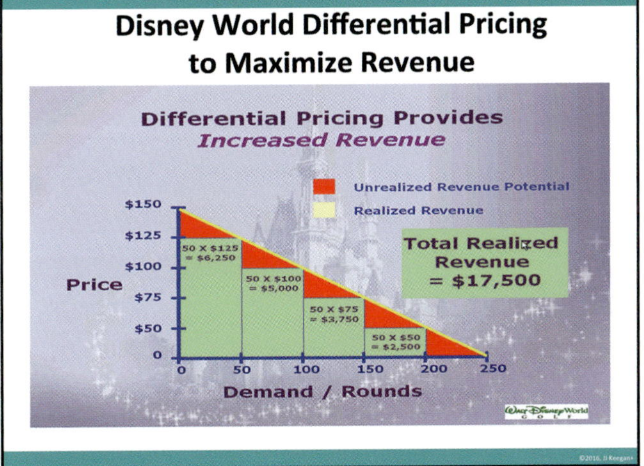

To recognize historical practices of booking seven days in advance, that practice can continue if you accept a credit card at the time of the reservation, with the card only charged on the day of play upon the appearance or non-appearance of the golfer.

Closer to the day of play, the demand to play at specific time increases. Therefore, the golf course would be wise to charge a higher price within 48 hours of the time reserved.

The benefits of revenue management techniques are demonstrated by Walt Disney World Golf, which creates up to six buckets for its rate various categories. Fifty rack rate tee times per day is its goal. Shown here is an example of how Disney attempts to maximize its revenue.

Walt Disney World Golf provides no discounts for rack rate rounds, fully paid packages, and groups. A 5% to 10% discount might be provided to the local community and corporations, AAA members, and other affinities. A 10% to 20% discount would be provided to annual pass holders, Florida resident golfers, and vacation club members. Deeper discounts would be allocated to commissioned business while the deepest discounts would be allocated to local hospitality and junior golf.

The key is that discounts are only provided when the rack rate demand doesn't first fill the times available. Disney uses a "wizard," a feature within its software, to ensure everyone reserves their tee times through the same booking engine where the yield management rates have been pre-established.

Technology to Optimize Price for the Golfer

With the increasing automation of the tee time reservation process and the growing use of the Web to book tee times, many golf courses have started implementing the dynamic pricing shown here.

What is intriguing and truly the introduction of revenue management at golf courses is where the golfer is provided the option of selecting his time by price using sliding bars on the online reservation system, adjusting by desired time of day and price, as shown here at Sewailo Golf Club.

These dynamic pricing models have been made possible by advances in technology that are being driven by third-party tee time firms, many of whom are engaged in barter. EZ-Link, Golf Channel's Golfnow.com, and Quick18, among others, are leading the development of software motivated to create dynamic pricing, including providing golf course mobile applications for their customers.

#Power In Numbers

With the continued evolution of software and its increasing sophistication, there is a new software company in the golf industry that promises great hope to the golf course operator: The ORCA REPORT. Tailored after the Star Report, which provides benchmarking and analysis for the hotel sector, the ORCA Reports provides key performance indicators for your golf course in comparison to your competitive set as shown here.

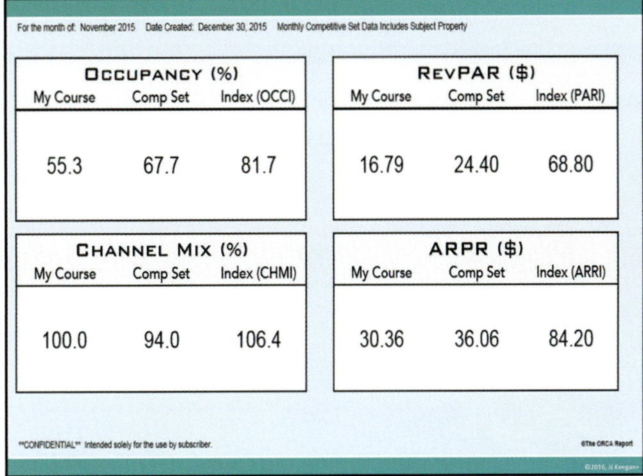
For the month of: November 2015 Date Created: December 30, 2015 Monthly Competitive Set Data Includes Subject Property

Occupancy (%)		
My Course	Comp Set	Index (OCCI)
55.3	67.7	81.7

RevPAR ($)		
My Course	Comp Set	Index (PARI)
16.79	24.40	68.80

Channel Mix (%)		
My Course	Comp Set	Index (CHMI)
100.0	94.0	106.4

ARPR ($)		
My Course	Comp Set	Index (ARRI)
30.36	36.06	84.20

CONFIDENTIAL Intended solely for the use by subscriber. ©The ORCA Report

©2016, JJ Keegan+

Utilization (**O**ccupancy), **R**evenue per available round, **C**hannel mix, and **A**verage revenue per round sold are key performance indicators.

The above information effectively presents the golf course owner vital information regarding the performance of their golf course. In this case, the management team felt that the market was vastly oversupplied and that it was necessary to keep prices low to attract golfers. The strategy was not effective as the lower prices were not being realized on increased revenue.

The result of this belief on annual revenues was costly, as reflected here:

For the trailing 12 months, the gross revenue generated was $855,531 less than competitors. The results, in this case, are stunning and reflect that a thorough examination of pricing strategies is warranted.

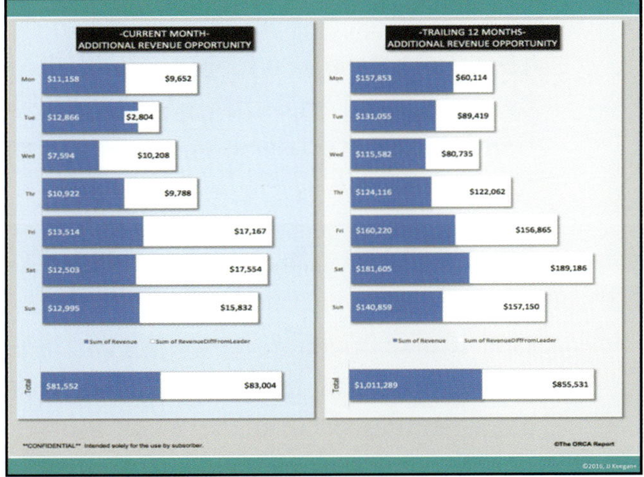

While all of the ORCA Reports provide value, the one that may have the biggest impact on the golf industry is the Channel

Distribution Report, with its ability to measure the cost of third-party tee time services. As reflected here for a golf course in Las Vegas, the opportunity cost of bartered times sold for 12 months was $110,123.

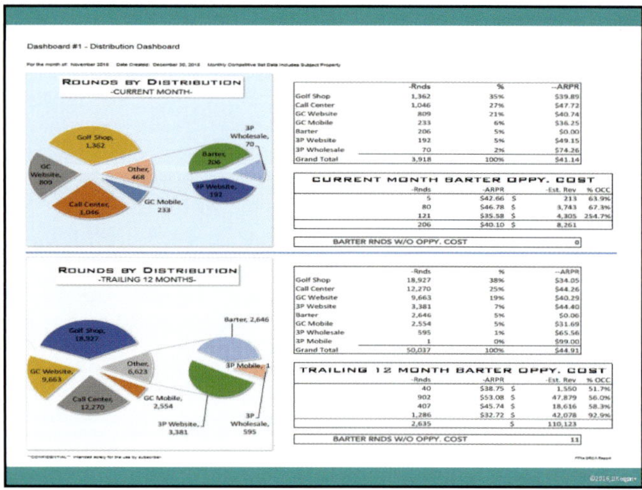

	-Rnds	%	--ARPR
Golf Shop	1,362	35%	$39.89
Call Center	1,046	27%	$47.72
GC Website	809	21%	$40.74
GC Mobile	233	6%	$36.25
Barter	206	5%	$0.00
3P Website	192	5%	$49.15
3P Wholesale	70	2%	$74.26
Grand Total	3,918	100%	$41.14

CURRENT MONTH BARTER OPPY. COST				
-Rnds	-ARPR		-Est. Rev	% OCC
5	$42.66	$	213	63.9%
80	$46.78	$	3,743	67.3%
121	$35.58	$	4,305	254.7%
206	$40.10	$	8,261	

BARTER RNDS W/O OPPY. COST	0

	-Rnds	%	--ARPR
Golf Shop	18,927	38%	$34.05
Call Center	12,270	25%	$44.26
GC Website	9,663	19%	$40.29
3P Website	3,381	7%	$44.40
Barter	2,646	5%	$0.06
GC Mobile	2,554	5%	$31.69
3P Wholesale	595	1%	$65.56
3P Mobile	1	0%	$99.00
Grand Total	50,037	100%	$44.91

TRAILING 12 MONTH BARTER OPPY. COST				
-Rnds	-ARPR		-Est. Rev	% OCC
40	$38.75	$	1,550	51.7%
902	$53.08	$	47,879	56.0%
407	$45.74	$	18,616	58.3%
1,286	$32.72	$	42,078	92.9%
2,635		$	110,123	

BARTER RNDS W/O OPPY. COST	11

These reports serve as an X-ray on the efficiency and effectiveness of golf course rate management programs and will greatly aid a golf course manager to set properly and dynamically adjust rates.

While this new service in 2016 is now serving over 120 golf courses in Arizona, California, and Nevada, the long-term success of this endeavor is unknown for several reasons:

1. The capitalization required in this entrepreneurial start-up is significant.
2. It is necessary to export data from various vendors' POS systems to the central database repository. Resistance from firms (e.g., GolfNow) is to be anticipated.
3. There is a natural skepticism amongst golf course owners to pool data for the collective benefit of the group.
4. Management companies whose influence is growing in the industry may be reluctant to adopt this service, because these reports will reflect the effectiveness of their rate management programs.

The ORCA Reports symbolize the challenges of the golf business. What should be obvious and implemented will meet with resistance masked with justifications that superficially appear to have merit but in substance have none.

How Much More Money Would You Like to Make?

Golf course operators in today's market should hope to achieve at least 66% utilization during the prime season. This is defined from sunup to two hours before sundown. Given that a golf course's most profitable customer is often the repeat customer, consider the following:

1. All green fees and tournaments should be prepaid at the time of reservation with credit card guarantees.
2. No "complimentary" rounds during prime time.
3. Golfers on Friday should be charged the weekend rate.
4. Tournaments should be booked for the "shoulder periods".
5. Tournaments should pay a premium of 25% over the standard green fees for prime time.
6. Carts should be mandatory for all tournament play.
7. Price and restrict a season pass to low utilization periods.
8. Introduce value pricing only during slack periods of time.
9. Use a "wave" or "crisscross" during prime times to increase revenue.
10. Put a winter enclosure on carts to encourage play during the shoulder seasons.
11. Don't participate in charity cards that give away golf.
12. Put your course brochures in the off-course golf shops.
13. Have the staff write a weekly golf tip for the local newspaper and make that tip a downloadable "gift" for registering on the website.
14. Minimize the downside of food and beverage. The food must be affordable, and a beverage cart and halfway house will increase revenue. By adding a phone to the ninth tee, phone orders will increase. Best practice is to have a barbecue at the turns. It creates a great smell and enhances the experience.
15. Selling bottled water rather than providing on-course water coolers.

Key Points to Remember

1) "Yield Management." While it sounds precise, it is very subjective. It requires a lot of guesswork initially before demand forecasts models can be constructed.
2) There is perhaps no more subjective area in the business of golf than determining green fees. Prices for green fees are sometimes said to be based on the ego of the management team and not on supply and demand.
3) Oftentimes, prices are set based on what competitors are charging.
4) Prices should only be set based on the value of the experience created. Green fees could be set based on the slope, strategic options, conditioning, grass texture, ambience, and customer amenities. Green fees could also be set, similar to other entertainment venues, based on an hourly fee.
5) Once the baseline rate has been established, the ability to adjust based on demand becomes viable.
6) The progressive golf course owner will begin a search for software that will provide for yield management and facilitate negotiated pricing of tee times. With these tools, the golf course owners are in complete control of reserving tee times and accepting or rejecting offers based on established criteria.
7) The daily fee golf business boils down to the simple fact that customer activity drives revenue.

Concluding Thought

The young man knows the rules, but the old man knows the exceptions.

Oliver Wendell Holmes

No man was ever wise by chance.

Seneca

Chapter 11

Golf Course Valuation
Step 4 of JJ Keegan+ WIN™ Formula (continued)

Work expands to fill the time available for its completion, the thing to be done swells in perceived importance and complexity.

Parkinson's First Law

Chapter Highlights

In entering into the golf business, the operative word is "business." In seeking a return from the investment in a golf course, understanding how golf courses are valued can ensure the acquisition is made wisely and that the sale optimizes the investment return.

Because this is a transaction an individual or entity makes infrequently, knowledge of the nuances of how a golf course is valued and the pitfalls of purchasing is essential. For the seller, just as a home seller prepares a house for showing, preparing the golf course for sale can help to ensure that fair value is received and that deductions for deferred capital expenditures are minimized.

This chapter focuses on the dramatic changes in golf course real estate transactions in a market that is now recovering from prices hitting bottom in 2012.

Abracadabra—Poof

Since 2006, the recession, which lasted until 2009, and the fact that golf course supply exceeds demand have changed the landscape of golf course real estate transactions. The major lenders focused on the golf market (such as Capmark, GE Capital, and Textron) have vacated, liquidating rather than expanding their golf course portfolios.

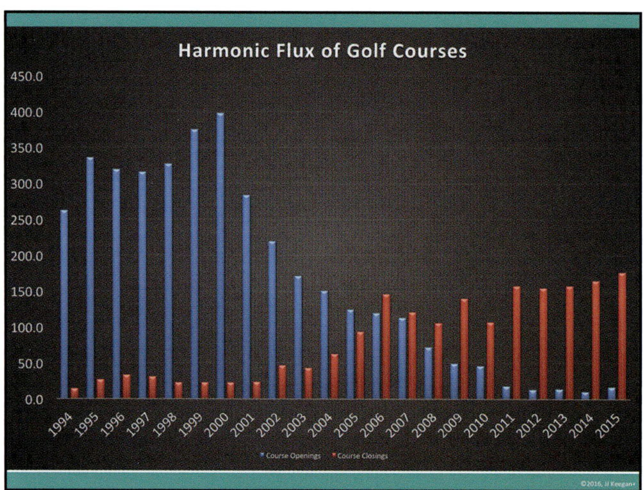

For the past decade, more golf courses have closed than opened. These changes in the dynamics of golf course real estate are shown in the figure shown here.

When demand exceeds supply, prices rise. The opposite has been occurring between 2006 and 2015; golf course sales prices have fallen 31.59% as shown here.

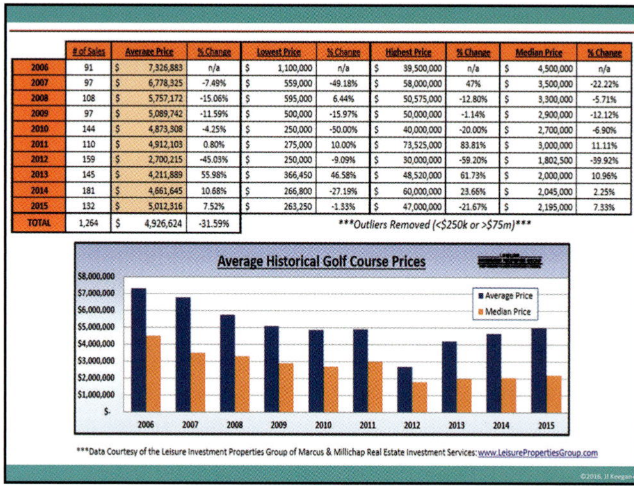

	# of Sales	Average Price	% Change	Lowest Price	% Change	Highest Price	% Change	Median Price	% Change
2006	91	$ 7,326,883	n/a	$ 1,100,000	n/a	$ 39,500,000	n/a	$ 4,500,000	n/a
2007	97	$ 6,778,325	-7.49%	$ 559,000	-49.18%	$ 58,000,000	47%	$ 3,500,000	-22.22%
2008	108	$ 5,757,172	-15.06%	$ 595,000	6.44%	$ 50,575,000	-12.80%	$ 3,300,000	-5.71%
2009	97	$ 5,089,742	-11.59%	$ 500,000	-15.97%	$ 50,000,000	-1.14%	$ 2,900,000	-12.12%
2010	144	$ 4,873,308	-4.25%	$ 250,000	-50.00%	$ 40,000,000	-20.00%	$ 2,700,000	-6.90%
2011	110	$ 4,912,103	0.80%	$ 275,000	10.00%	$ 73,525,000	83.81%	$ 3,000,000	11.11%
2012	159	$ 2,700,215	-45.03%	$ 250,000	-9.09%	$ 30,000,000	-59.20%	$ 1,802,500	-39.92%
2013	145	$ 4,211,889	55.98%	$ 366,450	46.58%	$ 48,520,000	61.73%	$ 2,000,000	10.96%
2014	181	$ 4,661,645	10.68%	$ 266,800	-27.19%	$ 60,000,000	23.66%	$ 2,045,000	2.25%
2015	132	$ 5,012,316	7.52%	$ 263,250	-1.33%	$ 47,000,000	-21.67%	$ 2,195,000	7.33%
TOTAL	1,264	$ 4,926,624	-31.59%						

Outliers Removed (<$250k or >$75m)

***Data Courtesy of the Leisure Investment Properties Group of Marcus & Millichap Real Estate Investment Services: www.LeisurePropertiesGroup.com

©2016, JJ Keegan+

Larry Hirsh, president of Golf Property Analysts and one of the industry's leading appraisers, estimated that nearly 500 golf courses are "eligible for purchase." As he commented while being interviewed for this book, "The golf course industry is akin to the Republican Party. Both have lost their constituencies and need to attract women, minorities, and focus on the family if they are to prosper."

As Hilda Allen, an industry leader in the sale and auction of golf courses and residential communities, stated, "I would speculate that 25% of the existing courses are for sale on some basis." She continued, saying,

"With so many facilities losing money, the net income multiplier or the income/capitalization rate valuation methods are no longer applicable. If there is a positive net cash flow, then the industry appraisers say 7 to 10 times multiple. If the cash flow is negative, then a gross income multiplier with consideration given to each profit center is used and is from .675 to 1.6 times gross income.

Owner financing is the key component; most buyers/investors have equity sources with debt participation. There are a group of new buyers with Wall Street hedge funds and some capital sources who are the 'kings' at this juncture as they can negotiate discounts from 10% to as much as 50%."

There clearly are some negative factors that weigh heavily on golf course values:

1. Lack of financing.
2. The size and scope of the courses and clubhouses built starting in the 1990s are very expensive physical assets to maintain, thereby impacting cash flow.
3. The second-home vacation market has vanished, with individuals preferring to pay a small premium for staying in luxury hotels rather than the constant cash outflow of second-home ownership.
4. Private clubs are saddled with refund liability on equity memberships (those who own stock in a club) and deposits (corporate-owned private clubs).

An Axiom

There is an axiom, "You make money when you buy, not when you sell." The focus of this book has been to demonstrate how golf course owners can maximize their return in the short term. Only by properly managing the business in the short term is its long-term value maximized, and that value is determined only when the golf course is sold. A golf course owner should always have an exit strategy, even if he or she never plans on using it.

Knowing the value of your golf course provides a useful snapshot of where the course currently stands, what options it has, and how it can improve long term. The valuation of your golf course is, in essence, a reality check.

Unfortunately, most golf course owners have a tough time determining value. Most golf courses will only pay for a valuation when it is required to obtain financing or because of some other kind of transaction, such as a divorce, death, or for estate planning purposes. These mandatory responses to outside circumstances often result in mistakes, which lead to flawed valuations. The value of a golf course can be determined much more accurately if the owner keeps a frequent tally of the market.

The process of selling a golf course involves the following steps:

1. Obtain an appraisal, which includes an opinion of the competitive market value.
2. Develop a strategy to sell, one that includes preparing a cohesive business plan that strategically positions the property. Such a business plan should include a realistic financial forecast, a list of potential buyers, and an investment analysis that reinforces the course's potential opportunity.
3. Find a real estate agent/broker who can represent the golf course.
4. Create a marketing program to contact identified prospects and to promote the opportunity.
5. Negotiate and complete the transaction, including reviewing offers, managing the due diligence, and ensuring a timely close through coordination with counsel.

While this five-step process seems simple, the sale of a golf course is a complex commercial transaction. The legal issues alone are daunting. Van Tengberg, partner of the law firm of Foley and Lardner, offers a list of the ten most important things that have to be addressed:

1. Title Survey

    a. Review and assess the impact of all exceptions to the title—covenant condition restrictions (CC&Rs), covenants, deed restrictions, and cost-sharing agreements.

    b. Determine the impact of all encroachments of golf course improvements onto adjoining properties.

2. Phase 1 and Phase 2

    a. Inspect the maintenance facility and confirm the existence, use, or discontinuance of underground or above-ground storage tanks, pesticides, fertilizers, fuel tanks, or oil drums.

    b. Determine the existence of any organized dumps on the property.

3. Memberships

    a. Review the seller's waiting list and determine the number of memberships on the list.

    b. Review all membership agreements regarding refund obligations.

4. Permits and Licenses

    a. Verify the existence of all required permits and licenses (health, resale, liquor, petroleum, storage tanks, pesticides, etc.).

    b. Confirm that all permits and licenses are transferable.

5. Leases—Purchase Contracts—Furniture, Fixtures, and Equipment

    a. Confirm that all contracts, agreements, and leases are transferable.

    b. Confirm the right to purchase leased furniture, figures, and equipment upon expiration of the lease (fair market value or fixed dollar amount).

6. Sensitive Habitat, Wetlands, Biological

    a. Determine what exists and its status.

    b. Analyze short-term and long-term maintenance, upkeep, and enhancement obligations.

7. Structural Issues, HVAC, Utility Accessibility, Irrigation Systems

    a. Itemize required repairs, replacements, or improvements.

    b. Determine what repairs, replacements, or improvements are mandatory for transfer or issuance of a certificate of occupancy.

8. Employees and Independent Contractors

    a. Review salary and benefits packages.

    b. Review all employment and independent contract agreements.

9. Irrigation Water

    a. Conduct a hydrology study and ascertain ownership of water rights.

    b. Confirm any alternative sources of irrigation water.

10. Surrounding Community Issues

    a. Review all golf course CC&Rs.

    b. Consider hours of operation and enforcement issues.[1]

Just from reading that list, buying and selling can seem to be overwhelming tasks.

But for those still inclined to sell, the first step is to learn the true value of the golf course. Seventy percent of all golf courses sold each year are transacted without being formally listed. This is often because the owners fear that nobody will want to play a course that's up for sale—all the more reason to have a thorough understanding of valuation.

Valuing the Golf Course

The value of a golf course is determined by an appraisal, a complex process no matter what form it takes. Golf courses are a mix of real estate and business, and before you can come up with a proper valuation, you have to understand the mix of the two.

Components that influence the value of a golf course include location, site configuration, population, topography, scenic appeal, course features, and amenities such as access to major highways and expressways. A comprehensive appraisal also looks at things like irrigation and pumping systems, cost and availability of irrigation water, drainage, ADA compliance, food and beverage operation, safety issues resulting from poor golf hole design, maintenance

1 Van Tengberg, "Buy-Sell Checklist," *Golf Inc*, March 2008, p. 33.

equipment, chemical and fuel storage, bridges, cart paths, utility of the clubhouse, maintenance barn, and pro shop buildings.[2]

At a minimum, the value of a golf course is worth the value of the land. Highest and best use, a term common in the real estate industry, is a wild card that can have a significant impact on value. This can be a big deal, especially at older clubs where the town has grown around the property, and the "highest and best use" of the real estate is a high-rise and not a golf course. For example, the raw land value of the Los Angeles Country Club, located in the heart of Beverley Hills, is estimated to be worth $20 billion. Would the course ever be sold? No. But for the vast majority of course owners, that sort of number gets your attention.

While the net liquidation of golf courses will continue, it is kind of ironic that the value of golf courses will likely rise, not for the intrinsic value of the investment return as golf courses, but for the value of the land for alternative uses.

Having a golf course valued, with all the variables and legal issues analyzed, can take 90 days or more and can cost anywhere from $5,000 to $50,000. A table of contents for a valuation would look similar to this:

Description	Page Number
Summary of Salient Facts	4
Client/Intended User(s)	5
Intended Use	5
Report Format	5
Analysis	5
Purpose of Report	5
Interest Appraised	5
Property Identification	5
Previous Sales	5
FIRREA Compliant	5
Scope of Appraisal	5
Tax Comments	6
Brief Property Description	6
Highest and Best Use	10
Valuation as a Country Club	13
Market Approach	13

2 http://www.gormangrp.com/golf_course_appraisals.html

Description	Page Number
Income Approach	20
Conclusion as a Country Club	27
Valuation as Vacant Land	28
Conclusion as Vacant Land	31
Highest and Best Use Conclusion and Final Value Conclusions	32
Definition of Market Value	33
Underlying Assumptions and Limiting Conditions	33
Certificate of Appraisal	37

While there are plenty of appraisers who will come up with whatever number you want, the talented business appraiser acts as a consultant, stripping down the numbers to determine real value. If really good, the appraiser will also provide suggestions to make the value higher.

Common mistakes in appraisals include valuations determined by price per hole, price per acre, replacement costs, and discounting cash flow during the first year with the assumption of gaining members at a rate that is not feasible. Also, comparative quotes may be two to three years old, using gross revenue methods of valuation. That is why it is important to use an appraiser who specializes in golf courses.

Valuation Methods

Appraisals are a subjective process. The range of values is determined by one of seven valuation methods:

Book Value: Assets (including cash, receivables, and property, plant, and equipment) minus liabilities and debt. This asset-based method could result in a number that seems too low because the intangible personal property is not valued.

Liquidation Value: This value is determined by asking, "How much money could be raised by selling all assets (receivables, inventory, and property, plant, and equipment) minus satisfaction of debt." This method also produces a value that seems low. It represents a worst-case scenario.

Excess Earnings: Tangible assets are multiplied by the standard return on equity. Any money earned above this value is considered excess earnings, which are then capitalized and added to the book value.

Multiple Models: This easy way to determine value is to take known value, earnings, or revenues and multiply that figure by the standard index. For example, the value of a business is worth between 6 and 20 times earnings or 1½ to 2 times revenues. The standard index for publicly traded companies is a price-to-earnings ratio of 15 to 1. This technique has some challenges because profits and revenues can prove to be erratic and this method often fails to recognize debt or other intangibles because of its simplicity.

Cost Approach: The cost approach is based on what an informed buyer would pay for creating a substitute property with the same functionality. Actual construction costs for a new golf course, as well as the furniture, fixtures, and equipment purchases costs, are determined.

Comparative Market Value: The value is determined by a locating a recent transaction involving the sale of a comparable course in a local market.

Discounted Cash Flow: A forecast of the amount of cash the golf course will be able to generate in future years discounted to present value based on competitive rates of investment.

Notwithstanding the popularity of these approaches, there are still plenty of intangibles: (1) each course provides a different experience, (2) the quality of management varies, (3) there are a plethora of different profit margins within the course's various departments, and (4) each course puts a different emphasis on strategies and tactics.

Additional terms used to value golf courses include:

Discount rate: The discount rate and the capitalization rate are similar but distinguishable. While both focus on the yield necessary to attract investors, the discount rate looks at projected cash flows, while the capitalization rate is based on data for a single period.

Net Income Multiplier: Revenues are multiplied by the standard multiple to approach the market value. It is a quick benchmark.

The appraised value of a golf course hinges on the number attributed to three factors—income stream, capitalization rate, and market value—that are closely interconnected. You merely need to know two of the three components to calculate the third. To illustrate,

Income = Capitalization Rate × Market Value

Capitalization Rate = Income/Market Value

Market Value = Income/Capitalization Rate

The interrelationship of these factors can be confusing.

As This Rate Becomes Larger	The Golf Course Market Value
Capitalization Rate	Decreases
Discount Rate	Decreases
Net Income Multiplier	Increases

Confusing, yes. Simplistic, yes. Subject to market interruption, absolutely yes.

Simply stated, divide net income by the capitalization rate to determine market value, as illustrated in the following table:

Net Income	Capitalization Rate	Market Value
$300,000	7.5%	$4,000,000
$300,000	9.0%	$3,333,333
$300,000	11.0%	$2,727,272
Note: Capitalization rate (or "cap rate") is the ratio between the net operating income produced by an asset and its capital cost (the original price paid to buy the asset) or its current market value.		

Today's Benchmarks—The Art of the Deal

For an appraisal, net income is not actually "net income" but rather a calculation that includes the following components: gross income minus collection losses, allowable expenses, replacement reserves, and real estate taxes.

Allowable expenses include management fees/expense, insurance, salaries, benefits, utilities, advertising, repairs, supplies, legal and accounting fees, and miscellaneous expenses. More important are the non-allowable expenses: depreciation, capital improvement, franchise fees and special corporation costs, owner's personal expenses, debt services, and payment on loans for capital improvements.

With numerous golf courses losing money, this standard formula for valuing a golf course, which hinges on the income stream, is currently not applicable.

The method of valuing of golf courses is gravitating toward a combination of discounted cash flow models, using capitalization rates and the creation of pro forma forecasts based on the probable income results with new management.

The capitalization rates are constantly changing in response to economic conditions and alternative investment opportunities. One of the reliable sources for current rates is provided by The Society of Golf Appraisers, an organization that provides information about financing and investment criteria, information that is instrumental in the evaluation of golf course–related investing and lending activity.

The 2015 SGA Survey reports the following benchmarks[3]:

Data Point	Average
Broker Sales Commission	3.20%
Capital Reserves as % of Gross Revenue	3.10%
Capitalization Rate – Overall (1)	10.60%
Capitalization Rate – Terminal (2)	11.40%
Debt – Loan to Value	60.00%
Discount Rate	14.10%
Interest – Prime Rate[4]	3.50%
Libor 1 Year[5]	1.22%
Management Fee as % of Gross Revenue	3.30%
Marketing Period	11.8 Months
Multiplier – Gross Income	1.60
Multiplier – Net Income (3)	8.60

Notes
1. Overall Capitalization Rate reflects going-concern operations.
2. Terminal or going out Capitalization rate
3. Net Income Multiple (Price/Net Income) is the inverse of the Cap Rate.

3 http://www.golfappraisers.org/SGAResources/AnnualInvestorLenderSurvey.aspx

The Process

Though not used in determining a value for real estate transactions, two benchmarks serve as an effective frame of reference as to the size and scope of a potential transaction: cost and replacement value.

When asked what it costs to build a golf course, the first question that must be addressed is, "What component?" The construction budget, land costs, water sources, power, clubhouse, parking, maintenance building, and the cost to grow the course between seeding and an opening are the principal components. Add the variables of the types of soil (sandy sites are less expensive), clearing and earth moving on the site, irrigation requirements, and the owner's vision for the course. With 140 to 180 acres of land being used to build a course, the cost of building a golf course can vary widely.

The American Society of Golf Course Architects[6] advised those desiring to build a course to proceed as follows:

a. Ascertain Project Feasibility
b. Choose an Architect
c. Site Selection
d. Land Planning
e. Land Entitlement
f. Financing
g. Construction Documents
h. Course Construction
i. Course Maintenance
j. Ownership and Operations

The process from concept to first tee shot can take more than two years: 6 to 12 months for permits, 3 months to select a contractor through a bid process, and 6 to 12 months to grow in the course before it can be opened.

---

4 http://www.bankrate.com/rates/interest-rates/prime-rate.aspx

5 http://www.bankrate.com/rates/interest-rates/libor.aspx

6 http://www.asgca.org/course-design

The cost per hole can vary from $100,000 to more than $500,000 for some upscale courses. The Golf Course Builders Association of America has constructed a cost template that will estimate the cost of the following: a full 18-hole renovation, a USGA green surface renovation, tee renovation, bunker renovation, irrigation renovation, and the cost to build a new golf course, as shown in the figure shown here.

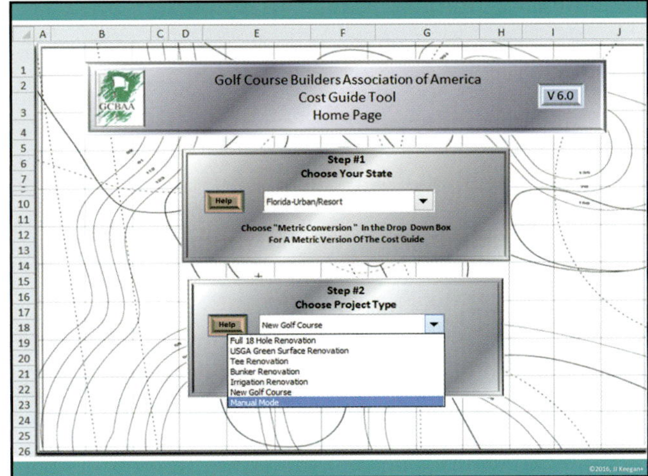

This template can be purchased at www.gcbaa.org. It was crafted based on a member survey. Recognizing the varying soil conditions and geographic climates in which a course might be constructed in the United States, it segments the estimated cost by 84 different regions (for instance, Oregon Coast, Oregon resort, and Oregon rural).

The template provides for the manual entry of other estimated costs, such as sediment traps, practice range netting, builder's risk insurance, growth in costs, architectural fees, restroom facilities, engineering fees, demolition of existing buildings, maintenance facilities, maintenance equipment, sand capping import, and topsoil import.

The estimated cost to build a new course in the United States is about $8 million, before the land and clubhouse, as illustrated here:

Category	Amount
Mobilization	$117,059
Clearing	285,000
Existing Grass Removal	221,400
Earthwork/Excavation	732,500
Shaping	185,000
Drainage	318,625
Storm Drainage	300,000
Irrigation System	2,343,000
Greens Construction	503,400
Tee Construction	402,575
Bunker Construction	445,825

Category	Amount
Cart Path Construction	577,875
Seed/Bed Preparation	315,000
Soil Amendments	101,250
Grassing	504,230
Specialist Items	168,750
Miscellaneous	399,500
Subtotal	7,920,989
Bonding	79,209
Total	$8,000,198

In undertaking a feasibility study, incorporating this forecasting tool is invaluable. The line-item detail the template provides is superlative; and it quickly summarizes the estimated costs.

The typical golf course generates slightly more than $1.65 million in revenue, with about $223,000 in earnings before interest, taxes, depreciation, and amortization. If for no other reason than the increasing costs, it is understandable that new course construction in the United States has ground to a halt.

In any event, owning a golf course is not for the faint of heart.

Government Gives, Government Takes

One area that is drawing increased scrutiny is the property taxes being assessed on golf courses. A potential reduction in real estate tax assessments is a fertile area in which golf courses can improve their bottom line.

The methods for calculating property tax assessments can vary widely between governmental jurisdictions. Some may use replacement costs while others may establish the annual tax based on fair market value, which could use comparable sales or income as alternative methods of valuation. With such a diversity of methods used, and with each often applied differently, the annual assessments create the opportunity for golf courses to review and protest property tax assessments.

A private country club in the Denver metropolitan area was awarded a six-figure rebate because its initial assessment included vacant land adjacent to the golf course that was zoned for future real estate development. We also know of farmland in the middle of nowhere in Nebraska that was valued as residential real estate, with a $150,000 annual property-tax bill on a golf course that generates $2.5 million in revenue per year. Left unchecked, and with governments seeking additional sources of revenue, property taxes are a likely source of government income, and the appeal process is complex and often requires the retention of specialists.

The process of protesting property taxes involves (1) assessment evaluation, (2) preparation of appeal, and (3) negotiation or litigation.

Golf Property Analysts recommends that golf course owners consider the following when appealing property taxes[7]:

1. What is the current assessment?
2. What is the operating trend of the club for the past three years?
3. Are there any items of deferred maintenance?
4. Are there bids to address these items?
5. Has the club been sold recently?
6. Has the property been marketed for sale?
7. Does the club have inadequate, adequate, or super-adequate equipment?
8. Is the club efficiently managed?
9. What is the appeal deadline, and has an appeal been filed?
10. If private, does the club have a full membership?
11. Is there a waiting list?
12. Are there any easements, covenants, or restrictions precluding alternative development of the property?
13. Is your state a "highest and best use" state, or are tax assessments based on the property's current use?

Appraisers can be retained based on a flat fee or an hourly basis to appeal property taxes.

There are specialists who will review a club's property tax assessment on a contingency-fee basis. Note that members of the Society of Golf Course

7 http://www.golfprop.com/sites/default/files/documents/Golf%20Property%20Tax%20Assessments%202014.pdf

Appraisers are precluded from accepting such contingency fee assignments, as they are perceived to compromise perhaps the independence of the appraiser in determining the valuation.

Playing With the Numbers

Each golf course should obtain an appraisal at least every five years. An appraisal provides an indication of a golf course's value and serves as a business tool that identifies weaknesses. Acting on the information gleaned from an appraisal; a golf course owner is likely to improve short-term income while increasing long-term value.

Key Points to Remember

1) A golf course appraisal can cost from $5,000 to $50,000, take upwards of 90 days, and consists of 10 very detailed steps.
2) There are seven valuation techniques: book value, liquidation value, excess earnings, multiple models, cost approach, comparative market value, and discounted cash flow.
3) The two most frequently used methods to value a golf course are the discounted cash flow (income approach) method and the comparative market value method.
4) The appraised value of a golf course hinges on the number attributed to three factors, all of which are interconnected—capitalization rate, discount rate, and net income multiplier.
5) The capitalization rate, discount rate, and net income multiplier are constantly changing in response to economic conditions and alternative investment opportunities.
6) A golf course owner should always have an exit strategy, even if he or she never plans on using it. Whether it be to sell the golf course to another operator or to a real estate or commercial office park developer, knowing the alternative that will produce the highest investment return is advised.

Concluding Thought

With good judgment, little else matters. Without it, nothing else matters.

Warren G. Bennis

A weak person has doubts before making a decision,
a strong person has them afterward.

Karl Kraus, Austrian author and journalist (1874–1936)

SECTION 3

Operational Execution
Chapters 12 through 18

From a broad overview of the golf industry in Section 1, we transitioned in Section 2 to understanding the numbers at a golf course, learning how to increase and maximize revenue, increase operational efficiency, and enhance customer service.

In Section 3, we narrow the focus even more to the golf course, daily operations, and the golfer. The factors that influence the financial success of a golf course are as follows:

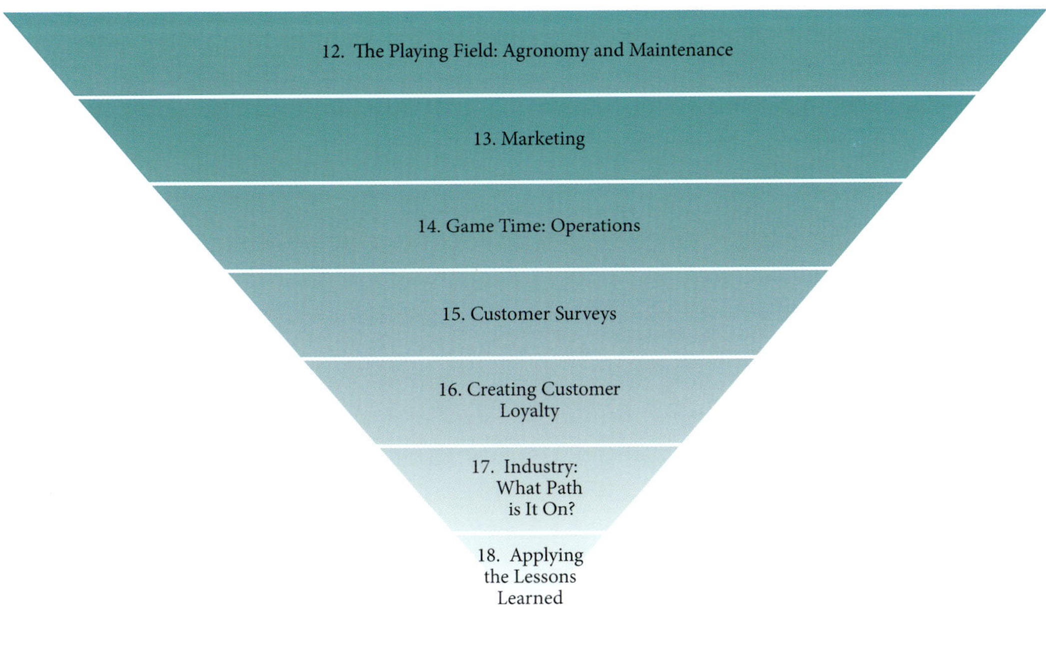

Knowing is not enough, we must apply.
Willing is not enough; we must do.

Goethe

Chapter 12

The Playing Field
Step 5 of JJ Keegan+ WIN™ Formula

A championship course is not a championship course until a championship has been played upon it.

Michael Bonallack, former Secretary of the Royal and Ancient Golf Club of St. Andrews

Golf is not a fair game, so why build a course fair?

Pete Dye, Golf Course Architect

Chapter Highlights

There are over 34,000 canvases of golf art in the world—golf courses created by artists who saw a vision on how to transform the land to entertain. No two canvases are the same, which makes the game special.

But unlike the great art works of the world that are on display in the Louvre, the Uffizi, or the Prado, golf courses are in need of daily maintenance. They are living entities with personalities of their own, and they change day by day.

How are operators keeping budgets in check and still meeting customer expectations? What is the life cycle of a golf course? And how does answering that question affect capital improvements, annual maintenance expenditures, and labor?

This chapter will provide those answers.

Types of Golf Courses

First, some basics on the type and nature of golf courses. Golf courses can be categorized as follows:

1. Ownership: private, daily fee resort, residential, military, private estate, industrial
2. Length: full-length, executive, par 3, pitch and putt, chip and putt, putting, Cayman
3. Design: core, integrated, hub, and spoke

One of the biggest factors that influence maintenance costs is the type of vegetation on a golf course.

Golf course settings include:[1]

1. Links golf courses are seaside courses that look like those in the east of Scotland, where the game originated. They are open grassy expanses, with rolling hills, deep roughs, and no trees.
2. Parkland golf courses are characterized by lush, manicured turf, favorable weather, and significant tree cover.
3. Heathland golf courses are inland courses that are characterized by low-growing shrubs, gentle slopes, and few to no trees. They are made to resemble the inland golf courses of England and Scotland.
4. Oceanside golf courses border the ocean, but unlike links courses they are well above sea level.
5. Mountain golf courses often aren't in the mountains but have a view of mountains.
6. Prairie golf courses are usually located in the flatlands of the Midwest in the United States. They are flat, have few trees, and have views of the prairie.
7. Desert golf courses are usually located in the arid regions of the southwest United States.

---

1 http://golftrainingaidandteachingtool.com/Golf_Courses_01.shtml, July 4, 2008.

Within the confines of these types of settings, the artists of the game, the architects, carve their masterpieces onto the landscape. Just as the paintings of Monet, Manet, and Picasso each have similar styles that can be identified, so do the works of classic architects such as MacKenzie, Ross, Tillinghast, or my favorite, Raynor. Add to those recent architects such as Dye, Nicklaus, Doak, Jones (Robert Trent and Rees), Coore/Crenshaw, and the very talented 200+ architects who are members of the American Society of Golf Course Architects.

Today's architects have become golf industry superstars. Architects of the past got very little attention. As Michael Young, an architect with Rymer/Young stated,

> "Golf courses were just places where you played golf. They weren't 'by' anyone and they weren't in any particular 'style.' Consider, for example, Bernard Darwin's famous *Golf Courses of the British Isles*, a book that brought attention to famous courses in England, Scotland, and Ireland for the first time. Golf architecture is central to the book. There is, however, not a single architectural attribution anywhere to be found."[2]

For the golf course owner, this current adulation of golf course architects often has significant financial consequences. Michael Young believes:

> "... all of this adulation has gone too far. As good as the Golden Age architects were, the reverence for them can sometimes be over the top. Their courses are sometimes treated like sacred texts. Every swale, tree, and ridge (or lack of the same) are taken as a sign of the master and invested with deep architectural significance.
>
> The sanctification of courses designed by these famous architects can get in the way of thoughtful restorations. I've had people tell me that an architect carefully placed a tree behind a green for depth perception. The tree would have been no more than a two-foot sapling when

2 http://www.mydgolf.com/blog/3

> the course was built in the 1920s. Swales in fairways, dug for drainage, are seen as marks of unsurpassed artistry. Odd bunker locations are taken to have deep aesthetic significance.
>
> Cults always get in the way of clear thinking.
>
> Thus, the relevance of all of this for today's golf course owner is simple. Golf course owners can waste hundreds of thousands of dollars while trying to restore a course to an image that even the original architect didn't have. With trees, shrubs, and ponds ebbing and flowing, perhaps those who attempt to preserve tradition take themselves too seriously and in turn fail to achieve their desired investment return."[3]

Thus, the clear lesson is that a golf course is a living organism that changes constantly based on the maintenance practices of the superintendent and is only as intended by the golf course architect on the day the course opened.

The Evolution of Architecture

Over the years, the artistic interpretations of golf course design have evolved and are fascinating. Today, the style of golf course architecture that is in vogue features the following:

- Minimalist design (natural and sustainable types of golf courses sporting strategic and playability options)
- Bunkers with fescue and Scottish broom
- Shots repelled from perched greens
- Closely cropped chipping areas
- Massive greens with many undulations and few areas for pin locations

These modern preferences make us wonder what were the primary factors influencing the architects. While we may view the evolution of golf course architecture as orderly and well-defined, it has been scattered and chaotic.

3 Ibid.

Golf courses in the United States were built as shown here.

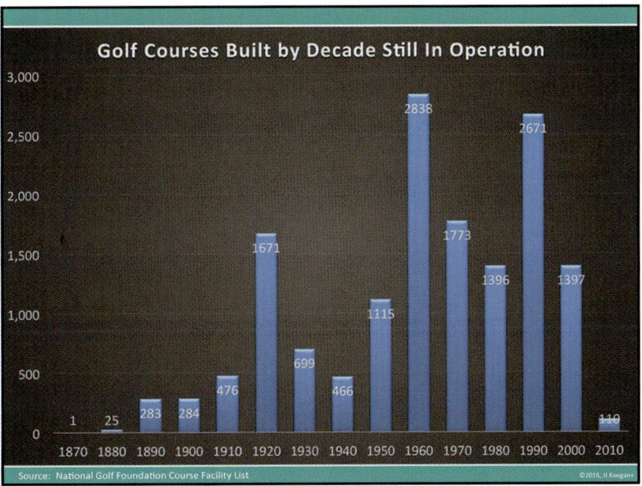

A detailed analysis of the golf courses listed above built in America since the first course was built in 1870 reveals:

- An architect is not identified with 4,321 of the courses.
- There are 775 18-hole golf courses of less than 5,000 yards.
- There are roughly 1,698 "unique" individuals designated as being golf course architects.
- Courses that are identified as having been built or renovated by members of the American Society of Golf Course Architects (ASGCA) number 5,386.
- 9,942 of the 17,816 courses built in the U.S. have been renovated at some time. Recall, only 15,204 are operating in the United States in 2016.
- Forty-seven architects are responsible for constructing 25.8% of all golf courses in the United States.

The next evolution of golf course design is likely to be evidenced by renovations rather than new course construction. The design will be kinder to the golfer, representing shorter courses with reduced slope rating. Kinder also to golf course owners as illustrated by a recent John Sanford, ASGCA, and Jack Nicklaus, ASGCA Fellow, redesign of the course at Naples Beach Hotel & Golf Club in Naples, Florida.

> "The green complexes are relatively small, and Jack wanted them partially open to running shots, so about 50-to-60 percent of each green is open to allow the ground game," said Sanford. "Of the 100 acres of turf, we will take 30-to-35 acres out of irrigation, resulting in unirrigated

natural areas. We end up with 65 or 70 acres of irrigated turf, which will reduce the watering requirement."[4]

The Endless Debate

One of the great things about the game of golf is the endless debate on which golf course is better. That answer speaks to the core of the connection between golfers and the course, of the bond that is formed. The discussion attracts people to the game, spurs many bar conversations, and serves as the incentive that drives certain golf course owners to seek and maintain excellence.

Many golfers and golf industry personnel attach great importance to the ratings given golf courses—the Top 100 in the World, the Top 100 in the United States, the Top 100 the Public Can Play, the Top 100 Golf Courses Prior to 1960, the Top 100 Golf Courses Since 1960; the list goes on and on.

The first of these lists was created in 1984 by George Peper, then editor-in-chief of *Golf Magazine*. In the March 2006 edition of *Links Magazine*, Peper writes,

> "Hey, it seemed like a good idea at the time. The magazine got great publicity and sold more ads and copies, and I was proud of our biennial list, the first to rank courses from one to 100. Over time, however, I realized I'd created a monster.
>
> 'You've done our club a tremendous disservice,' Pine Valley president Ernie Ransom told me after we pegged his course as No. 1 in the world. "Everyone wants to play here now, and 99 percent of the requests can't be granted."[5]

For a golf course, being ranked can have significant monetary benefits, from establishing lofty membership fees for the private club to attracting golfers at high green fees at the public facility. Being ranked also often enhances the brand image of the course.

4 http://asgca.org/images/stories/by-design/2016/By_Design_-_Issue_27_Spring_2016.pdf

5 George Peper, "Out of the Shadows," Linksmagazine.com, March 2006, p. 45.

The relevance of a top ranking is that it has positive financial implications for the golf course owner. All golf courses that are so ranked have one element in common—the maintenance conditions of the golf course are usually superior.

The Impact of the Evolution of Golf Clubs on Course Design

One of the things presumed in designing or renovating a golf course, but rarely expressed, certainly not among the players, is the influence of today's golf clubs and balls on new course construction and renovations on the safety of the players.

Golf course architects create safety corridors for each hole which start at the tee and encompass an area on either side of the fairway centerline and continue to beyond the green.

Kevin Norby, ASGCA, principal of Herfort-Norby Architectural firm, believes,

> "In the 1990s, we were designing golf holes with landing areas at 250 yards from the back tees of most public golf courses. Today, we are typically positioning landing areas at 270 to 310 yards from the back tees.
>
> It is my belief that not only are today's golfers bigger and stronger than 20 years ago, but the impact which technology has had on the game is profound.
>
> Today's golfers are not only hitting the ball further, but they are hitting the ball further off-line. Every situation is different, but it's possible to have corridors more than 400 feet—particularly on short par fours or par fives where the golfer may not exercise good judgment.
>
> As technology continues to impact and change the game, many courses will need to adapt or face growing concern for public safety."[6]

Another important factor is cost. In a survey done on 26 golf courses in Melbourne, Australia, it was confirmed that "the cost of maintaining the golf course

---

6 Kevin Norby, Herfort Norby, "Safety Corridors for Today's Golf Courses," March 15, 2013.

increases by about 2% percent for each 100 meters of additional length, which is about the distance of two 'extra' holes."[7]

Conversely, if courses were shorter, savings would be likely. Jeff Brauer, ASGCA, president of GolfScapes, believes,

> "It may be time for golf courses to re-think the one-size-fits-all mentality moving forward. If we admit that we have all the championship courses we need for the 40-something men's pro tournaments annually, we would nicely accommodate more than 97% of the players on courses with maximum yardage of about 6,800 yards. In this age of belt tightening, wasting resources on so few in so many places just doesn't make sense."[8]

Armen Suny, a partner in the architectural firm of Suny-Zokol, believes,

> "Most golf course architects are missing the single most important facet of golf course design—golfers. Anyone can create a golf experience that is extremely difficult; it takes little skill to do that and has been part of the ruination of our sport ever since Pete Dye popularized the notion that difficultly equates to great. What takes skill is to embrace golfers of all skill levels while challenging the best."[9]

The acceleration of costs in maintaining a golf course to the level shown on television, with lush manicured fairways and slick putting surfaces, is a formula that, if it is followed by the vast majority of golf course owners, is sure to lead to diminished profits.

In 2016, that trend seems to be fortunately reversing.

Maintaining the Playing Field

Turfgrass is a living, breathing entity that will not stop growing. Courses face the challenges of proper staffing levels, adequate equipment to maintain prescribed

7 Jeff D. Brauer, Golf Course Industry.com, "Should Future Courses Be Shorter?" June 2010, p. 26.

8 Ibid.

9 Armen Suny, Suny Zokol Golf Course Design, "*The Anarchist's Guide to Golf Course Architecture*," March 21, 2013.

levels of conditioning, and a budget that facilitates turf conditions and will attract play throughout the calendar year.

An average 18-hole golf course covers 150 acres, of which only 100 acres are maintained turfgrass,[10] and includes the following:

		Acreage	%
Turfgrass	Rough	51	34.0
	Fairways	30	20.0
	Driving Range/Practice Areas	7	4.7
	Greens	3	1.3
	Tees	3	1.3
	Clubhouse House	3	1.3
	Nurseries	1	.7
	Total	100	63.3
Non-Turfgrass	Non-turfgrass landscape	24	16.0
	Water	11	7.3
	Building	6	4.0
	Bunkers	4.5	2.9
	Parking Lots	4.5	2.9
		50	33.1
Note: In published report, averages were utilized, which don't necessarily sum to the total.			

The quality of the playing field can be reduced to four principal elements: (1) labor, the largest expense; (2) water, fertilizer, chemicals, and utilities; (3) capital improvements; and (4) equipment required to maintain the facility.

The cost of maintaining an 18-hole golf course can range from $200,000 to more than $2.5 million. *Golf Course Industry* magazine reported the following maintenance expenses in 2015:

	2012			2015		
	All	Non-Private	Private	All	Non-Private	Private
Total	651,392	458,071	848,951	697,000	487,000	940,000
Water	16,499	12,484	20,390	22,800	17,400	28,600
Fuel	289,174	22,260	33,876	29,200	22,900	36,200
Mowing/Cutivating Equipment	37,644	25,335	50,649	31,300	25,700	37,700
Handheld Equipment	3,066	1,702	4,419	2,410	1,720	3,180
Course Accessories	4,561	3,804	5,294	4,410	3,030	5,970
Electricity and Natural Gas	19,048	17,990	20,088	21,300	18,200	24,800
Shop Tools	2,568	1,878	3,284	2,860	2,160	3,620
Irrigaton Parks, Heads, and Maintenance	7,918	5,948	9,876	84,100	6,880	10,170
Fungicides	33,461	22,163	44,478	34,100	20,900	49,000
Herbicides—preemergent	6,369	5,109	7,603	6,370	4,880	8,010
Herbicides—postemergent	3,869	3,613	4,144	4,260	3,500	5,120
Insecticides	5,141	3,694	6,570	6,190	3,580	9,160
Granular fertilizers	17,723	15,203	20,244	20,300	16,800	24,300
Liquid fertillizers	10,231	7,315	13,088	12,100	9,000	15,500
Wetting agents	4,399	3,129	5,669	6,150	3,500	9,120
Plant Growth Regulators	5,151	4,309	5,982	4,570	3,230	6,050
Seed	4,620	4,127	5,136	7,390	7,030	7,780
Aquatic Weed Control	1,890	1,635	2,145	2,570	1,500	3,710
	473,332	161,698	262,935	302,380	171,910	287,990

The investment to maintain the course annually contains many elements as shown that vary greatly based on geographic location.

10 GCSAA, "Golf Course Environmental Profile," 2007, p. 12.

The Natural Replacement Cycle

Because a golf course is a living thing, creating a capital budget and providing an annual reserve to replace the vital components is prudent.

Unfortunately, as golf courses begin losing money in a competitive market, the first cuts are always made by deferring capital expenditures. While understandable because of the large investment, these cuts are often made without the continuing recognition that the condition of the golf course remains the number one requirement of golfers.

The Golf Course Superintendents Association of America estimates that the amount of capital improvements required as part of a golf course's natural replacement cycle is $2,952,215, and that a prudent golf course should create an annual capital improvements allowance of $132,038.

Renovation Cost and Annual Capital Reserve

Component		Years Minimum	Years Maximum	Estimated Cost to Replace	Annual Capital Reserve
Greens		15	30	775,000	25,833
Bunker Sand		5	7	44,800	6,400
Irrigation System		10	30	314,000	10,467
	Irrigation Control	10	15	171,000	11,400
	PVC Pipe	10	30	329,600	10,987
	Pump Station	15	20	425,000	21,250
Corrugated Pipe		15	30	398,180	13,273
Cart Paths	Asphalt	5	10	93,350	9,335
Cart Paths	Concrete	15	30	146,685	4,890
Practice Range Tees		5	10	37,680	3,768
Tees		15	20	150,720	7,536
Bunker Drainage Pipes		5	10	65,000	6,500
Mulch		1	3	1,200	400
Grass		Varies	Varies	N/A	
Total Deferred Capital				2,952,215	132,038

The table here provides the estimated life spans of the various components of a golf course, as estimated by the GCSAA and Golf Course Builders Association of America.

Very few golf courses budget for capital improvements. Most courses incorrectly wait until the capital project is mandated and then often borrow to fund the costs.

The Equipment

Most golf courses operate with a potpourri of equipment. Looking for a standard equipment list for your 18-hole golf course? The following list of equipment has been compiled to meet the general needs of a high-end public or an average private 18-hole golf course and should be used as a **minimum guideline** for reviewing equipment inventory.

Pieces of Equipment	Department	Total Cost
17	Greens	$ 87,500
2	Tees	24,000
4	Fairways	70,000
6	Rough	112,000
6	Transportation Vehicles	25,000
5	Tractors and Trucks	117,000
12	Sprayers and Spreaders	50,800
9	Utility Equipment	56,000
14	Tools and Small Equipment	850
	Total	$543,150

Keep in mind that a standard equipment list is as challenging to define as a "standard" golf course. Variations may occur, or additional pieces of equipment may be needed, depending upon an array of factors including golf course terrain, maintenance standards expected, and a range of regional requirements.

It is suggested that 10% to 15% of the total equipment replacement value be spent toward purchasing new machinery each season to avoid losing valuable staff time and, potentially, top course conditions due to down time.

To Preserve and Protect: Agronomy 101

Of all those involved in the business of operating a golf course, who is the one person that is most vital? It would be easy to make the case that it is the superintendent. Without the proper construction and maintenance of a golf course, the playing field doesn't exist.

Superintendents are not only the stars of the golf course industry but perhaps the most unheralded group of industry professionals. As a group, their technical knowledge is rooted in chemistry, physics, agronomy, and other scientific disciplines. Their superlative expertise is both a blessing and sometimes a curse.

Members of board of directors, owners, general managers, and those employed in the golf shop lack the detailed knowledge of what is required to maintain properly a golf course. Many probably water their lawns, see the grass grow, mow it, and think it is a simple process. Not really. Because superintendents prefer to work outdoors, relating to those indoors can cause communication barriers.

It is the goal herein to provide a background so that the barriers that may exist are removed by an understanding of the complexity of a superintendent's role.

To illustrate, the golf course superintendent has an incredible impact on one of the most important elements of the game—pace of play.

Research by the Golf Course Superintendents Association of America revealed that pace of play is largely a management issue. Maintaining proper fairway widths and rough heights, trimming underbrush, marking the course, having tees properly positioned, rating the greens with a fair stimpmeter, and making sure pin positions are appropriate for the type and volume of play are all controllable factors for the superintendent.

The superintendent deals with many challenges, including types of grass, controlling water expenses, understanding chemicals, and battling turf diseases.

The primary role of a superintendent is to ensure a consistent playing surface, whether on greens, fairways, or tees. Every element of a course is fraught with challenges, as shown in the picture here on the approach to a green at a Top 200 golf course in the United States.

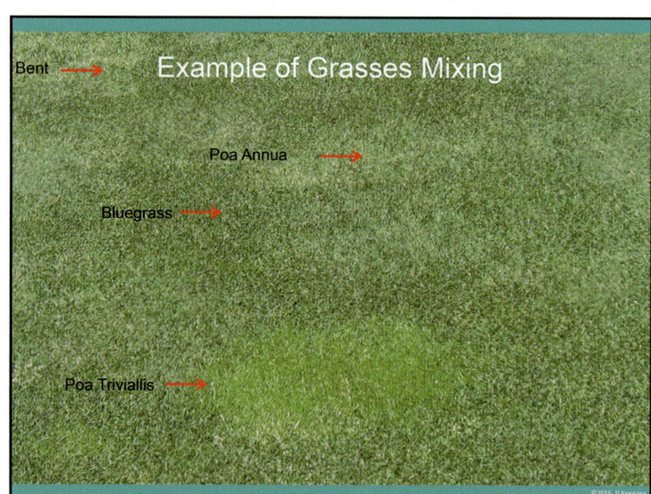

There is always a story. In the case of the grass pictured at this course, the greens were to be bentgrass and the fairways Kentucky bluegrass. A collar that was installed around the circumference of the green was insufficient when a heavy rain storm came right after the green was seeded. The seed washed into the fairway, causing the problem noted here.

The varieties of grasses used on a golf course are diverse, but each offers different playing characteristics. Golf courses can have many different types of grasses with wildly varying growing tendencies as illustrated in the following table with the popular grasses used on northern courses:

Feature	Bentgrass	Bluegrass	Fine Fescue	Poa Annua	Poa Triviallis
Best use	Greens	Fairway	Fairway	Greens	Noxious
Color	Gray to Blue green	Mid Green	Dark Green/ Brownish	Light Green	Light Green, shiny
Height	0.12	0.5	0.5	0.15	0.15
Blade	======	|||||||||	|||||||||	======	======
Ball	Tight Lie	Ball Sits Up	Ball Sits Up	Tight Lie	Tight Lie
Strength	Moderate Weak	Strong	Strong	Weak	Weak
Weather – Hot	Dies	Thrives	Thrives	Struggles, especially if kept wet	Can go off color; dies
Weather – Cold	OK	Excellent	Dies	OK	OK
Challenges	Crowds out bluegrass in summer	Long germination period	Crowds out bluegrass	Vibrant and patchy	Vibrant and patchy

This chart indicates that bentgrass greens are a poor choice for courses in the Deep South. The hot weather kills the blades. Courses in transition areas in the country, such as North Carolina, find that bentgrass is a preferred putting surface February through June and September through October, but that it often burns out in the height of the summer. MiniVerde Ultradwarf is preferable in this region.

Each type of grass reacts differently to the environment. Bentgrass thrives with much more water than bluegrass. Bluegrass has a 21-day germination period while rye has a 4-day germination period. Which grass would you prefer to plant on a heavily used range? Rye is often the choice for tees and ranges, to facilitate the repair of divots. Poa annua and Poa triviallis are difficult to kill selectively in Kentucky bluegrass and bentgrass. Fescue grass uses 80% fewer chemicals than bentgrass. Seaside Paspalum, the drought-resistant strain, thrives on saltwater and provides a surface almost as smooth and fast as bentgrass or rye. Bermuda grass is popular in the warmer climates of the southern United States because its coarser blade provides heat tolerance.

One of the big differences in the maintenance practices of low-end courses when compared to elite golf courses is how often they aerate, verticut, and top dress the greens. An elite golf course will top dress bi-weekly and may even drill press the greens annually, removing up to 20% of the underlying surface matter on a green. The goal is to improve the quality of the putting surface and reduce the cost of watering by improving drainage, reducing soil compaction, and controlling thatch development.

Fertilizer, herbicides, and pesticides are the magic chemicals that can be used to create great and consistent playing conditions. They are defined as:

> Fertilizer:[11] a chemical or natural substance added to soil or land to increase its fertility.
>
> Herbicide:[12] a substance that is toxic to plants, used to destroy unwanted vegetation.
>
> Pesticide:[13] a substance used for destroying insects or other organisms harmful to cultivated plants or animals.

You can't be around two superintendents for long before one asks the other, "How much 'N' are you dropping on the greens?" Nitrogen (N), phosphorus (P), and potassium (K) are the primary ingredients that are mixed and mingled in what seems to a lay person to be a witch's brew to stimulate the growth of grass. These major nutrients, known as NPK, usually are lacking from the soil as grass requires large amounts for its growth and survival. Each plays a major part in the health of turf.

With turf health, comes disease. The chemicals used to eradicate as summarized below:

Chemicals	Purpose
Barricade	Pre-emergent herbicide broadleaf weeds and grassy weeds: crabgrass, goosegrass, and Poa annua.
Beacon	Post-emergent grassy and broadleaf weeds for agriculture.
Certainty	Post-emergent grassy and broadleaf weeds with excellent control of both purple and yellow nuts edge.
Echelon	Pre-emergent control for Poa annua.
Primo	The purpose of pre-stress conditioning is to prepare turf grass for extreme conditions before they hit. Using Primo growth regulator before the onset of stresses like heat, drought, disease, and traffic can strengthen the turf, and therefore allow it to withstand ongoing stresses throughout the season.
Rodeo	Top choice for emerged aquatic vegetation control, i.e., cattails. Broad-spectrum grass, broadleaf weed, and brush control.

---

11 http://oxforddictionaries.com/definition/english/fertilizer?q=fertilizer

12 http://oxforddictionaries.com/definition/english/pesticide?q=herbicide

13 http://oxforddictionaries.com/definition/english/pesticide?q=Pesticide

Chemicals	Purpose
Roundup	The most commonly applied weed killers in use today. These herbicides are used by everyone.
Tenacity	A herbicide for the selective contact and residual control of weeds in ornamental turfgrasses.
Velocity	Velocity can gradually eliminate both Poa annua and Poa trivialis from creeping bentgrass at tees and fairways and effectively transition a Poa-dominated mixed stand of turf to pure bentgrass.

Finally, a primer of golf course maintenance must mention the importance of water conservation if for no other reason than water's escalating cost in many parts of the United States has the risk of financially undermining many courses. Though the average water budget in the United States is $88,552, it soars to $173,901 in the Southwest and $244,513 in the Pacific region.[14]

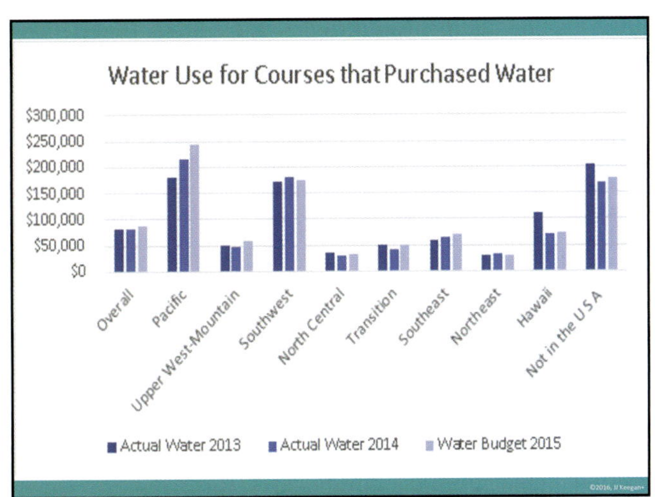

A Beacon for Change

For the golf course industry to continue to be a vibrant business, it is important to grasp that a golf course can't continue to maintain 150 or even 100 acres of pristine, well-manicured turf. Because of this, the industry needs to consider a redefinition of the maintenance standards for golf courses.

Leaders in the golf industry need to become aware of the different maintenance standards in the rest of the world, particularly Great Britain, where facilities are maintained for far less money than U.S. courses. While the greens are routinely good, fairways, teeing grounds, and the rough are maintained at far lower standards.

Such should be the mantra for courses in the United States.

14 GCSAA, "2015 Maintenance Survey," p. 8.

Key Points to Remember

1) Being ranked a Top 100 golf course has a financial benefit in terms of brand and fees that can be charged.
2) Golf courses are unique and can be classified by five categories: ownership, length, vegetation, design, and landform.
3) The typical golf course encompasses 150 acres, of which 100 are maintained.
4) Maintenance budgets within regions average from $200,000 to over $2 million.
5) It requires over 12,000 man-hours to maintain a golf course that is open 32 weeks a year. A course in operation 52 weeks per year would likely require over 30,000 man-hours to maintain.
6) Golf courses have 11 depreciable components that require an annual investment exceeding $125,000.
7) The cost of an minimum equipment fleet to maintain a golf course exceeds $500,000.
8) The golf course superintendent should be an active participant in all management and board meetings.

Concluding Thought

For every complex and difficult issue, there is always an answer that is simple, easy, and wrong.

H. L. Mencken

It is not the me same thing to talk of the bulls as to be in the bull ring.

Spanish Proverb

Chapter 13

Marketing, the Internet, and Social Media

Step 6 of the JJ Keegan+ WIN™ Formula

Wear the right costume and the part plays itself.

Ely's Law

It takes 20 years to build a reputation and five minutes to ruin it.

Warren Buffett

Chapter Highlights

Most golf courses market the "what," but few golf courses market the "why."

There are numerous ways to convey the brand message of a course. Many golf courses use a shotgun approach to marketing, causing their efforts to be diffused and ineffective. Because golf courses are rarely adept at marketing, third-party marketing firms (last-minute tee time programs) have become a significant influence in the golf industry, changing the competitive landscape.

The key to marketing is creating a brand impression through a repetitive and consistent message.

This chapter explores the more effective marketing alternatives and provides guidance regarding the application of evolving social media to a golf course's arsenal of marketing tools.

Making the Complicated Simple

Golf is not a "Field of Dreams." Just because you build it doesn't mean they will come. Millions of dollars have been invested in the course and the clubhouse, the management and staff have been hired, and the maintenance and cart equipment have been purchased. But until a customer walks through the door, the effort is all for naught.

The brand you create and the methods by which you market may be the key to your ultimate success. A brand image, once established, will attract customers even when the experience at a given moment in time may not reach the aspirational level conveyed.

Unfortunately, most golf course operators seem to believe that marketing consists of placing print ads in a local golf magazine, an advertisement in the Saturday sports section of the local newspaper, participating in coupon books, using third-party websites, and blasting e-mails containing discounted coupons to a database that is not properly segmented.

Most golf course marketing programs are created without accurately answering a simple question, "What customer segment are we trying to target?" What is needed is a highly targeted marketing approach that focuses, based on priority, on the following groups:

Let's start with the basics.

Marketing 101

Most golf courses spend about 2% of revenue on marketing. Most businesses spend about 5% of revenue on marketing. With the average daily fee course grossing about $1.2 million, the proper marketing budget should be $60,000.

Marketing has both an outbound and inbound component. We believe that resources should be allocated evenly.

Outbound marketing comprises three elements:

- Advertising
- Public relations
- Promotion

Advertising is the foundation of a marketing campaign and has two components: awareness and recall.

Awareness is simply making a favorable impression on as many consumers as possible. "Just do it," "Don't leave home without it," "Mmm, mmm good"—these immediately bring to mind Nike, American Express, and Campbell's Soup, respectively.

Awareness, for a golf course, is creating sizzle by featuring the course's architect, the history of the course, the championships conducted there, the family experience, the best greens, and the unique selling proposition for the golf course. Awareness is getting your tagline firmly embedded in the minds of the golfers. When you realize that 90% of all marketing and advertising is rooted in exaggeration, identifying the fundamental truth about your facility is important.

Fifty to sixty percent of the marketing budget should be allocated to the following electronic forms of advertising:

- Website – costs range between $3,000 and as much as $10,000 and should include Sumo.me as a list building tool with its welcome mats with the site built on a WordPress platform.
- Loyalty programs

- E-mail and text messaging marketing campaigns using Constant Contact, Vertical Response, or Sharp Spring.
- Social media via blogs, Facebook, Google+, Instagram, Linked-In, Pinterest and Twitter using Hootsuite, Sprout Social, Marketo or Hubspot to communicate to the vast majority of platform simultaneously.

Ten percent of the budget could be allocated to what is becoming dated forms of communication: press releases to leading local golf publications, participation in the local golf consumer shows, and brand advertisements in regional and local four-color publications.

The best advertising programs are those that allow the customers to be actively engaged through an emotive message rather than the presentation of a fact or statistic.

As part of **public-relations**, an advertorial focuses on a supposedly disinterested third party who independently hails the benefits of your product. Because many publications and media outlets are at any given time seeking content, advertorials lessen your cost. Such publications will probably consume approximately 10% of your marketing budget. Public relations include sponsoring charity events and hosting writers and other groups to establish a basis for the message you are disseminating.

The final outbound marketing piece is **promotion**, which is used to stimulate play on a specific day. Ten to twenty percent of a facility's marketing budget should be used for promotion, for example, a closest to the pin contest on Thursday in August with the winner getting a driver, or a hole-in-one contest with an automobile as the prize.

An additional 20% to 30% of the budget should be allocated to inbound marketing, leveraging the evolving technology that monitors customers' behavior when viewing e-mails you have sent or visiting your website.

The guesswork of any golf marketing plan is determining how to allocate finite resources to each of these categories to achieve the optimal result with advertising, public relations, and promotion—different tools for different purposes.

The trial, repeat, tracking, and evaluation of a marketing program are necessary to position the course's brand.

Rich Katz, managing director of Buffalo Communications, summarized it best:

> "Businesses frequently impart too many conflicting messages about their products, services, value proposition, culture and more. Audiences are left feeling burdened and confused. If you can relate, the time is now to develop an easy-to-understand and compelling core message. Identify three simple points of distinction that elevate your brand to world class, and support them with succinct sub-messages and attention-grabbing imagery.[1]"

Boring – It Is So Predictable

The process of marketing begins with the course's name. And, out of the gate, this is where most courses begin their path to failure. The vast majority of courses are identified by either color, land feature, type of tree, direction, or location. It is hard to believe, but just 28 words are used as part of the name in 7,176 of the 15,204 golf courses in the United States, as shown below.

Color	Frequency	Direction	Frequency
Green	356	West	186
Black	88	North	142
White	87	South	133
Red	85	East	55
Land Feature	**Frequency**	**Tree**	**Frequency**
Hill	1019	Oak	440
Lake	856	Pine	368
Creek	703	Cedar	93
Ridge	507	Willow	92
Valley	496	Maple	49
River	389	Elm	41
Brook	212	Cypress	28
Animal	**Frequency**	**Miscellaneous**	**Frequency**
Eagle	165	Old	175
Deer	94	Indian	119
Fox	90	New	105

Names that convey emotion or images are much more effective at creating interest in a facility. The Bandit, Cape Kidnappers, Coffin, Galloping Hill, Man of War, Powderhorn, Rainmaker, Sanctuary, Wildhorse, and Wizard—all of these are names of golf courses in the United States, and all are names that would be likely to entice golfers.

1 Rich Katz, "Golf-Lifestyle_PR Update," May, 2013.

The Wheel of Fortune—Website: It Starts Here

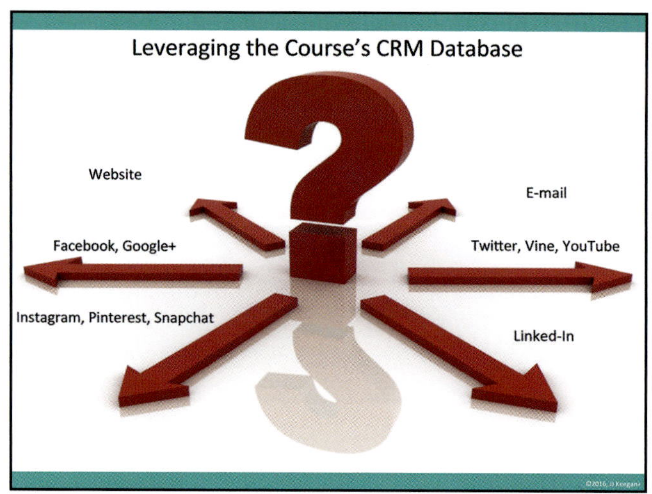

In today's electronic world, a golf course has many avenues to broadcast its message, as illustrated here:

Internet marketing is one of the most cost-effective, accurately targeted, and measurable ways to attract new golfers, retain existing customers, and reconnect with defectors. It is becoming the **most important** component of a golf course marketing effort.

It is our belief that a course's website is the entry door to its facility. A golf course website should contain a statement that emphasizes customer benefits by creating a community of dedicated visitors who have the opportunity to transact business on the site.

The website should be focused on what entertainment and value the customer will derive both from that particular golf course and from the amenities that are available there.

A website must be consistent with the corporate strategy and do more than repurpose existing static content. Quality execution in graphics, writing, and navigation are fundamental. Think of the website as a newspaper whose content is frequently changed not a book with fixed content.

The highlights of a successful site will facilitate the creation of a customer database and include:

- The "why" statement, i.e., brand message, prominently displayed.
- The phone number on the top right banner
- Rotating images of simply yet elegant graphics of the facility. The saying that a picture tells a thousand words is true.

- The ability to initiate a reservation on thc home page by entering the date, time, and group size desired.
- The opportunity to register for events, purchase merchandise, and pay online.

Mechanically, the website will have:

- A hierarchical scheme that makes navigation intuitive to the end user.
- Very fast speed in downloading images. It cannot be quick enough.
- Have meta and title tags properly code to facilitate search engine identification and placement of the course.
- The ability to quickly process transactions.
- The transmission of the transaction information along with the secured credit card data to the golf course owner.
- No meaningful content should be below the fold.
- Will properly display on desktop computers or mobile devices.

In 2015, the websites of many large corporations changed from basically a "table of contents" or index of the services provided to a graphic presentation with spectacular images of the qualities of their brand-defining their "why."

Why?

The website provides the opportunity to place an emotive aspirational message differentiating one's facility to motivate a customer to visit. This message, described by Simon Sinek, is the "why" statement—people don't buy what you do, they buy why you do it. Each course is unique and appeals to a narrow set, not to "everyone."

Let's explore possible "why" statements. They might include the following:

A municipal or daily fee course:

Option 1: "We deliver a convenient and affordable recreational experience for those who play just for fun."

The subtle message here is that frequent customers who act as though this is their private club should sense the equality in the message and perhaps play elsewhere if they don't want to encounter beginners. And conversely, beginners and many women might feel more welcome reading this "why."

Option 2: "We are here to provide a cauldron to allow you to learn how good you are at golf and how you much you appreciate the traditions of the game."

This would be appropriate wording for a course with a slope rating greater than 130. The subtle message here is to bring your game, and that this is not the facility for rank amateurs who don't appreciate the challenges golf offers and the respected traditions that shape the culture of the game.

Exclusive private club:

Option 1: "We celebrate the privileged lifestyle of those who have achieved success in their personal and business lives."

The not-so-subtle message is that this is the enclave for generational wealth and blue-bloods.

Option 2: "We welcome families and encourage them to share their diverse recreational and social interests in a warm and engaging community environment."

The subtle message is that this is a home away from home for you and your family.

Resort:

Option 1: "We offer an oasis from the daily hassle of life, a place to restore your soul."

The message is that this is a vacation hideaway where you can decompress and focus on what is important in your life.

Option 2: "Every day we provide the opportunity to form new friendships, strengthen old friendships, and add to family bonds."

The message is that this is a comfortable, friendly environment that encourages social interaction.

The "why" is simply a well-crafted vision statement that conveys to the customer the experience offered. There are many different "why" statements for golf courses.

A location that understands its "why" is Las Vegas, with the marketing moniker, "What happens in Vegas, stays in Vegas." The message implied is provocative and engaging: Be naughty and no one will know.

In its simplest form, a golf course could market value, experience, or price—the three components that determine customer loyalty.

Most golf courses attempt to compete on price. The more astute golf courses market the experience: the history, the architect, the course layout, the course conditioning, the clubhouse, amenities, practice facilities, GPS, etc.

Here are the some examples of how leading golf courses have applied this concept marvelously.

> **Bandon Dunes: "This is golf as it was meant to be.[2]"**
>
> "Bandon Dunes is true to the spirit of Scotland's ancient links. Here, players immerse themselves in the traditions of a timeless game and the grandeur of Oregon's rugged coast. Sweeping, untamed shores stretch for miles. Primeval grassy dunes roll to the sea. Five distinctly different courses have been conceived in harmony with the natural environment. They combine with all the essential elements to reveal a new golf experience every time you play. The soul of the game resides here. Players walk. And at the end of the day, gracious hospitality comforts each guest like a warm, friendly embrace. This is Bandon Dunes. This is golf as it was meant to be."
>
> **Torrey Pines: "Welcome to the nation's foremost municipal golf course."[3]**
>
> "Situated atop cliffs towering above the Pacific Ocean in San Diego, California, golfers marvel at the views of the coastline, deep ravines, and classic championship golf holes.

---

2 http://www.bandondunesgolf.com/

3 http://www.torreypinesgolfcourse.com/_tpgallery/gallery.htm

Torrey Pines is the beautiful site of one of the most memorable battles in golf's history—the 2008 U.S. Open. While taking in the views and gorgeous weather, discover our award-winning golf shop where you can take home some of the magic.

Live close by and want to improve your swing? Or perhaps you're visiting San Diego on your dream golf vacation. In either case, our popular player development programs will get you smiling about your game in no time."

What is interesting is that the Torrey Pines statement several years ago was displayed on its home page. In Spring 2016, the visitor to their website is greeted with music and stunning images that make Torrey Pines special. It is very well executed.

Another website that is compelling is St. Andrews with its message, "You've arrived – The Home of Golf."

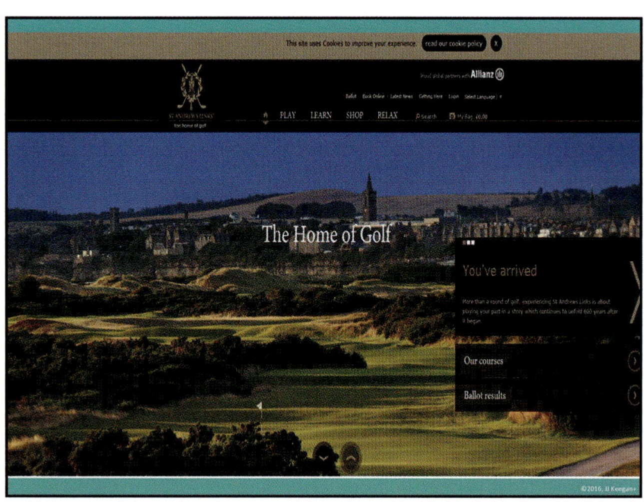

While you might question the commercial advertising on the home page above, with references to Callaway and Allianz, the St. Andrews website is elegant with the minimal "play, learn, shop, relax."

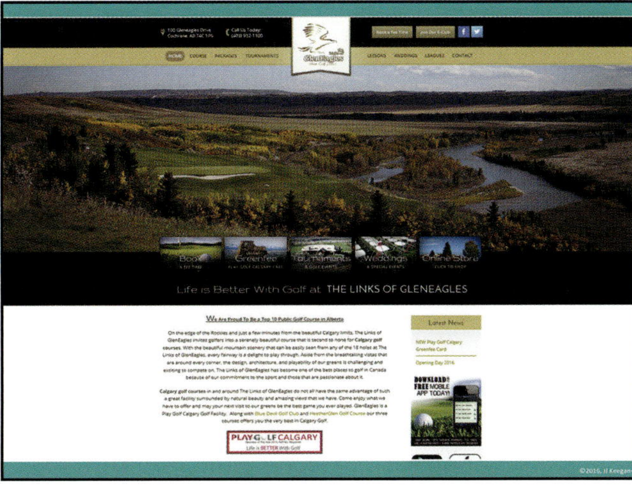

Disappointing are the websites created by templates from third-party firms. Many of these look identical. Although a golf course may save a few thousand in development costs, it costs itself tens of thousands in revenue by not having a compelling website. The easiest path is rarely the best.

That is why sites such as Play Golf Calgary, which include the Links of Glen Eagles in Calgary, Canada, shown here, are so appreciated as they incorporate the "why" message (creating memories worth repeating), facilitate on-line booking, and accelerate customer segmentation.

Although some of the academic discussion about technology is overwhelming, there are some easy, small progressive changes that can be made now that will have an immediate benefit.

Regarding tee time reservations, there is a lesson offered by the airlines, hotels, and car rental companies that every golf course should adopt. The real estate on the home of your website has different values. As people read from left to right and from the top down, the most important items should be in the upper left corner of the website. If you go to the websites of Orbitz, United Airlines, and most car rental companies, you will see their booking engines on their home pages in the upper left corner.

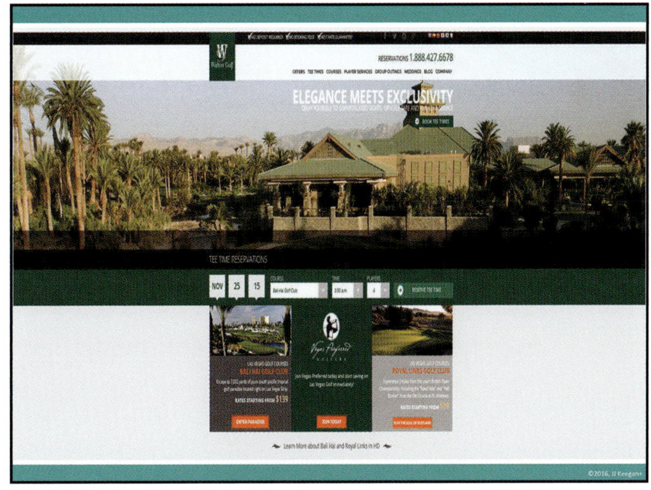

Astute golf course owners will ensure that their websites enable customers to book on their home pages, as shown on the Walters Golf website in Las Vegas.

The functionality of this website is marvelous. Rotating banners of the different courses with the "why" statement featured—"Elegance Meets Exclusivity – Treat Yourself to Sophisticated Sites, Upscale Fare and Five-Star Service." This is a really good example of website design for a golf course.

The Web Is the Spider. The E-mail Is the Fly.

From surveys conducted by JJ Keegan+, it was interesting to note that e-mails and a facility's website remain the primary ways golfers find information about the course and the specials that may be offered.

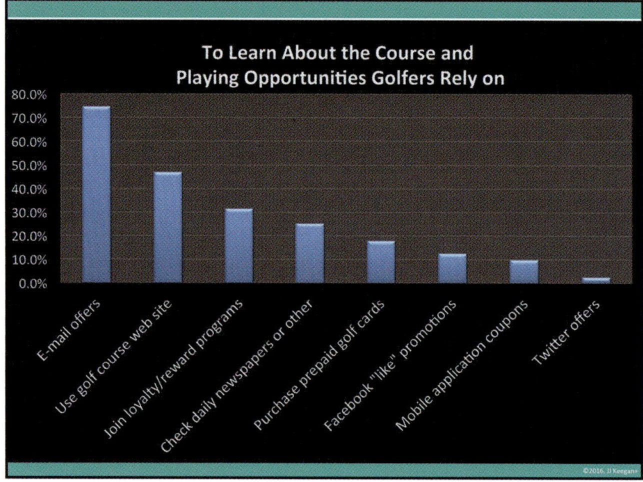

Golfers prefer e-mail messages, appropriately spaced—preferably every two weeks. The core tag line should be consistent while the subject line may vary as it features promotions.

The subject line is tricky. First, it should be written with less than 100 characters to pique the reader's curiosity enough that the e-mail is opened and to ensure that the subject line can be posted to Facebook and Twitter, as the latter limits the message to 140 characters.

It is estimated that only 80% of readers read the subject line. A reader who is familiar with the sender merely clicks on the e-mail to open it without reading the e-mail. Thus, it is a prudent practice to enter the subject line also as the first sentence of the text.

The Rules of Thumb

The typical golf course has built an e-mail database through registration of golfers at their point of sale terminals and from their website. But there is a wide disparity in the size of the e-mail databases that golf courses have been able to aggregate, as shown in the following figure:

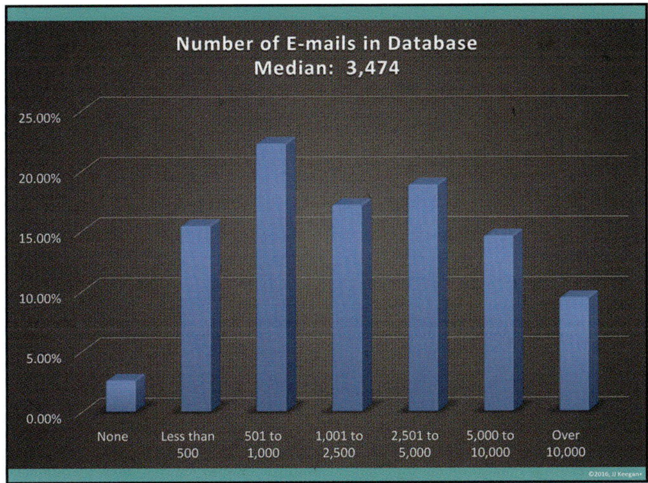

There is a science to the madness of e-mail marketing as 78% of all e-mails are spam—94 billion are sent daily.[4]

The open rates, click-through rates, soft and hard bounces, and unsubscribe rates vary widely by industry and by the device received on.

Here are some statistics regarding e-mail marketing tactics and trends:

- "The average e-mail open rates have risen from 18.35% to 21.47% in the last 12 months.
- The average person checks his or her smartphone 34 times per day.
- E-mails sent on Saturdays and Sundays have higher open, click-through, and transaction rates.
- Subject lines with 30 or fewer characters performed above average.
- Personalized subject lines are 22.2% more likely to be opened.
- 64% of recipients open an e-mail based on the organization that sent it.
- Only 26% open an e-mail based on the offer."[5]

4 http://www.slideshare.net/michaeljbarber/email-marketing-trends-tools-and-tactics-for-2014-and-beyond/42-DSD14MICHAELJBARBER_42PervasiveWe_are_reading_emails

5 http://www.business2community.com/email-marketing/23-tweetable-stats-on-email-

Here are the basic rules:

Lesson 1: Repetition ad infinitum is vital. If you are so sick of the message you want to barf, it is just beginning to become effective. "The Friendly Skies," "The Pause That Refreshes," "Squeezably Soft" are brand messages that will resonate in our minds—forever—testaments to the power of repetition. Repetition of the time sent is also recommended. Choose a standard day of the week and time of day for release (perhaps Wednesday at 6:00 a.m.) to set a standard of consistency that customers can anticipate.

Lesson 2: Fine-tune your marketing message using A/B testing or multi-variant testing. The essence of this method is that the call to action (the enticement for the customer to act) is different even though all other elements of the e-mail's copy and layout are identical. By monitoring which campaign produced the highest click-through rate, you will be able to communicate more effectively in future campaigns.

Not Only "What?" But Also "How?"

E-mail requires work. Every time an e-mail is sent, you need to manage the bounces and unsubscribes and reclassify the prospects who purchased. The following chart illustrates the response rates to JJ Keegan+ e-mails during the first 24 hours after release on opens, click-throughs, and the percentage who responded, bounced, and unsubscribed.

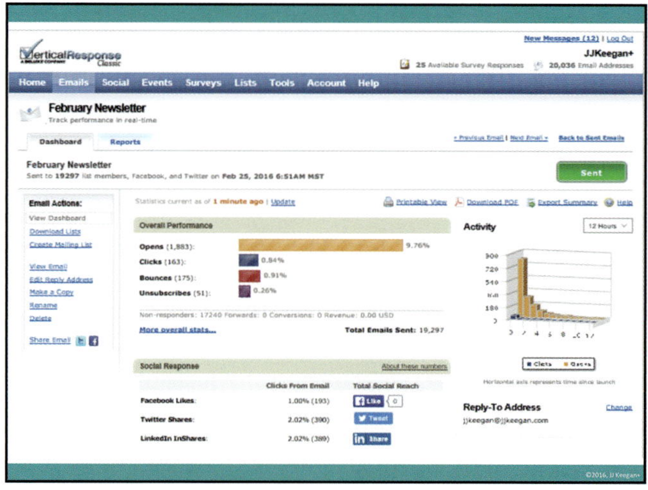

"The Science of Email Marketing," a webinar by Hubspot's Dan Zarrella, produces many insights for the golf course owner:[6]

6 Dan Zarrella, "The Science of Email Marketing," 2012 Edition, Slides 7, 8, 9, and 33.

- 80.8% read e-mail on mobile devices.
- 65.0% prefer HTML image-based e-mails.
- 88.0% percent of individuals with e-mail accounts do not maintain separate business and personal e-mail accounts.
- 58% maintain a separate junk inbox to trap "blast" e-mails.

In studying more than 9 billion e-mail messages delivered by Mail Chimp, Zarella noted that e-mail messages were opened as follows:

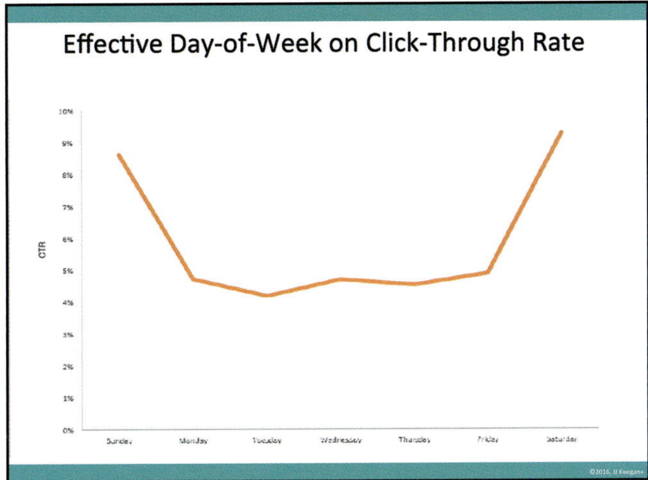

The highest unsubscribe rates were on Tuesday, and the highest click-through rates were on e-mails sent between 5:00 a.m. and 6:00 a.m., as illustrated here:

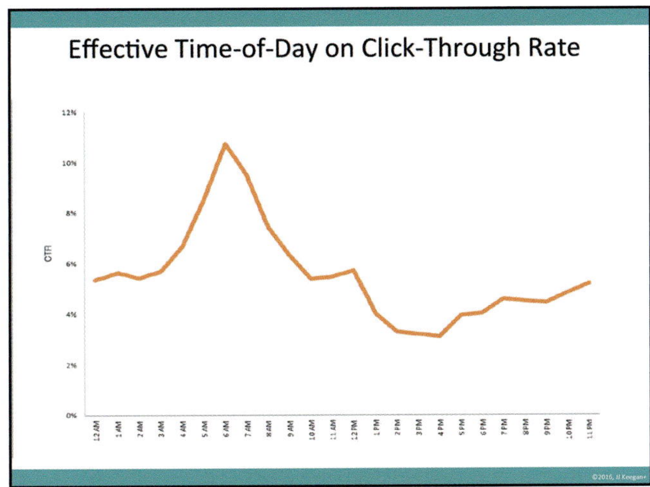

The buzz today is all about social media—Facebook, Google+, Instagram, Linked-In, Pinterest, Snapchat, Twitter, Vine, and YouTube. Shown here are the various popular platforms: all command the masses in varying degrees, but only a few should attract the attention of golf courses in marketing their facilities.

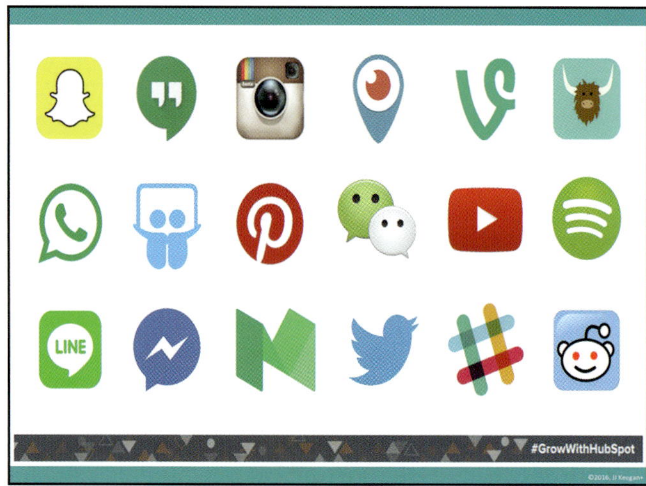

The first concept to grasp is that social media has not killed off e-mail. As reported,

> "With Facebook boasting over 1 billion active users per month and Twitter boasting 255 million, we certainly couldn't blame you for being persuaded to focus a large portion of your marketing efforts on social media.
>
> But what you don't see so frequently touted are the statistics on email usage. According to Radicati, the total number of worldwide email accounts was 3.9 billion in 2013 and projected to be 4.9 billion by 2017.
>
> To put this in perspective for you, there are 3x more email accounts than there are Facebook & Twitter accounts combined.
>
> From a marketing perspective, though, it's the statistics on reach and engagement that show the real story. Did you know that organic reach on Facebook (i.e. the number of your fans who see your posts in their Newsfeed) is only 6%?

On the contrary, open rates for email marketing messages are generally in the 20 – 30% range, meaning your message is 5x more likely to be seen through email than Facebook.

Similarly, click through rates from email are generally in the 3% range, while click-through rates on Tweets are generally in the 0.5% range. This means you are 6x more likely to get a click-through by email than you are from Twitter."[7]

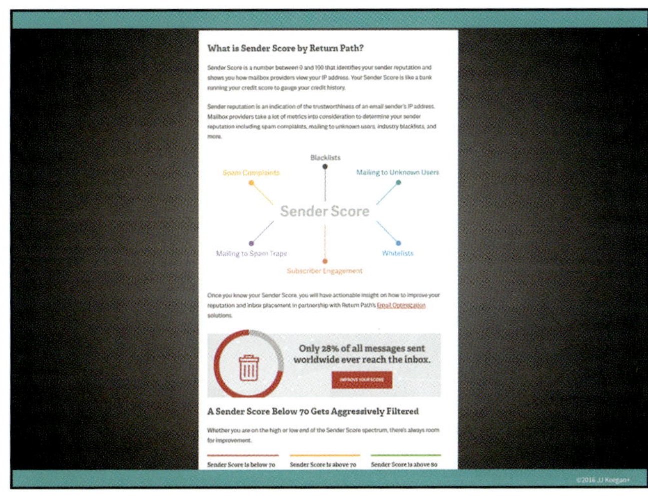

With confusion abounding, which are the best tools for you to use to monitor the effectiveness of your marketing?

With respect to e-mail, a complimentary service, Sender Score by Return Path, is valuable as it monitors the deliver rate of the e-mails you send as shown here.

Ultimately, the effectiveness of a facility's website can be measured by various indices.

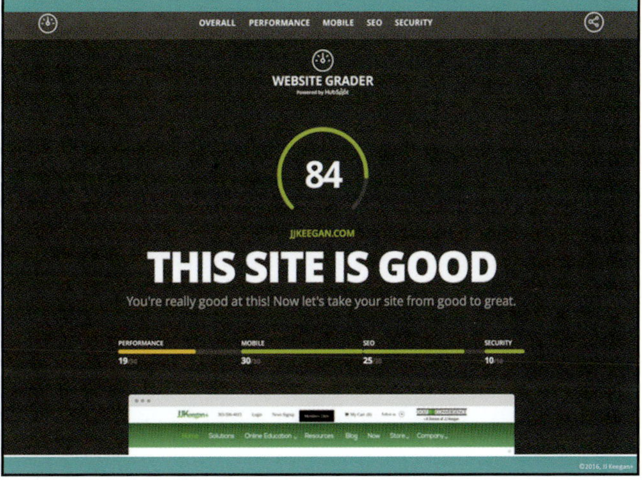

Google Analytics reflects the geographic location of individuals viewing a website. The Google Analytics tool identifies the number of site visits, new vs. returning visitors, how long customers remain on a site, the pages on the site that are being viewed the most frequently, how users enter and leave the site, what Internet browsers they are using, their age, gender, geographic location and many other meaningful metrics including whether your site was viewed from a desktop, mobile phone or iPad.

7 https://www.campaignmonitor.com/blog/email-marketing/2014/07/email-marketing-vs-social-media/

Website Grader by Hubspot evaluates your website by its performance, whether it displays properly on mobile platforms, whether you have optimized search engine optimization, and the security of your site. Shown below is the score www.jjkeegan.golf received upon launching its revised site April 16, 2016.

For performance, it measured browser caching, page redirects, compression, and render blocking of javascript and CSS code. For search engine optimization, it evaluated page titles, meta descriptions, heading, and whether the site had a sitemap.

In that most golf courses have their website developed by a third-party firm, website grader provides you an easy tool to measure whether the firm you retained is creating a site of value to you.

To determine the popularity of your website vs. your competitors, Alexa (www.alexa.com) provides traffic statistics and search analytics, identifies the audience and linked sites, and provides reviews and contact information.

Another marketing service growing in popularity, particularly among the leading management companies, is Google AdWords, which has attracted the attention of Billy Casper Golf Management, OB Sports, and Troon Golf.

Google AdWords is pay-per-click advertising in which course operators can determine how many searched for golf or discounted golf in their local market. Rick Katz, managing director of Buffalo Communications, comments that "You can turn on or off Google AdWords based on weather, time of the day, day of the week, and month of the year and on and on. That way, you can mitigate your risk of waste."[8]

It is common for a golf course operated by a management company to invest between $300 to $900 monthly on this form of promotion via Google AdWords or Facebook. The best return from these activities is from reservations made by groups, leagues, banquets, and weddings.

What is assured is that properly leveraging all of the software marketing tools is a time-consuming task. One service, Hootsuite, can rein in the chaos by providing you the ability to manage all of your social networks and schedule messages

8 Steve Eubanks, "Marketing Mix," Golf Business, April 2013, p. 30.

for future publishing by connecting you with 35 of the most popular social networks.

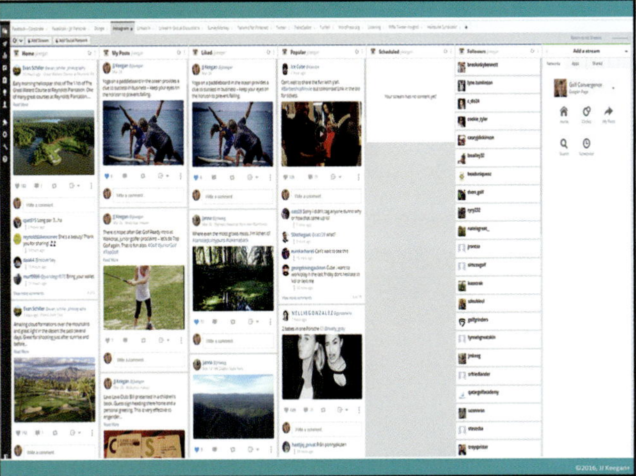

Hootsuite's social media analytics give you an in-depth view of how well your social media efforts are being received. You can learn what your audience is saying about your brand and engaging them. Radian6 and Brandwatch are two other services that monitor your brand. The dashboard is illustrated as here.

The dashboard displayed was configured to post simultaneously to the following: Facebook corporate page, Facebook personal page, Google+ corporate page, Google+ personal page, Instagram, Linked-in home page, 17 Linked-in discussion groups, Riffle, Survey Monkey, Trendspottr, Tumblr, Twitter, Word Press, Riffle, and Hootsuite Syndicator.

The time saving is enormous, and the ability to expand one's marketing presence is available. We have noted a definite increase in the "social media chatter in the forms of likes, new followers and comments regarding our postings" since subscribing to these service in March 2016. The key is not to sell our products or services but provide quality content that will assist the viewer in the conduct of their own business. The hope is that by demonstrating our expertise the viewer becomes a client. For a golf course, Hootsuite would be very effective for creating a community of interest.

Inbound Marketing

Instead of blasting out interruptive ads and trying to pull people to your company, inbound marketing uses helpful content to attract visitors and get them to engage of their own volition. This marketing approach takes longer but is far more effective as meaningful information is provided to the perspective client, usually in exchange for an e-mail address, in which a naturally flowing conversation can be developed ensuring the customer's needs, interests, and desires are being met shown here:

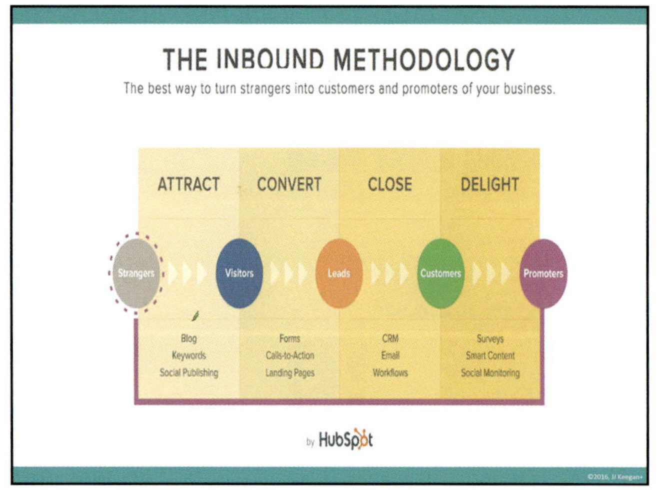

Hubspot advocates the formula is "attract – convert – close - delight" by turning your website into a magnet. Create content, optimize it for search engines and share it on social media. Then engage your prospects with landing pages, calls to action, personalized email and a personalized website.

At what may be perceived as "entry level" inbound marketing is Sumo.me. This analytical instrument monitors every click on a website. Based on that click, various pop-ups are invoked to encourage the viewer to register for newsletters and upcoming webinars, or being able to download content immediately. The following is a heat map of where viewers clicked most frequently on the home page at www.jjkeegan.golf.

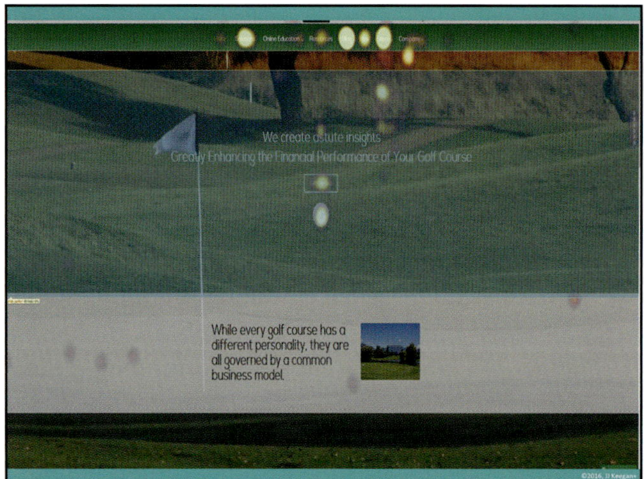

If you are looking to build an e-mail list, Sumo.me or Sharp Spring are effective places to begin.

Two of the more advanced inbound marketing automation programs are Hubspot and Marketo. The concept of these instruments is to help you master the art and science of digital marketing to engage customers and prospects.

A final recommended tool is Leadlander. If you like the concept of "big brother is watching you," you will be excited about the potential of this web software program. Leadlander enhances the ROI of your marketing automation efforts by showing you who is visiting your site and the articles that they are viewing and downloading as shown above.

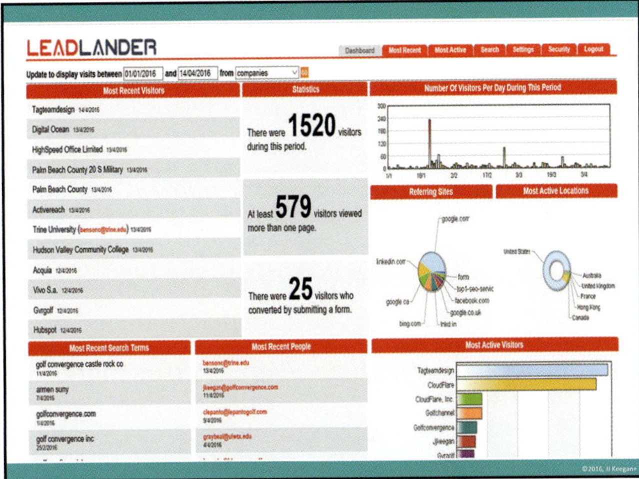

The software can be configured to send you an alert if an individual has clicked on a certain number of pages or a specific page. Thus, if a potential member was reviewing the membership plan or a bride who was planning her wedding wondered what services you provided, the ability to immediately contact them is fabulous.

Regardless of the marketing programs created, the ultimate key is to realize the long-term value of the relationship. Focusing on the customer experience and providing a personal touch should drive the message.

Key Points to Remember

The strategic vision for a golf course operation creates awareness of its brand image.

Tactical planning for marketing focuses on the allocation of resources between advertising, public relations, and promotion.

Operational execution is dedicated to measuring the efficacy of each marketing effort as it relates to the return on investment.

To ensure that a golf course's marketing efforts are effective:

1) Develop a compelling "why" statement that is consistently articulated in all advertising, public relations, and promotional efforts.

2) With the assistance of the accounting department, create a matrix of each expenditure that is related to marketing.

3) Measure the rate of return on each marketing initiative qualitatively regarding community brand recognition and incremental sales.

4) Select three marketing activities that produced a low rate of return or for which the rate of return cannot be measured. Sunset those expenditures, and reallocate those dollars to new promotional efforts.

Concluding Thoughts

The greatest deception men suffer is from their own opinions.

Leonardo da Vinci

Twitter is a gun without a safety release.
You have a great chance of killing yourself if you don't use it carefully.

Jim Rome, Sports Broadcaster

Chapter 14

Game Time

Step 6 of JJ Keegan+ WIN™ Formula (continued)

The journey of a thousand miles begins with a single step.

Lao Tze

It is our choices that show what we truly are, far more than our abilities.

J. K Rowling

Chapter Highlights

The golf course experience could be viewed as an "assembly line."

The sun rises, the gates open, management and staff arrive, and another day begins. The golf course is like an amusement park that winds the customer from the entrance around a series of themes to a thrilling conclusion upon departure.

Every point of contact is important. The design and layout of the clubhouse and pro shop define the experience likely to be encountered. The bag drop, obtaining a cart, the range, starter, golf course, cart return, and the restaurant and bar—all are elements that provide the opportunity to define the customer experience.

Creating the superior customer experience through consistent execution is the only way to guarantee survival in today's competitive market.

Making the Complicated Simple

Golfers race from the parking lot and hastily put on their shoes, perhaps not even stopping to tie them. They walk into the pro shop looking at the staff person behind the counter and think, "They work at this beautiful golf course, play all the time, and are accomplished golfers. They have it made. What a life!"

Few golfers know how much hard work is needed to create that efficient golf operation. The person behind the counter plays infrequently and rarely has time to hit balls at the range before or after his or her shift.

The Home Team

A golf course staff combines the talents of many different individuals. Staffing at a golf course, regarding the quality of the personnel retained and the number of individuals, both full- and part-time, can vary widely. The following table lists the typical positions filled at the golf course and the number of staff hired, both full- and part-time, for the peak season.

Job Title	Function	Minimum	Maximum
Bag Drop	Check in golfer to course	0	4
Starter	Start golfers on course	2	8
Ranger	Pace of play	0	4
Pro Shop Staff	Collect fees/act as starter	4	12
Director of Golf	Oversee golf operation	1	1
Assistant Golf Professionals	Customer service in pro shop	0	6
Director of Tournaments	Organize and administer golf programs	0	1
Director of Instruction	Create instruction programs	0	1
Teaching Staff	Teach customers	0	6
Food and Beverage: In Clubhouse: F&B Director, Chef, Sous Chef, Waiters	Sell food	4	8

Job Title	Function	Minimum	Maximum
Food and Beverage: On Course	Sell limited items from cart	2	2
Catering Manager	Arrange banquets and special events	0	1
Tournament Director	Groups and outings	1	3
Reservation Agent	Book individual times	1	5
Merchandise Manager	Select, arrange, and monitor inventory	1	3
Purchasing Agent	Purchase inventory	1	1
General Manager	Oversee general operations	1	2
Membership Director	Recruit members	0	2
Personnel	Retention of personnel	1	4
Controller	Monitor cash flow	0	1
Bookkeeper	Account for activity	1	4
Receptionist	Handle telephone calls	0	1
Systems Administration, sometimes outsourced	Oversee systems	0	2
Superintendent	Oversee the turf	1	1
Grounds Crew, Mechanic	Maintain the turf	6	30
Total Staff		25	113
Note: Several of those positions, depending on the size of the operation, can be performed by the same individual; thus some golf courses might operate with as few as ten people.			

These averages of personnel retained vary widely between municipal, daily fee, resort, and private clubs. For example, at the Reignwood Pine Valley Golf and Country Club in Beijing, the grounds crew totals 292 people to maintain a 45-hole course. Why such a large crew? The average annual salary is only $2,750, and staffing levels have been suggested by the Chinese government.

The challenge is selecting, training, and educating both full- and part-time staff members. Most managers underestimate the complexities of the golf business. The motivations of the food and beverage personnel, the golf shop personnel, and the tournament coordinators are all different.

The key to the daily operation of a golf course is creating a "culture of discipline." When expectations are clarified, and the commitment conveyed, individuals will take their responsibilities seriously. The key for each employee is to turn common sense into common practice.

The communication of the mission statement and management's expectations can be summarized on a small card that is carried within the wallet of each employee. Such is done at The BROADMOOR Hotel in Colorado Springs, Colorado, which has the very clear mission statement, "Above and Beyond Guest Expectations.[1]" The card that each employee carries includes its 16 guidelines for interaction with guests:

1. Make eye contact, smile, and greet the guest or employee immediately.
2. Use the guest's or employee's name.
3. Escort guests or employees to their requested location when possible.
4. Immediately approach a guest or employee who seems to be lost and offer assistance.
5. Learn what is expected from your department so you can anticipate the needs of the guests and employees you service.
6. Follow up on requests, even when it is not a duty of your department.
7. Never say: "I don't know." Say: "I'll find out."
8. Never appear hurried, even if you are very busy.
9. If unable to comply with a guest's wishes, offer an alternative. Avoid negative expressions like: "That's against hotel policy," or "This is not my table."
10. Keep The BROADMOOR spotless! If you see something that's out of place, pick it up! Remember, we are all part of The BROADMOOR Beautification Committee.
11. Act professionally in public areas at all times. Stand erect and avoid leaning against walls or furniture.
12. Always recommend The BROADMOOR restaurants and shops to our guests before suggesting other alternatives.
13. Take "ownership" of a guest's problem. Ensure the matter is resolved and that the guest is satisfied with your solution.
14. Respond to a guest's request within 10 minutes.
15. Know the services the Hotel offers and the location of the banquet facilities and meeting rooms.
16. Go the extra mile!

---

1 The BROADMOOR Management, "Exceptional Services Begins with Exceptional People."

The Assembly Line of Golf

What differentiates one course from another regarding a customer experience?

What follows is a template by which golf course personnel can ensure that they enhance the customer experience on the "assembly line"—regardless of whether the economy is robust or languishing.

Step 1—Motivating the Golfer to Select Your Course

Each touch point defines the total golf experience and starts with a golfer's decision about "which course to play."

What Motivated Me to Play Course	Yes	No
Website "why" statement		
Social media messages		
Word of mouth from "respected friends."		
National ranking in *Golf Magazine*, *Golf Digest*, or *Golfweek*		
Yellow pages		
Literature at airport		
Literature at kiosk in hotel		
Phone listing on hotel phone		
Concierge		
Billboards		
Local referrals		
Invitation from friend to play		

Though many golfers have a "home course," they are often influenced by other factors.

The billboard shown here is a good example of eye-catching advertising. This billboard is effective for many reasons: (1) an appealing photograph that entices the avid golfer; (2) a sensational tagline—"Golf Heaven"; (3) announcement of the opening of the new course; and (4) information that you are only 34 miles away from "Golf Heaven."

Most resort billboards are merely informational, providing contact information or directions. Some have compelling pictures, but few have compelling taglines.

Step 2—Making the Reservation Process Seamless, Quick, and Informative

The customer's first experience with the golf course usually comes when reserving a tee time. In most instances, the customer is put on hold—not a great first experience. We monitor the following when evaluating the process of reserving a tee time:

Reservations—Making the Process Easy	Yes	No
Was phone answer by pro shop staff?		
Did phone ring more than three times?		
Was there a music-on-hold system that played a message about course information?		
Are touch-screen kiosks available?		
Can a golfer book on-line?		
Was credit card guarantee required?		
Did agent get all players' names and e-mails?		
Were directions to a course offered?		
Were the fees discussed?		
Were the amenities mentioned?		

There are many golf courses that do a fabulous job at booking tee times, but none that exceeds the quality of the customer experience at Bandon Dunes.

These written confirmations are effective because they (1) provide details as to time and cost of pending reservations; (2) provide the opportunity to upsell; and (3) provide a link for directions to the facility.

When Darla Hamblin, who oversees reservations at Bandon Dunes Golf Resort, was asked how many reservations are booked without any changes, she chuckled and said, "Less than 5%." Thus the importance of the e-mail confirmation.

Step 3—Providing Directions to the Golf Course

One of the great frustrations in playing golf at a course for the first time is finding it quickly and easily. Notwithstanding the use of Google Maps, MapQuest, or Siri, there is a high probability you will circle some golf courses for 10 minutes trying to find their entrances. Thus, having some of the following signage is highly recommended.

Guiding the Golfer Smoothly to the Golf Course	Yes	No
Billboard on the interstate?		
Sign on nearest exit?		
Directional sign at 5 miles?		
Directional sign at 2 miles?		
Directional sign at 1 mile?		
Flowers at the entrance?		
Directional sign to facilities at club entrance?		
Sign for a parking lot or valet?		
Sign for bag drop?		
Direction sign to clubhouse entrance?		
Welcome sign at clubhouse entrance?		

An example of the proper use of signs follows:

With a tee time reservation in hand, the thought of being late because you got lost is aggravating. The golfer's goal should be to arrive 45 minutes before the scheduled tee time to practice, putt, and hit some range balls, especially when the golfer is playing a high-end daily fee course where the green fee is north of

$100. Removing that angst from the golfer by providing directional signs creates comfort. Also, these signs serve as "advertisements" for the golf course for every car that passes.

Step 4—First Impressions Are Lasting

Another first impression is created at the entrance to the property. From attractive entrance signs welcoming golfers; flower gardens that are well maintained; directional signs for the bag drop, parking, and clubhouse entrance; to staff in uniform with name tags—all these indicate the experience is likely to be a good one.

In arriving at a golf course, the following are observed:

Club Entrance: The Bag Drop Area	Yes	No
Is staff in uniform?		
Does the desk say "guest services"?		
Is attendant available?		
Does attendant provide guidance as to next steps?		
Is bag tag affixed to the bag?		
Is the bag tag personalized?		
Is course condition displayed as to green height, green speed, etc.?		

Golf courses that have a theme and execute that theme throughout the property always heighten the customer experience. The following photos depict the bag drop area and clubhouse at the Wizard Golf Course in Myrtle Beach. The neighboring course, Man of War, has a "horses" motif that is consistent with its branding. Wizard and Man of War are great names for a golf course and are compelling.

The entrance to Yalong Bay on Hainan Island has this very innovative entrance shown on the next page.

In the middle of China on a remote island, this course features its website address in the flower garden at its entrance. How creative!

Another opportunity for great marketing and brand recognition comes from the creation of a fabulous logo. Can you think of any course with a great logo? Think of Pebble Beach with the Cypress tree and Kapalua with the butterfly blended into a pineapple.

As for great experience, the arrival at Shanqin Bay sets a level of expectation that is amazing, from the general manager to the staff of the course to the fine dining. There is a reason this is one of the Top 100 golf courses in the world.

Staging the experience is an important element to a successful and profitable golf course. One of the great advertising marketing opportunities that is often lost is putting a bag tag the arriving golfer's clubs. Not only does it make each golfer feel special, but it also provides a "souvenir" of the experience. It's great "free" advertising. The average golfer plays four to seven different courses a year. Bag tags beg the question: "How was your experience there? Is it a must-play course?"

Step 5—We Are Here to Enhance Your Experience

Golf has so many unwritten rules regarding etiquette and proper decorum that most players have a feeling of apprehension the first time they visit a course. Welcoming guests with warmth alleviates that anxiety and makes them feel welcome and refreshed.

The following are opportunities for a golf course to distinguish itself as the golfers enter the clubhouse before proceeding into the pro shop.

Clubhouse: Celebrate the Traditions as Golfers Enter Your "House"	Yes	No
Flowers at entrance door?		
Symbol of pride and tradition by the front door?		
Welcome mat?		
Mission statement displayed by the front door?		
A sign that "dress standards apply"?		
Soft spike facility sign?		
Signage as to where soft spikes can be replaced?		
Plaques indicating heritage of course?		
Audubon Society awards displayed?		
Pictures of animals to be seen on course?		
Display case with championship trophies?		
Display case with merchandise inventory on mannequins?		
History of the site in the hallway to POS area?		

As one enters the Hawk Hollow Golf Course in Bath, Michigan, the mission statement is displayed. The statement is a great reminder for the staff as well as displaying a course's commitment to the guest. Little things do matter. Hawk Hollow also constructed a white picket fence between the highway and several adjoining holes. The white picket fence extends from the club entrance to near the clubhouse, perhaps ¼ mile. Expensive, probably, but it creates a special feeling about the upcoming experience.

A picture is worth a thousand words. The following was located inside the men's locker room at the famed New South Wales Golf Club in Sydney, Australia. It highlighted the club's regulations on trousers, shirts, shorts, course shoes, socks, and shoes permissible within the clubhouse. The pictures left no ambiguity as to acceptable attire.

Step 6—Mi Casa Es Su Casa

If entering the clubhouse creates an anxious moment, entering the pro shop is even more intimidating. A lot of this phobia stems from the attitude of the golf staff. If you are greeted with, "Welcome, glad to have you visiting with us. How may I help you?" anxiety will evaporate like morning dew. But too many golf employees are unwelcoming. Many women comment that they feel like they are an imposition on the young male staff pounding the computer at the check-in station.

Grayhawk Golf Club is Scottsdale, AZ, makes you feel comfortable by the ambiance as you walk into the pro shop and witness the marvelous apparel for both men and women that they have assembled:

The following is a checklist used to measure the customer friendliness of the pro shop experience.

The Pro Shop: Welcome with Warmth	Yes	No
Does the pro shop have a theme?		
What ambiance is created within the shop to hold the customer?		
PGA plaques of staff behind the counter?		
Course awards displayed behind the counter?		
The name entered into the computer?		
Were you upsold: merchandise, membership, range?		
Yardage book?		
Tip sheet on how to play the course?		
Are tees colored to represent a theme?		
Logoed balls?		
Logoed merchandise?		
Logoed gloves?		
What is the distribution of soft goods (men's and women's) versus hard goods?		
Women's inventory commensurate with the percentage of rounds played?		
Fees posted?		
Two POS registers available?		
Was there a wait at the counter?		
Candy bin upon departing?		
Customer service monitor poll?		

Making the pro shop warm and welcoming is an understandable challenge. Undertaking a repetitive task 300 times a day is boring to nearly everyone. How can you make what is a repetitive experience enjoyable for the staff? The image shown here from Chateau Whistler reminds the staff as to their role in serving the customer.

Shakespeare stated in "As You Like It," Act 2 scene 7,

"All the world's a stage, And all the men and women merely players. They have their exits and their entrances, And one man in his time plays many parts. . ."

The previous sign serves as an effective and tactful backstage reminder that the staff of the golf course is on the "world's stage."

One of the best gestures of warmth displayed within a pro shop was evidenced at Lost Tracks in Bend, Oregon. Brian Whitcomb, the owner and former president of the PGA of America, has the philosophy that a golf course is his home, and those who visit are treated with the same respect as those who visit his house. Brian loves candy. At the exit of his pro shop, he offers his "house guest" a big vase of Tootsie Rolls to select from. The total cost of giving away candy? Brian indicated it was less than $200 per year.

Step 7—Chariots of Fire: Earth Calling Satellite

Although the best golf experience is found while walking with a caddie, carts have become de rigueur, both for their economic benefit to the golf course and their convenience to the golfer. Because of carts and the mobility they provide, some who otherwise might not play the game have the opportunity to enjoy the sport.

Any golfer will surely expect water, ice, towels, and tees in the holders once the price of the green fees exceeds $100. The fundamental cart services and provisions should be as follows:

Carts	Yes	No
Cart wash and cleaned?		
Clean towels in the cart?		
Seed mix bottle full?		
Full ice chest?		
Scented towels available in the ice chest?		
Tees in rack both long and short?		
Bottles of water?		
GPS?		
Carts reflect the theme of course?		
Golfer's name in placards when advanced reservations have been made?		

Although GPS has been a fixture in the golf industry since the early 1990s, the technology has advanced remarkably since those days. The golf course GPS that began life as a toy has evolved into a business tool that some courses find indispensable. The technology has evolved to assisting pace-of-play, fleet rotation, and customer-to-pro shop communications.

As the technology is expensive, with the annual cost exceeding $50,000, the introduction of advertising on the GPS has been incorporated to lower costs. The course and the GPS vendor split the advertising revenues after an agency fee is paid.

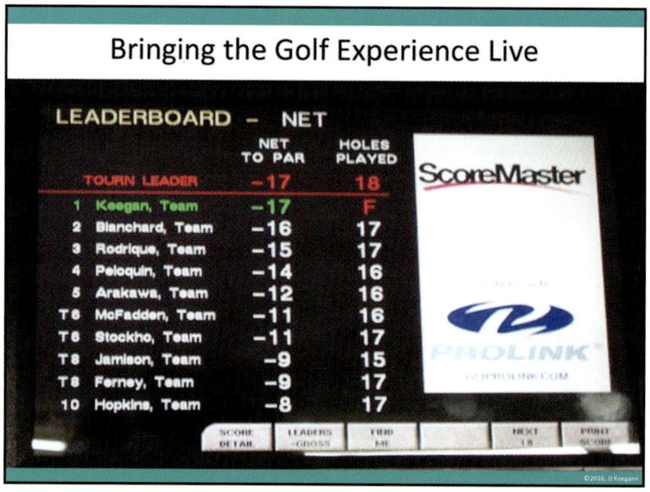

GPS is almost "standard" for golf courses whose green fees exceed $100, especially those that are resort-oriented. Unfortunately, GPS is of limited value on golf courses that require golf carts to stay on the path. Carts on paths only increase the length of the round and create golfer frustration. GPS, when used correctly, however, enhances the golf experience by allowing the golfer to select the proper club quickly, order food, and record their score.

Carts will remain a mainstay of a golf operation because they can generate revenue and are used by upwards of 75% of golfers.

Step 8—Fire Until the Blisters Burn

A golf course that has a well-designed range and short game area can be a pleasant addition to the golf experience. At the range, having golf balls aligned, tees available, and a bucket of water and a towel to clean your clubs all adds to a pleasant golf experience. Such is the case at the BROADMOOR, where two individuals "walk the range" and clean the golfers' clubs while they practice.

The following criteria are used to evaluate the adequacy of the range and practice facilities:

The Range: Warming Up to Chill Out	Yes	No
Stations with benches properly spaced for safety?		
Stations frequently rotated to ensure good turf conditions?		
Range in the aggregate in good condition, level teeing grounds with identifiable greens and target flags?		
Type of golf balls and color—good quality, white?		
Balls aligned—course logo foil used?		
Free tees?		
Correct distances to flags displayed from current tee markers?		
Driving range fees assessed by minute or number of balls? Or not at all?		
Putting green available?		
Short game area with bunker available?		
Seed mix in buckets on the range?		
Water bucket/club cleaning machine?		
Clock on the range?		

At the home of golf, St. Andrews, the importance of pace of play is first subtly communicated to the golfers by the imprinting on the range balls, which notes the pace of play goal. Pebble Beach also stamps its balls with the desired pace of play. The time on its golf balls is 4 hours 30 minutes, which says something about the different cultures. It makes you wonder how many more people would play if a round could be completed in less than 4 hours.

It is always a mark of distinction when a golf course makes the effort to indicate accurate yards to the various flags on the range, based upon a range finder that a staff member uses each day to measure distances from the hitting

stations. Having a clock prominently displayed on the range also tends to ensure a smooth flow of players to the first tee.

One of the best range experiences can be found at Diamante in Cabo San Lucas, Mexico. Each foursome is grouped together, with tables fully stocked, i.e., sunscreen lotion, tees, divot repair tools, and your choice of music: Sade, Sting, Bono, etc.

Step 9—Get Ready, Get Set, On Your Mark, Go!

Can I see your receipt? Where are the other players? I need to see their receipts now. You have to play in 4 hours and 30 minutes. Keep up the pace. Keep you carts on the cart path. Wave to the group in back of you on Par 3s. Fix your ball marks. Replace your divots. Rake the bunkers. And oh, by the way, have fun.

How many starters come across as drill sergeants? Way too many.

Don't you wonder why a golf course puts its most inexpensive labor (likely a volunteer who is working for perhaps minimum wage and for the opportunity to play golf for free) as the key customer contact before teeing off?

Imagine if you were to hear "Welcome, it's great to have you here today. Thank you for coming. You're going to have a great time. This is an exciting course. The architect is ____. His philosophy was _____. I want to ensure that you have a fabulous time. Here are my suggestions for your consideration: ____."

The opportunities to make favorable impressions are endless. So why do so few courses avail themselves of the opportunity?

The following checklist can be used to measure the friendliness of the experience.

The Starter: Welcome with Warmth	Yes	No
Sharpie and ball mark provided?		
Divot repair tool?		
Free fruit, water?		
Scorecard: color printing?		
Scorecard: routing map of course?		
Scorecard: slope, the pace of play, etc.?		
Instructions on the pace of play, rules of course given?		
Is starter wearing a headphone connected to POS counter?		
Does the starter recognize the golfers by their first names?		
Does the starter take the receipt and enter it onto the tee sheet?		

On the first tee at the Old Head of Kinsale, in Cork Island, Ireland, a ritual "stone of accord" is displayed bearing the following account:

"In ancient times when Celtic people (the Eire-ann) lived on this headland, friendships were acknowledged, arguments settled and bargains and marriages were sealed by joining hands through the Stone. This tradition may be up to 6,000 years old and can still be practiced. As we set out to enjoy the Royal and Ancient game let us continue this ancient tradition by shaking hands through the Stone to symbolize camaraderie and goodwill."

In Korea, caddies often take the foursome through some yoga stretching exercises before teeing off, where the order of play is determining by drawing chopsticks.

The little things often make a big impression.

As one approaches the first tee at Circling Raven, the Coeur d'Alene tribe, the Schitsu'umah, talk about the history of their tribe and that, "Since time began, we have shared our wealth and welcome strangers. Here, today, we welcome you" as shown here.

Step 10—18 Tees, 18 Fairways, 18 Greens: The Thrill Ride

The golf course is like a great book. It excites in the beginning, engages throughout, and disappoints and brings heartache when least expected. As the end approaches we hope for a fabled ending, and even if the fable isn't to be told on that day, the golfer, upon completing the round, immediately wants more.

Golf courses are, in essence, history museums.

At West Point, there is a plaque at each hole describing a battle in American History.

How better to convey that thought than to design a golf course that describes and demonstrates the theories of the world's great golf course architects. The Architects Golf Club in New Jersey uses those theories of the greatest architects and educates the golfers as they play the course.

Not only is the round fun, but it's also highly educational, as the golfers gain an appreciation for the game and its complexities. Thus courses that have a theme that is carried throughout, like an entertainment park, should be celebrated.

Each golf course should tell its story and provide bookmarks on which your enjoyment can be measured as shown here at the Cowboys Golf Club.

Below is a checklist to ensure that your course is unique.

The Tract: Each Course Is Unique	Yes	No
Tee signs with yardage guidance?		
Unique tee markers depicting a theme?		
Elevated multiple tees with "sticks" indicating tee positions?		
Tee signs suggesting where a golfer would have the most enjoyable round?		
Flowers on some tee boxes?		

The Tract: Each Course Is Unique	Yes	No
Seed mix on every tee next to tee markers?		
Food and beverage cart available?		
Lightning warning signs and notification of what to do?		
Heart defibrillator available at the course?		
Pace of play clocks on the golf course?		

The concept of creating a unique experience is illustrated at Lost Tracks where they bought an abandoned rail car and then furnished it as a dining parlor. In putting up a bag tag, this became a place where every golfer would leave their own personalized bag tag showing the club they came from, reflecting the path from which they have traveled.

Step 11—When You Have To Go, You Have to Go

Is there anything more disgusting than a filthy bathroom? Is there anything more disgusting than a golf course where you pay $78 in green fees and are required to use a porta-potty, or worse yet, one that hasn't been cleaned recently?

A golf course restroom should not resemble that found at a run down gas station. Bathrooms are graded based on the some of the following criteria:

Bathrooms: The Dump Should Not Be a Dump	Yes	No
Fragrance acceptable?		
Carpeted?		
Toilets clean and modern?		
Paper toilet seat covers available?		
Lockers available?		
Flowers by basin?		
Candles by basin?		
Soap fresh?		
Cloth towels?		
Sunscreen?		
Deodorant?		
Mouthwash?		

The importance of bathroom facilities is recognized by some. The on-course restrooms at Red Sky Ranch in Vail cost nearly $1.5 million each. Whistling Straits is to be lauded for hiding its bathrooms within the dunes on the course.

At Diamante in Cabo San Lucas, consciousness of branding extends even to the men's bathroom as shown here:

Step 12—The Mad Dash to the Finish Line

What seems so simple can be such a confusing process for the customer. Upon completing the 18th hole, do I drive the cart to the car and unload? Are the carts even allowed in the parking lots? Whose liability is it if the cart is damaged in the parking lot? If I return the cart to the clubhouse, is there an attendant on duty to clean the clubs? If the round cost more than $200, should I tip the attendant or presume that it is included in the green fee?

The process can be simplified for the golfer with signage from the 18th hole directing the desired flow of carts and with a clean staging area with logical "parking" positions for the carts. A tip jar sends a clear message as to whether gratuities are appropriate. More than half the golfers in America do not tip. That lack of response from the golfers could reflect their frustration with their game, their desire to quickly depart, or the realization that the clubs aren't going to be cleaned very well. Most golfers have experienced all of these.

What if an attendant asks, "How was your round and what could we do better to heighten your customer experience?" Rarely is that second question asked, but what better time is there to get a snapshot of the golfer's experience?

More checkpoints for a course to consider are:

The Finish Line	Yes	No
Free club cleaning?		
All clubs cleaned or just the irons?		
Garbage cans nearby to allow customers to dispose of "junk" while gathering belongings?		
Carts allowed in the parking lot?		
Clear signage where to return carts?		
"Thank you" sign for playing?		
Sign showing the replay rate to encourage further incremental play?		
Upon departing property: "thank you" sign and directions to other courses?		

When the golfer returns the cart and gathers belongings, the course has one last opportunity to make a favorable impression. Look at the following photograph to see how Hualalai creates a lasting impression. The cart return attendant has cool, moist towels ready for the golfers as they return to the staging area as they approach. What a nice customer service gesture.

Of all the closing guest experiences, one of the most impressive is at Coeur d'Alene, Idaho. The 14th hole on the golf course is a floating island to which golfers are shuttled by boat. At that course, a walking caddie is assigned to the foursome. Upon completing the round, players who make par are presented with a certificate.

This touch demonstrates that when a guest's expectation is exceeded, the story gets retold many times as free advertising as shown here.

Step 13—Chow Time

No aspect of a golf operation is as scattershot as the food and beverage experience.

Some courses confuse food service with selling implied sex masquerading as "marketing." At these courses, skimpily clad ladies parade around the course in beverage carts, offering beer that is often warm and coffee that is often cold.

Other golf courses provide grilled brats and hamburgers at the turn. Is there a better smell to stimulate a golfer's appetite?

With respect to restaurant dining, Castle Pines Golf Club has great milkshakes; turtle soup is a staple at Pine Valley; Southern cooking is available at Sage Valley; fish chowder is in the house at the turn at Caledonia Game and Fish Club; fish tacos are almost obligatory at the Ocean Course at Cabo del Sol, Baja California Sur, Mexico; or the gamed waffle and cream showed here at Bro Hof Slott in Sweden:

The key to a food and beverage operation is to have sufficient tournaments and a catering operation to create the volume necessary to provide the economies of scale in a food operation.

Items to watch for at on-course food service include:

Fine Dining or Chow Time?		Yes	No
Sign that states "Guest Services" rather than "Halfway House"?			
Ability to pre-order food mid-round to keep from delaying the round?			
Four essentials available (club sandwiches, burgers, hot dogs, and salads)?			
Outside grill with brats, dogs, and burgers being cooked?			
Diversity of beverages, from athletic to soft drinks to beer?			
Crackers, snacks, and a small assortment of candy?			
Ice machine to allow carts to refill ice buckets?			
Chilled bottled water available?			

But in looking for the best on course dining, Shanqin Bay deserves much consideration for its bountiful spread:

The Customer Experience – Consistency in Execution Ensures Success

The process of creating the perfect golf experience for the customers seems never-ending. Like football, in which every play has the theoretical possibility of resulting in a touchdown, the operational plans created by a golf course are implemented in the form of numerous make or break moments.

For an impressive experience in customer service, Haesely Nine Bridges and Nine Bridges on Jeju Island set the international standard with their personalization of bed pillows, napkins, and other items, as illustrated here:

Another great off-course experience is available at Bandon Dunes by visiting its labyrinth in the forest:

This memorial was visioned by Mike Keiser to his good friend Howard McKee. As you enter the area, a message on a stone reads,

> "The labyrinth is a metaphor for our journey through life. Its path leads toward an inner light, to the center of our self and the center of the sacred, one and the same. Its directions, at times, is confusing,

> taking us around, and then back again. Yet, it is through this circular journey of discovery and growth that we reconnect where we once began."
>
> In memory of Howard McKee, whose own journey through the labyrinth contributed to the vision and experience that is Bandon Dunes.
>
> This is a replica of the labyrinth in Chartres Cathedral, France dated 1194–1220."

I would guess that less than 5% of Bandon's visitors know the labyrinth exists and far fewer has visited it. It is truly special.

This kind of creative thinking meets and exceeds the expectations of customers, creating valued memories and the likelihood of more guests wanting to return.

Key Points to Remember

1) Creating a superior customer experience requires careful thought, preparation, and consistent execution.
2) Eighty-eight percent of golf courses do not secret shop their customer to ensure the consistency of the experience provided. To do so produces valuable insights.
3) The staff at a golf course can vary widely from as few as 16 individuals to upwards of 200, depending on the diversity of activities and service level objectives.
4) Disney has seven keys to success that should be emulated at a golf course:

    a. The competition is anyone the customer compares you with.
    b. Pay fantastic attention to detail.
    c. Everyone walks the talk.
    d. Everything walks the talk.
    e. Customers are best heard through many ears.
    f. Reward, recognize, and celebrate.
    g. Everyone makes a difference.

5) The golf course experience is like an assembly line and comprises these steps:

    a. Motivating the golfer to select the course
    b. Making the reservation process seamless, quick, and informative
    c. Providing clear directions to the course
    d. Creating a positive first impression
    e. Welcoming the guest into the pro shop
    f. Creating a department store, not a penalty box
    g. Carts: clean, properly stocked
    h. Range: a place to learn and practice
    i. The warm start

j. Ensuring the golf course is like an amusement park thrill ride

k. Keeping the bathroom facilities consistently comfortable and clean

l. The finish line: greet, serve, and ensure a friendly departure.

6) To follow the current best management practices observed, go to www.instagram.com/jjkeegan.

Concluding Thoughts

If you're not stubborn, you'll give up on experiments too soon. And if you're not flexible, you'll pound your head against the wall, and you won't see a different solution to a problem you're trying to solve.

Jeff Bezos

Ten percent of your clients give you 90 percent of the grief.

Mendelson's Law

Chapter 15

Who Are Our Customers?

Step 7 of the JJ Keegan+ WIN™ Formula

There are some people that if they don't know, you can't tell them.

Louis Armstrong

Chapter Highlights

This chapter explores golfers' habits and their psychology and how these can be studied.

The choice is everywhere, and barriers are prolific. There are at least five potential barriers to playing golf—lack of need, money, desire, time, or trust that the experience will be enjoyable. Why do golfers make the choices they do? How do they differentiate between all of the alternatives? What influences them?

Recent studies indicate that most of those who choose this sport play because of the level of affiliation and engagement they derive. Social connection drives choice, which provides sound guidance on attracting and retaining millennials.

An X-Ray of Who Plays Golf

Understanding the underlying motivations of golfers is essential. You must identify the real reason a consumer decides to come to a golf course to spend upwards of six hours of their day: for sport, for competition, for exercise, for leisure, for recreation, for networking, or merely to enjoy the outdoors.

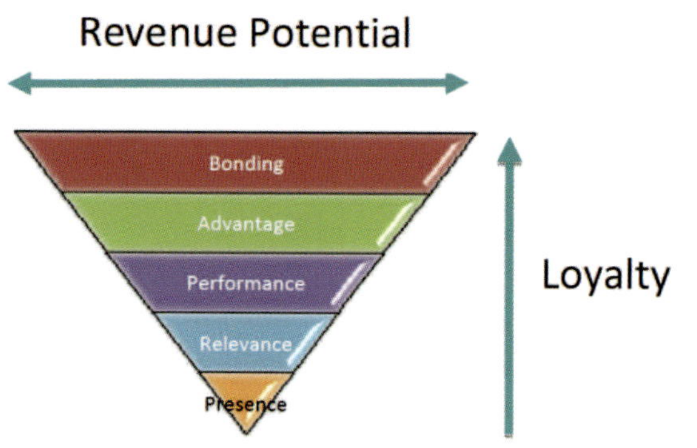

Those who come to the course seek to play the game of golf; the mission of those who are employed at the course is to build customer loyalty to enhance the facility's revenue potential.[1]

To build loyalty you first must understand exactly who your customers are by their income, age, and ethnicity. Then grasping their wants, needs, and desires are vital.

PARTICIPATION BY INCOME

	<$35K	$35K-$74K	$75K+
% of Population	35%	31%	34%
% of Golfers	16%	29%	55%
Golfers (MM)	3.0	6.9	14.8
Golf Part. Rate	3.9%	7.9%	13.6%
Est. Pop Growth (Next 5 Years)	-4.5%	-0.5%	+17%

Source: NGF golf participation study

It behooves one to understand the distribution of golfers by income as shown here[2]:

Thirty-four percent of the population generates 55% of the golfers. It bodes well for the industry that the estimated population growth of 17% will occur in income segment of $75K+ that golf attracts.

Regarding age, there are encouraging signs that the highest participation rate is actually among those 30–39 years of age shown on the next page[3].

1 https://www.mindtools.com/pages/article/brand-pyramid.htm

2 National Golf Foundation, "State of the Industry – the NGF Perspective: 2015," slide 13.

3 National Foundation, "State of the Game and The Business of Golf, May 2014," slide 9.

One of the concerns regarding the potential growth potential of golf is discovered in an analysis of the ethnicity of those who play—largely Caucasian as illustrated by the graphic below:[4]

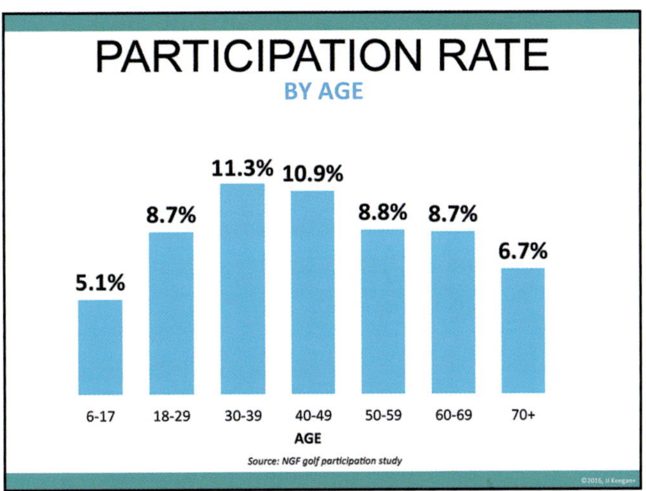

The NGF research has documented that the participation rate of Caucasians is 12.0%, Hispanics, 7.7%, Asian-Americans 8.9%, and African-Americans 3.9%.[5] With the increasing diversity of population in the United States as reflected by the non-Caucasian sector growing by 60% during the next decade, the participation rate for golf is likely to fall.

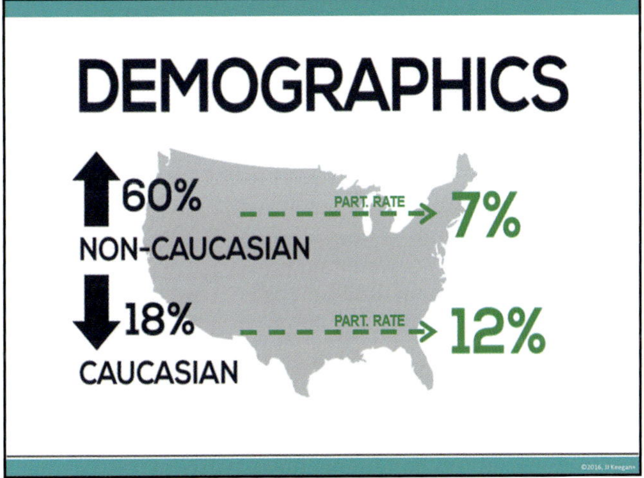

In 2012, the National Golf Foundation examined what attracts individuals to commit to the game. The NGF redefined the standard classifications of golfers from occasional, core, and avid into the following segmentation[6]:

- **Nuts:** I'm a "golf nut"; I love the game and it's my favorite activity.
- **Hooked:** I guess you could say I'm hooked. It's certainly *one* of my favorite things to do.
- **Fun:** It's fun—one of the several ways I like to spend my recreational time.
- **OK:** Golf is okay, but I often choose to do something else with my recreational time.
- **Nots:** I don't consider myself a golfer; I play rarely and usually only at the urging of others.

4 National Golf Foundation, "Golf and the Millennial Generation," slide 5.

5 National Golf Foundation, "Minority Golf Participation in the US," 2010, p. 3.

6 National Golf Foundation, "The State of the Industry – NGF Perspective – 2015," slide 17.

There was a clear connection, as would be expected, between an individual's self-description and their likelihood of continuing to play. The retention rate of the "nots" was only 16% while "nuts" were 96% likely to continue playing.

The research by the NGF determined that the secret sauce that attracts and retains golfers is the correlation between the fun the golfer has in playing reflected here:

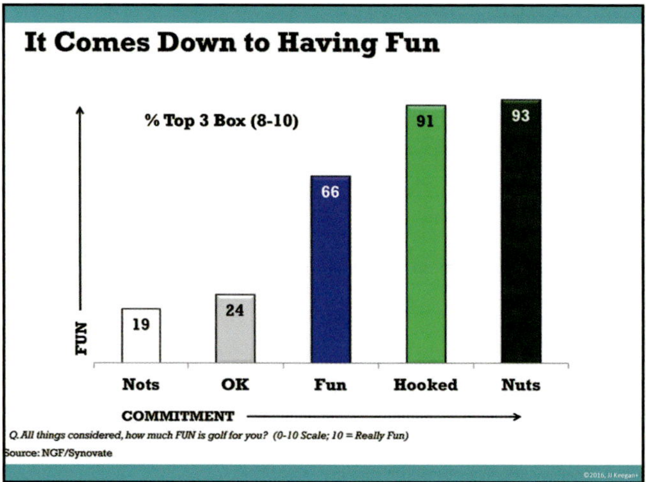

Market Dynamics

Understanding who is utilizing the facility and the actual potential for rounds and revenue allows one to tailor the products and services to the specific needs, wants, and desires of the customer.

Billy Casper Golf Management,[7] a golf course management company that serves more than nearly 200 public golf courses, has identified certain predictable characteristics as to the volume of individual customers at a golf facility and their behavioral tendencies:

7 Peter Hills, Billy Casper Golf Management, "Programming for Profit," presented at NGCOA Multi-Users Conference. Statistics updated as of June 21, 2016.

1. A golf course, on average, has 8,000 distinct customers, from a minimum of 3,500 to a maximum of 11,000. Many believe, incorrectly, that a golf course may serve upwards of 17,500 customers.
2. 22% of those customers are "initiators" and reserve the tee time for their group.
3. 60% of those customers play the course merely once per year.
4. 50% of those customers will not return next year.
5. Only 11% will play six or more times.
6. Customers average 3 1/2 rounds per year rounds played at a specific course.
7. A golf course will have a 18% wallet share of core golfers who each plays 40 rounds per year.
8. Customers become at risk of not returning when they haven't played your course in 120 days.
9. The response rate from customers offered a 20% off coupon, a 10% off coupon, or merely acknowledging that they are missed is nearly the same.

Gathering the demographics of the golfer is a very manageable process due to the small number of unique individuals that a golf course serves annually. Unfortunately, this is one area where golf course operators have struggled. A survey of 994 golf courses by JJ Keegan+ concluded that although 94% of golf courses maintain a database of customers' names, only 8% of those golf courses were able to capture more than 50% of the e-mail addresses of golfers who played their golf course.

The challenges to creating a customer database can be traced to several sources: use of a cash register, lack of an integrated tee sheet, and the attitude that the facility didn't feel identifying customers was important or thought the process was too cumbersome for staff and inconvenient for the customer.

We are always humored by how difficult golf course staff can make a simple task. Note how efficiently a golfer's e-mail address can be captured as illustrated here:

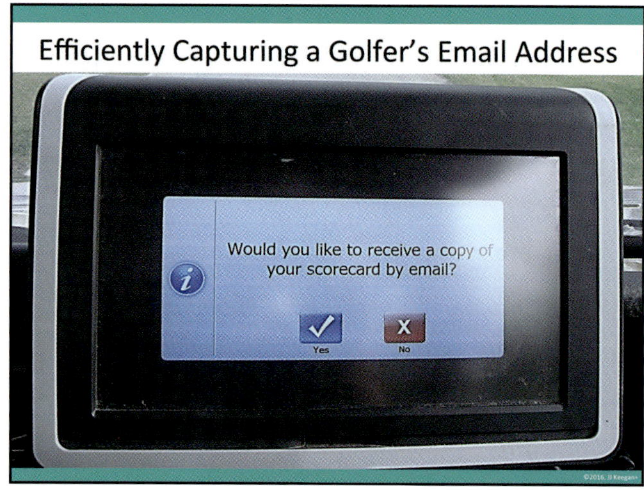

Framing the Survey

Information about your golfer's preferences can be learned in several ways, among them customer surveys, volunteer programs, and advisory councils. All three are vital and augment the value of an integrated golf management solution described in Chapter 7, Technology—The Foundation.

There are many ways to construct, issue, and tabulate surveys. They can be lengthy paper forms that are manually tabulated. But long and cumbersome surveys come with many inherent risks. Satisfied customers are not likely to invest the time to complete them, and the results tend to be skewed towards the dissatisfied customers when the overall response rate is low.

The most efficient survey method is to create a brief, 25-question survey that is electronically distributed from one of the many Internet survey sites (such as Survey Monkey or Survey Gizmo).

Another effective technique is to retain a third party to undertake a survey on behalf of the course. The fees assessed (between $1,500 and $3,000) are reasonable. The use of the third party eliminates survey bias as customers can be completely candid because the promise of treating their responses confidentially is more credible.

Using a third party has another benefit—they can often add to your customer database a large sampling (5,000 to 10,000 golfers' names within 10 miles of your facility) through acquisition via third parties on a one-time use or by obtaining the cooperation of nearby golf courses to participate in the survey and provide confidential access to their customer database. The ability to compare and contrast the views of your patrons with the views of area golfers is often very informative.

The purpose of a survey is to be able to draw conclusions about a population with a reliability and credibility that will facilitate decision making. The process involves the following:

Step 1: What Is Your Population?

For a golf course, the population consists of two subsets: those golfers that frequent your golf course and, for municipal, daily fee, and private clubs, golfers within a 30-mile radius, whether or not they have visited your facility.

Step 2: How Accurate Would You Like to Be?

The answer to this question has two components: the confidence interval and the margin of error. What you are trying to determine is how much risk you are willing to take that the answers you get from the survey are accurate because you haven't surveyed the entire population.

The confidence interval is an indication of how representative the answers of the survey respondents are of the population not surveyed. The most commonly used confidence interval is 95%; decreasing it to below 90% is not recommended.

The margin of error is the risk you are willing to assume that the answers reflect the views of the population. For example, if the survey responses indicate that the typical golfer plays six different courses per year, with a margin of error of 5%, the range of golf courses played would be between 5.7 and 6.3 courses per year.

Although 5% is the most commonly used margin of error, depending on the size of the population, you might come up with between 1% and 10% for a margin of error.

Step 3: Determining Sample Size?

Having determined the population size, the confidence interval, and the margin of error desired, the required sample size can be determined, as illustrated in the following chart.

Population	Margin of Error Confidence Interval					
	90%/10%	90%/5%	90%/1%	95%/10%	95%/5%	99%/1%
100	41	74	99	50	80	99
500	60	176	466	81	218	476
1,000	64	214	872	88	278	906
5,000	67	257	2,876	95	357	3,289
10,000	68	264	4,036	96	370	4,900
100,000	68	270	6,336	96	383	8,763
1,000,000+	68	271	6,719	97	384	9,513

To determine the sample size required, numerous complimentary websites are available to guide you, including Raosoft, Inc. at http://www.raosoft.com/samplesize.html.

Step 4: Response Rate

The response rate represents those who return the completed survey. A certain percentage of those surveyed must respond to achieve the level of accuracy sought.

In conducting the Canadian financial benchmarking survey in 2013, the challenges to achieving an appropriate response were evident. It was hoped that the survey would reveal meaningful financial information by which courses could compare their operating performances to their peers, both regionally and locally. For that to happen, sufficient responses needed to come from each province. Although a confidence level of 94% with a 6% margin of error was achieved nationally on 325 respondents, as illustrated below, parsing the data further by province could have easily produced some incorrect conclusions.

PROVINCE	Population (Number of Courses Located in Province)	Actual Sample Size	Statistical Sample Required to Achieve 90%/10%	Actual Confidence Level and Margin of Error
British Columbia	311	56	56	90 | 10
Alberta	313	43	56	90 | 12
Saskatchewan	165	11	48	90 | 25
Manitoba	133	14	47	90 | 21
Ontario	841	149	62	95 | 7.5
Quebec	367	10	57	90 | 26
New Brunswick	56	8	31	90 | 28
Nova Scotia	72	13	35	90 | 21
PEI	30	4	21	90 | 18
Newfoundland	22	1	17	90 | 90

Only in the provinces of Ontario and British Columbia were the response rates high enough to generate a statistically valid response.

Response rates vary widely depending on factors such as the relationship with your target audience, the length and complexity of the survey, incentives, and the topic of your survey.

For online surveys in which there is no prior relationship with recipients, a response rate of between 10% and 20% is considered to be highly successful. When sampling golfers, a response rate of upwards of 40% is often achieved, but the relationship of the target audience to the survey greatly influences the outcome.

Step 5: How Many People Should the Survey Be Sent To?

Divide the sample response desired by the anticipated response rate. If you are seeking to achieve a 95% confidence level with a 5% margin of error, and you anticipate a 20% response rate, with a population size of 5,000, the survey should be sent to 1,795 individuals (357/.20%). Contests and awarding some complimentary rounds to respondents can stimulate the response, although those efforts may slightly compromise the validity of responses received.

There are a couple of "catches" in undertaking surveys.

First, the completion rate. The goal is that 90% of the respondents will complete all questions. The probability of achieving that completion rate is dependent upon the length of the survey and the form of the questions. After 25 questions, that completion rate starts to drop. Yes, No, and Multiple-Choice questions are preferred over essay questions for two reasons: they are easier to answer and far easier to tabulate the responses in a meaningful format for analysis. Also, when the survey is released, there will be an initial surge of respondents who believe they can answer the questions quickly to qualify for the prize. They tend to drop out after 10 questions.

Second, while Yes, No, and Multiple-Choice questions are preferred, they can produce serious flaws as to the internal validity and create a ceiling effect. The answers to some questions on a survey need to be measurable on a 5-point or 10-point scale to undertake the meaningful statistical analysis.

Third, when you ask customers questions about policies and procedures (rates, tee time access policies, credit card guarantees, etc.), they will respond not from the perspective of what would be equitable for all parties but solely from personal self-interest. Although you hope that they will respond with an amount that represents the fair market value of the experience received, they don't want to look cheap but also want to ensure the lowest rate possible. Their answers reflect what they hope the new rate will become.

One of the effective ways of minimizing the respondent bias in a survey is to use multiple collectors where analysis can be conducted based on various "self-interest" groups. For example, for a client in 2015 the principal question was to determine the support for a renovation of up to $4 million for a golf course that is encased within a very impressive residential development in which various collectors were utilized shown on the next page.

Learning how the neighborhood that bordered the course felt vs. the community at large was important. By accessing the golf course database, the city's park and recreation database, as well as the city's database a representative sample of the various groups was able to be achieved.

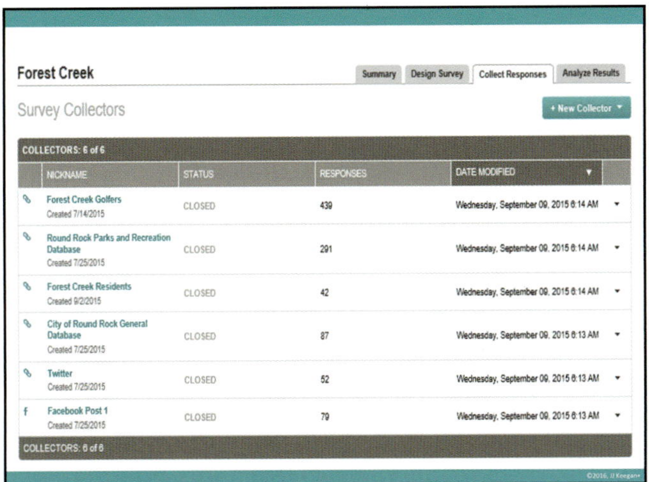

NICKNAME	STATUS	RESPONSES	DATE MODIFIED
Forest Creek Golfers Created 7/14/2015	CLOSED	439	Wednesday, September 09, 2015 6:14 AM
Round Rock Parks and Recreation Database Created 7/25/2015	CLOSED	291	Wednesday, September 09, 2015 6:14 AM
Forest Creek Residents Created 9/2/2015	CLOSED	42	Wednesday, September 09, 2015 6:14 AM
City of Round Rock General Database Created 7/25/2015	CLOSED	87	Wednesday, September 09, 2015 6:13 AM
Twitter Created 7/25/2015	CLOSED	52	Wednesday, September 09, 2015 6:13 AM
Facebook Post 1 Created 7/25/2015	CLOSED	79	Wednesday, September 09, 2015 6:13 AM

Questions to Pose

A customer survey should comprise four components, (1) learning about the golfer, (2) where they play, (3) their opinion about your facility, and (4) their golf spending habits and practices.

A well-crafted survey will incorporate “skip logic” to ensure that the respondent can complete the survey in less than 10 minutes. For example, if they haven’t played the golf course in the last two years, the logic would be to have them skip over any questions evaluating the course, the food service, and the staff.

One of the great options a survey provides is the ability to filter responses to a given answer by gender, ethnicity, income, playing frequency, etc. Some amazing insights can be obtained by drilling into the detail if the survey has attracted a sufficient number of respondents.

Questions about gender, age, household income, ethnicity, education, zip code, how many times they play golf each year, their barriers to playing more often, how many different courses they play annually, and the factors that they consider important in selecting a golf course are usually included in the survey’s first section.

To begin the second section of the survey, the question “Would you recommend the following courses to a friend, colleague, or family member?”

should be asked. A 10-point rating scale ranging from “Extremely Likely” to “Extremely Unlikely” is appropriate. Which courses in the area are their favorite, and which courses they play most often also provide insights as to their playing patterns. Their ideal length of the golf course and how they rate a competitive set of golf courses based on conditioning, course layout, customer service, food and beverage, merchandise, practice facilities, and price and value provide insights regarding how the customer perceives the attributes of your course vs. your competition.

The third section of the survey provides the opportunity for respondents to opine on the facility as to how they rate the various specific aspects of your golf course: condition, layout, customer services, food/beverage, merchandise, pace of play, price, proximity to home/work, range, tee time availability, etc. Their evaluation of course conditions can be further analyzed by their opinion on the condition of bunkers, fairway, greens, rough, and tees. Questions asking how many times they have played your course, whether they are likely to play the course again, and the primary barriers to playing there more frequently provide insight on challenges to increase rounds and revenue. Obtaining feedback on all aspects of the facility including the restaurant, staff, their preference for making tee time reservations and their preferred communication (e-mail, website, social media) are frequently asked.

For a private club, the questions can be expanded when facing financial challenges as to what is the member’s desired preference: capital assessments, operational assessments, increase in monthly dues, course renovations, or closing various amenities offered. For a municipal, daily fee, or semi-private facility, changes regarding season passes programs as the perceived value can be vetted through a survey.

Finally, learning what golfers perceive to be a good value, whether they make tee times on the Internet, and where they search for special prices are beneficial.

Following are the results from four randomly selected questions that highlight the disparities that can exist between a facility, the local market, and national averages.

The first question usually pertains to gender. Nationally, according to the NGF, the distribution of players is 78% male and 22% female, compared to the national population of 51% female and 49% male.

What Is Your Gender?	Atlanta	Denver	Grand Rapids	Pacific Grove	San Antonio	Winnipeg
Male	92.80%	83.10%	52.30%	79.90%	91.60%	77.5%
Female	7.20%	16.90%	47.70%	20.10%	8.40%	22.5%
Only Grand Rapids mirrors the national market while Pacific Grove and Winnipeg resemble the typical gender demographics in golf.						

Age is another factor that determines playing frequency; the older the clientele, the greater the probability that they will play more rounds per year.

What is Your Age?	Atlanta	Denver	Grand Rapids	Pacific Grove	San Antonio	Winnipeg
Median	45.83	48.80	44.71	53.76	54.08	49.46
It should be noted that the golfer survey is likely to indicate that the average age of a golfer is 12% higher than the results of the geographic local market analysis discussed in Chapter 5.						

The third criterion is to measure the annual income of the golf course's customers, as reflected in the following table:

What Is Your Income?	Atlanta	Denver	Grand Rapids	Pacific Grove	San Antonio	Winnipeg
Median	136,441	118,723	67,366	118,179	79,238	95,952

The fourth fundamental question regarding playing frequency highlights the potential opportunity to increase rounds.

How Many Rounds Do You Play Annually?	Atlanta	Denver	Grand Rapids	Pacific Grove	San Antonio	Winnipeg
Median Rounds Played	34.73	31.32	24.42	42.09	45.32	20.98

In conducting surveys an obtaining a zip or postal code is appropriate. There are complementary software tools available to help you map the geographic distribution of your respondents: Microsoft Bing Maps and Google Earth Pro.

Where pictorial representations are handy is best illustrated here where we conducted a survey for the Trails at Chickasaw Point of 14,000 public golfers within the Anderson-Clemson-Westminster, South Carolina market.

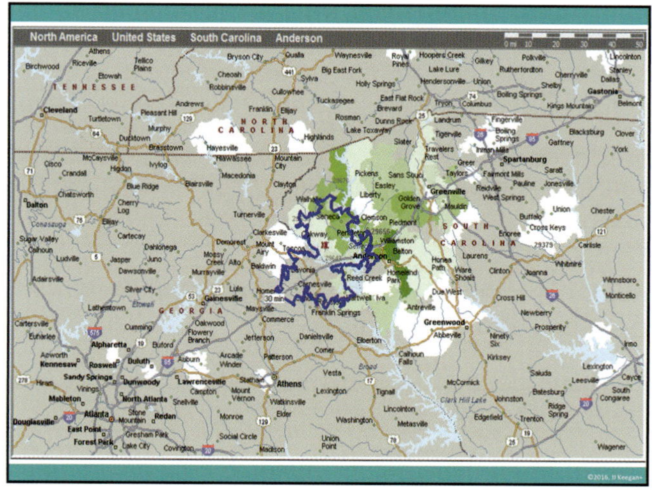

The distribution of public golfers outside the 30-mile drive time circle (jagged blue line), indicates the challenge the course will have in attracting and retaining public golfers. The opportunity for growth at this golf course is based on the 1,600 lots and 400 homeowners and ensuring their expectations and satisfaction are in balance.

Volunteers and Advisory Councils

Another form of feedback that is available comes from volunteers and advisory councils.

The concept of the volunteer program is valid if properly implemented. Usually, a volunteer program provides free or discounted golf during non-peak times to individuals who perform valuable services for the golf course. From a volunteer program, management can also garner meaningful feedback on the strengths and weaknesses of the operation.

A typical volunteer program includes:

- To be eligible for discount golf, an individual must volunteer for a minimum of eight hours per week. A formal time-keeping system to measure hours worked is usually necessary; the "honor system" often leads to chaos.
- The number of volunteers should be limited to 15.
- For working such hours, volunteers are provided the opportunity to play golf at a 50% discount off the established rates at off-peak times. It should be noted that volunteers should pay the posted golf cart rates.
- Volunteers should only be able to play on a walk-up basis, occupying a tee time that would otherwise not be sold.
- Volunteers, if they play in regular groups or outings, should be required to pay the same green fees that a regular patron would pay.

Volunteers do come with risks, starting with the IRS because of Federal wage and withholding guidelines. Further, volunteers are difficult to hold accountable and keep responsible. Volunteer programs can also create a sense of entitlement. Individuals can be difficult to terminate, they sometimes discuss the course's business with the customers, and managing them can be like herding cats.

Another kind of volunteer program is the Golf Advisory Council. The concept of this body is to advise golf management on plans, policies, and procedures, thereby providing an effective forum for customer feedback before the implementation of major initiatives.

Councils also come with risks, as members of the Golf Advisory Council often perform frequent oversight of the facilities, asking questions and perhaps even giving orders, thereby taxing the resources of the staff who must attempt to respond courteously. We have too often seen where the director of parks and the director of golf at municipal golf courses becomes an employee of these voluntary councils, having to answer their numerous demands and requests. We believe the risks far outweigh the benefits of a formally established Golf Advisory Council.

Implications for Today's Golf Course Manager

Customer feedback that is unbiased is of tremendous value. This feedback reveals:

- Why golfers choose a golf course.
- How your course stacks up against the competition.
- The fair value of your course.
- Your unique value proposition message to your customers.
- Your competitors' weaknesses.
- At what price points your competitors' customers become your loyal customers.

Online tools make surveys easy, and they make it possible for you to measure the successes and failures of your relationship with your customers quickly.

Key Points to Remember

1) Understanding who your customers are—their needs, wants, and desires—allows a management team to craft a value-based experience that will produce an appropriate financial return for the facility.
2) Customer feedback can come from volunteer programs, advisory councils, or surveys.
3) Although volunteer programs and advisory councils can be beneficial, both have significant risks.
4) Obtaining customer feedback is essential to create a valued experience for the golfer. Eighty-two percent of golf courses DO NOT conduct an annual survey. By doing so, you will gain a competitive advantage over your competition.
5) Although many golf courses maintain a customer database, most are lacking sufficient names to make this a valuable tool.
6) Electronic surveys are very cost effective.
7) There are four required questions in each survey: gender, age, income, and frequency of play.
8) A survey of customers regarding potential course policy usually reveals that they will be self-serving in their answers.

Concluding Thoughts

A guest sees more in an hour than the host in a year.

Polish Proverb

It is not necessary to understand things to argue about them.

Pierre Beaumarchais

Chapter 16

Creating Customer Loyalty

Step 7 of JJ Keegan + WIN™ Formula (continued)

You don't have to explain something you never said.

Calvin Coolidge, President of the United States

Chapter Highlights

It is easy to believe that satisfied customers are valid predictors of future customer behavior. Such is not the case.

Customer satisfaction may be a short-term reaction, and it doesn't predict whether the loyalty intrinsic to a long-term relationship will be established. The fundamental characteristic of loyal customers is that their positive opinion of your business is communicated to family, friends, and associates. Loyal customers are advocates. They are uncompensated promoters of your business, and everyone they talk to knows they are expressing their true endorsements, not their paid-for opinions.

This chapter emphasizes the concept of customer loyalty and the importance of segmenting customers to enhance the brand image of the golf course and stimulate revenue.

Do Loyal Customers Really Matter?

Consider the following[1].

- Only 4% of dissatisfied customers voice complaints, but 91% never come back.
- 24% of customers have posted comments on-line.
- 80% of tweets regarding customer service are negative.
- It takes 12 positive experiences to make up for one negative one.
- It is six to seven times more expensive to acquire a new customer than it is to retain an existing one.
- The probability of selling new customers is 5% to 20%. The probability of selling existing customers is 60% to 70%.
- Loyal customers are worth 10 times their initial purchase.
- 70% of a buying experience is based on how the customer feels they are being treated.
- 75% are more likely to buy a brand that they follow on Twitter.
- 90% of customers will pay a premium for superior customer service.

If customer loyalty is that important, where it does start, how is it built, and how is it sustained?

Every customer touch point provides the opportunity to build brand loyalty over the entire process of pre-purchase, purchase, and post-purchase, as illustrated in the following figure[2]:

1 http://downloads.helpscout.net/Help-Scout-75-CustServ-Stats-eBook.pdf

2 http://www.slideshare.net/Michael_Hinshaw/measure-understand-and-improve-customer-experience-mcorp-consulting?utm_source=slideshow01&utm_medium=ssemail&utm_campaign=share_slideshow, slide

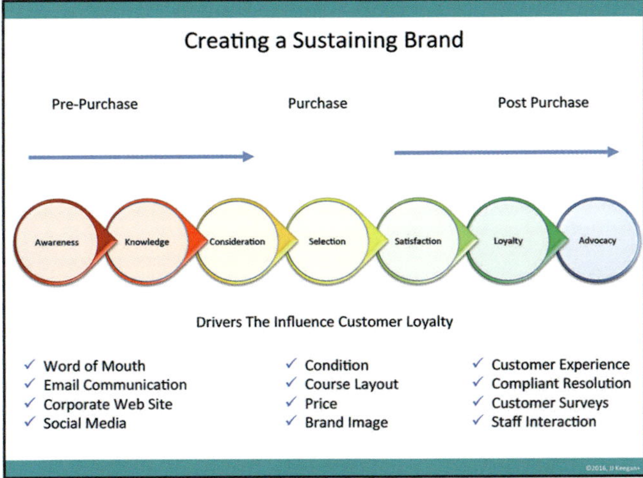

You can't shortcut the relationship. It takes the time to develop customer frequency, duration, and interaction—all of which the customer controls and all of which combine to become loyalty.

A golf course achieves customer loyalty not because of what you do (sell a green fee, cart, merchandise, food, and beverage) but because you establish an emotional connection to the customers through every step of the purchase cycle. Their loyalty becomes a sphere of influence that gets your facility repeatedly chosen over the competition, not once or twice but consistently.

Some may confuse the recent emphasis on customer loyalty with the evolution of social media and the connected customer. However, customer relationship management came to the forefront of every smart business owner's conscience when it was introduced in 1993 by Don Peppers and Martha Rogers, Ph.D., who are recognized as founders of that discipline. Their book *The One to One Future* revolutionized marketing when it was first published.

Simply stated, customer relationship management is a system for managing a company's interactions with current and future customers.

Informal methods to win repeat business have been built around marketing incentives for over 100 years, evolving from tangible goods, to cash incentives, to a loyalty system, to virtual rewards, all illustrated by the following graphic.[3]

3 http://www.slideshare.net/alexdrozdovsky/how-game-thinking-is-changing-brands#btnNext, slide 41.

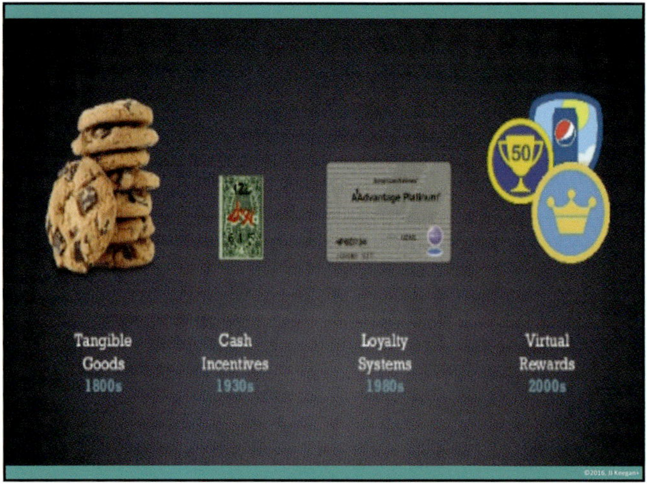

All loyalty programs involve around points, discounts, rebates, or privileges.

While these retention/reward programs may increase transaction frequency, it is important to differentiate between rewards programs, which stimulate additional purchases, and loyalty programs, which often cause the customer to become a promoter of the company, regardless of spending habits.

Many rewards programs are merely another way of describing a discount program. The virtual rewards systems of today are so compelling and addicting that they create behavioral habits around which frequency of purchase, if not loyalty, is built. It becomes a game to achieve a certain status with an airline, to be rewarded with increased benefits that make travel easier, or to get "a star" downloaded while you wait for your morning Skinny Vanilla Latte or an afternoon Java Chip Frappuccino.

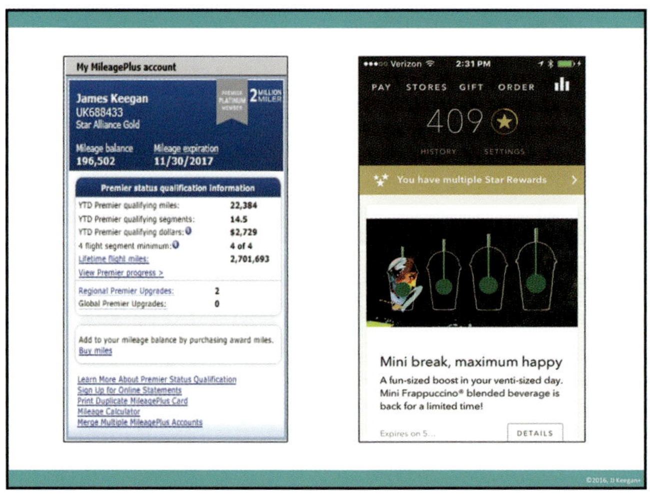

The success of Starbucks' loyalty card program is attributed to its mobile rewards app, which customers can use to pay for their orders by smartphone. Over 7 million mobile users have the Starbucks' mobile rewards app[4] and check their loyalty program account information in real time on their phones. Additionally, the app delivers special promotions to users, and, of course, it locates Starbucks stores. At 6 million average weekly transactions in the United States, it now accounts for a full 15% of transactions made at the U.S. Starbucks-operated stores.[5]

The process of implementing a customer relationship management system to build brand loyalty includes implementing technology to efficiently track customer transactions, measuring the customer touch points to ascertain which ones have value, and assessing the overall rating against industry peers.

Implementing a CRM System

Very few golf courses effectively engage in customer relationship management. Facilities have historically faced four barriers:

1. Lack of segmentation of their customer database, if they have one.
2. Inadequate tools to cost-effectively market.
3. Marketing inexperience.
4. Inconsistent execution of programs.

Building customer loyalty in the golf business is straightforward. A customer relationship management program involves four steps: collecting data, analyzing the data, executing a marketing program, and monitoring the results. For the golf industry, those steps mean to proceed as follows:

- Install an integrated tee time reservation system that interfaces with your POS system.
- Use the software to build a customer database that tracks customer frequency, spending, and preferences. Note that developing an accurate customer database is not without challenges. One of the problems is that

4 http://www.mobileworldlive.com/money/news-money/over-7m-users-for-starbucks-payment-app/

5 http://www.businessinsider.com/starbucks-mobile-payments-app-2014-9

courses often collect "data" only from the golfers who make the tee time, especially if they check in and pay for the foursome. If the other golfers check in separately, then there's the delay of getting names (spelled correctly), phone numbers (repeated for accuracy), and e-mail addresses, which are a pain because many are "cutesy" and thus hard to listen to and type into a computer. Utilizing a registration system separate from the POS process is an effective way to overcome this potential bottleneck.

- Construct a website that can do the following:
  1. Allow the golfer to book a tee time on the home page of the website or via a mobile application in three clicks. Few golf courses have websites or mobile applications that are this efficient.
  2. Permit the customer to self-register for tournament opportunities, merchandise specials, and tee times that are priced consistent with the course's yield management strategy. Fortunately, more courses are beginning to provide this functionality.

With the information collected, custom-tailored e-mail and social media messages are sent to your demographically profiled customers on a bi-weekly or customer-requested frequency to win and build loyalty.

It should be cautioned that the data collection and filtering process must be accurate. Poor data will lead to poor decisions about how to manage the customer experience. Nothing is more frustrating than getting an e-mail from a company to purchase products you have already purchased from them or receiving an invitation to play in a tournament for which you are not qualified.

The key to success in building loyalty is crafting messages to golfers based on their preferences and their degree of loyalty. Identifying core, new customers (acquired) and defectors (lost customers—those who haven't played in 90 days) are essential. In Chapter 8, you learned about the key reports that should be included in your golf management system to achieve the recommended segmentation.

We don't recommend a reactive philosophy of only serving customers upon their arrival. We like to see a proactive philosophy of "hand picking" your customers based on their spending profiles.

At an NGCOA Annual meeting, Peter Hill, chairman of Billy Casper Golf, commented that software may evolve to a point at which the more favorable tee times will be made available to those with the highest spending patterns per transaction, who are qualified loyalty club members, and who prove they are advocates by bringing new players to the course. That would be the ultimate in customer relationship management.

Measuring Customer Touch Points

Secret shopper services or electronic surveys, are two effective ways to measure the perceived value the customer has experienced.

Two different questions can be posed to measure that value. Utilizing A/B testing, the first question offers a five-point rating scale. Each of the touch points are listed with descriptors that are appropriate for this facility's vision, as illustrated in the following table.

Rating the Customer Touch Points

Touch Point	Excellent	Very Good	Good	Fair	Poor
Reservations: courtesy, efficiency, and helpfulness					
Club Entrance: welcoming ambience including signage and flowers					
Bag Drop: presence of staff, greeting, assistance, and guidance					
Locker Room: friendliness of staff and availability of amenities					
Pro Shop: atmosphere, appearance of staff, greeting, friendliness					
Range: quality of balls, turf quality, directional yardage, safety					
Starter: welcoming, playful, creates positive anticipation, helpful					
Course: conditioning, price, layout					
Beverage Cart: properly stocked, professional yet engaging					
Half Way House: good selection, quality of food, engaging staff					
Cart Return & Club Cleaning: warm, efficient, offers assistance					
Locker Room: encouraging, tidy, respectful					
Bar/Restaurant: appealing, likeable, quality					

A second question is designed to measure the relative value perceived by the golfer based on each of the touch points encountered. Asking, "Please rank (from 1 being extremely important to 10 being extremely unimportant) what is important to you in determining the value of your experience at our facility" would be insightful.

Responses to this question provide data as to value perceived measured against the cost of providing the touch points. When the customers' perceived value is low and the cost of administrating that touch point high, modifying the touch point becomes a suggested course of action.

Determining Your Loyalty Score

The value of any business to ensure sustainable growth is based on the promoters, which can be identified by using the "net promoter score." This index measures the relative strengths of a facility's franchise. Developed by Fred Reichheld, a fellow at Bain & Company, it is now a widely used measurement by many industries and companies, including Intuit and Costco. This metric of customer loyalty has shown that companies with high customer loyalty typically increase revenues at twice the rate of competitors.

To refresh this material, in Chapter 15 we covered the following question posed to the customer:

> Based on your playing experience over the last 12 months, how likely it is that you would recommend the following courses to a friend, colleague, or family members? (Rate your likelihood on a scale of 0 to 10, with "10" being "Extremely Likely" and "0" being "Not at All Likely.") If you did not play a course, please indicate by circling "N/A."

The net loyalty score is obtained by subtracting the detractors from the promoters. With the possible range of answers from 10 (strong promoters) to 0 (strong detractor), usually those answering 1 to 6 are subtracted from those answering 9 or 10. Note that Reichheld would consider scores of 7 and 8 as "passive" respondents.

The following is an illustration of a loyalty rating:

What is both amusing and heartening is that golfers are very sincere and accurate in their responses. In the survey conducted using the Minneapolis Park and Recreation database, their customers indicated that of the top five courses they were loyal too, four were those of competitors. The highest rated course, Keller, has just completed a marvelous renovation where the master plan was done by Herfort-Norby Architects and the field work by Richard Mandell & Associates.

Why are those loyalty numbers important? Loyalty correlates to wallet share, which represents the percentage of a golfer's money spent at each golf course versus the total amount spent annually by the golfer. The percent of wallet share a course receives is a highly predictive factor of success which translates into net income.

Segmentation: All Customers Don't Have the Same Value

Segmentation of customers can be based on many different criteria: demographics, geography, attitudinal affiliations, transaction value (recent historical value, historical total cumulative value, and future lifetime value), motivations (impulse, early adopter, status seeker, and bargain hunter), or lifestyle.

For golf courses, the transactional value of recent, total, and lifetime customers are the most appropriate benchmarks. For example, where segmentation beyond transaction history would be of value in the golf industry would be in identifying those who make the tee time (called "Captains") versus the remaining group members and defectors (those who haven't played in 90 days).

It should be noted that for resort golf courses, the number of unique golfers who play the course is higher, and their repeat frequency is far less. Tailoring communication to those golfers at appropriate longer intervals will justify loyalty on subsequent travel.

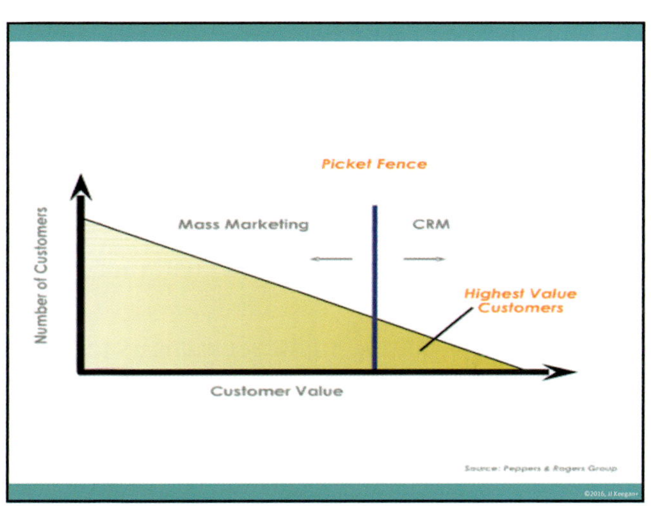

To effectively market to these groups, Peppers and Rodgers created the Picket Fence concept shown in the figure on the next page.[6]

6 http://www.slideshare.net/vdimitroff/customer-segmentation-principles, slide 6.

What is interesting about their Picket Fence concept is that it introduces customer segmentation to perhaps the top 33% of the customer database that has the greatest value. Peppers and Rodgers carry that concept deeper by addressing the customers according to their differentiated value, as shown below.

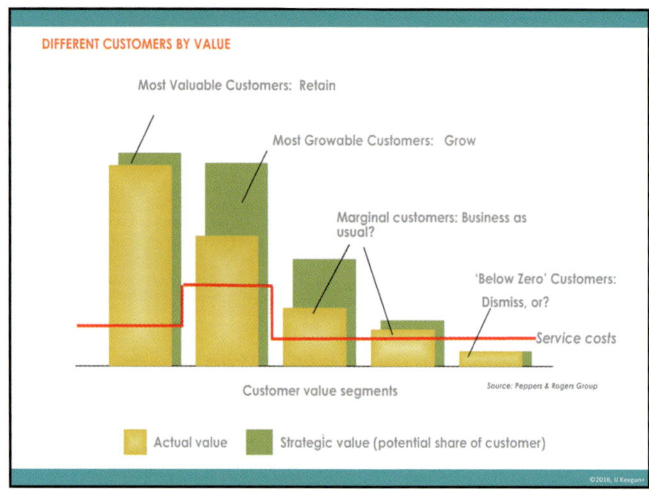

A lot of maxims ring true for the operation of any business or golf course. For the golf course, a strategic but often overlooked maxim is that each customer has a different value. While all customers have "cash value," some customers may also have strategic value. For example, the director of marketing for a corporation may have huge strategic value. By identifying such customers quickly and courting them wisely, you can capture their corporate outing business.

The idea of dismissing customers who bring in less revenue than the cost to serve them is a good one. Unfortunately, most municipalities are precluded from engaging in the productive business practice of shooing away the season pass holders who dominate the tee sheet and behave as if they own the course. Daily fee golf courses get caught in the trap of the upfront annual revenue from season pass holders to even cash flow requirements and are reluctant to dismiss the frequent but difficult customer.

Thus, a course might segment its ideal customer profile as follows:

- Best Customers: enjoy the experience, interaction is good, low service requirements.
- 2nd Quartile: pay top dollar, but the cost to serve is high in demands made of staff and complaints registered.

- 3rd Quartile: very price-sensitive but have few special demands and are easy to serve.
- 4th Quartile: leverage buying power to achieve low price with lots of services required.

All of this academic theory is great, but it will remain largely pointless for the golf course industry unless achieved through execution. Change in the golf course industry seems to occur either almost accidentally or traumatically. Just as a trainer can't make someone lose weight or a counselor can't force a client to quit the excessive use of alcohol or cigarettes, it is a foolhardy to think that demonstrating the benefits of customer segmentation will bring about the implementation of new management practices.

Comprehensive customer segmentation is one of the new frontiers for golf course managers. Golf course owners and managers that invest the time in the short term will reap financial and psychological rewards in the intermediate and long term.

How Social Media Is Changing Customer Loyalty Programs

Social media are changing the way human beings communicate, expanding the historical one-way communication (vendor to the client) to two-way (vendor and client) to multi-dimensional (vendor and client and client to friends and the world).

Social media is facilitating creating a personal bond with the customer through faster communication that is timely and important to them through understanding their buyer behavior.

The impact of the digital age will be felt even more in the future, as the costs of administering loyalty programs fall and the importance of customer increase is recognized, as shown in the figure on the next page.[7]

It is within the human gene that we seek to be part of a community, an entity larger than ourselves. Social media provide golf courses with a way to improve

7 http://www.slideshare.net/alexdrozdovsky/how-game-thinking-is-changing-brands/42-Objectiveswhattheplayer_has_to_achieve

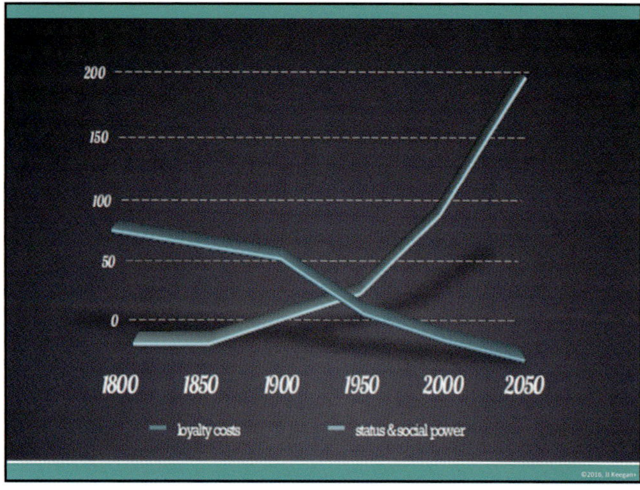

the quality and timeliness of communication, from static pages to dynamic, interactive tools of cross communication. From these communications, emotional bonds can be formed. For example, soliciting input on a master plan via blog posts would attract interest. Are there golfers who don't fancy themselves as golf course architects? Not likely. Offer a wine-and-dine, a ladies event via an alert; create that emotional bond.

Smartphones give companies a 24-hour window through which to connect with their customer base. I'm always amazed at how the distribution of world news and sports via alerts provides an immediate connection to that information. With mobile phones outselling PCs six to one in 2015, 1,946,546 vs. 316,689[8], golf courses need to focus on not only the message and the distribution channel but also the manner of communication—shorter messages and multiple channels will prevail.

The risk of social media is that multiple-channel communications provide customers the ability to vent not only to course personnel but also to broadcast their displeasure globally. Monitoring the "social chatter" regarding your golf course has become important. Radian 6, Brandwatch and Mention are software platforms that can help with media monitoring.

Timely management of a customer's complaint is more vital than ever, not only to ensure that the customer is satisfied and that the problem is rectified, but most importantly before the customer's frustration level builds enough to cause them to broadcast their complaint to their social network. The average customer expects a response in six hours. Presented in the graph on the next page are the response times of the leading retailers.

8 http://www.extremetech.com/computing/185937-in-2015-tablet-sales-will-finally-surpass-pcs-fulfilling-steve-jobs-post-pc-prophecy

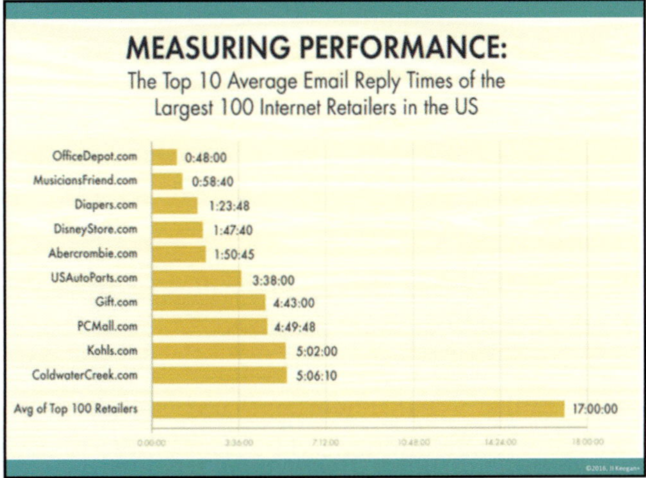

By really listening to complaints, by actually looking for them regularly on social media, then apologizing and implementing corrective action quickly, you may stop the bleeding, even though you may feel as though you have fallen on your sword.

Creating a Coherent Strategy

Many opportunities exist to implement a successful strategy aimed at creating customer loyalty. Marketing programs (outbound) and revenue strategies (inbound) enable the value chain (operations, information systems, personnel, and capital investment) to define the brand.

Whereas plastic cards, print coupons, or punching holes defined loyalty programs in the past, creating a multi-prong strategy of a website, Facebook, Google+, Instagram, Pinterest, Twitter, and YouTube to create a community of interest now form the basis of future success.

After that, a smartphone-based loyalty program can simplify the customer connection in the following ways:

- Better tracking of golfer buying behavior.
- Earning and utilizing reward points becomes hassle-free. A golfer can flash his phone at a point of sale (POS) and get instant credit in the loyalty program.
- Information captured via mobile loyalty programs can be used to strengthen customer affinity by facilitating engagement at a more personal level.

- Personalized incentives and offers can be delivered easily to complement customer purchases; a club purchase might result in 50% off the price of a lesson.
- Ability to broadcast events such as last-minute tee time specials, clearance discounts on merchandise, and even Happy Birthday or Happy Anniversary wishes all create a great bond.
- The great advantage over texting is that the lifespan of a cell phone number is far greater than that of an e-mail address.

During the next one to three years, "winners" and "losers" in the facility management arena will be strongly influenced by their ability to manage and build customer franchises.

Key Points to Remember

1) Managing the customer experience through the touch points is the most cost-effective way to drive customer satisfaction, customer retention, and customer loyalty. Not only do loyal customers ensure sales, but they are also more likely to purchase ancillary, high-margin, supplemental products and services.
2) Loyal customers reduce costs associated with consumer education and marketing and are likely to become net promoters for your organization.
3) Retaining customers is less expensive than acquiring new ones.
4) Considering the highly competitive golf market today, customer segmentation is an effective way to differentiate your course from the competition.
5) The challenge of customer relationship management is registering the customer by capturing the requisite and relevant demographic information.
6) Customer franchise analysis involves four steps: collection, analysis, execution, and monitoring.
7) Most golf course managers don't fully comprehend how much the balance of retained, acquired, and lost golfers affects the volatility of their revenue base.
8) The identification of customers as core, acquired, or defectors with timely and precise e-mail and text messages to those customers can impact positively gross revenue.
9) The simple formula for a customer's repeat purchase is that Motivation = Engagement + Loyalty.

Concluding Thoughts

Human beings are distinguished from animals much more by the ability to rationalize than by the ability to reason.

Milton Friedman, Economist and Nobel Laureate

We focus so much on our differences, and that is creating, I think, a lot of chaos and negativity and bullying in the world. And I think if everybody focused on what we all have in common – which is – we all want to be happy.

Ellen DeGeneres

Chapter 17

The Industry—What Path Is It On?

A Future Perspective

The further away the future is, the better it looks.

Finnegan's Law

Chapter Highlights

What do we need to do, as an industry, to preserve the traditions of the game of golf while also offering recreational entertainment to match the evolving interests of a diverse society? Is it possible to achieve both?

The golf industry is in flux based on changes in societal factors. These changes are likely to influence the ownership, management structure, and operational policies of golf courses as the competing forces of adherence to tradition vs. a more casual style ebb and flow based on perceptions of what will produce the highest investment return.

This chapter explores how the golf experience may need to evolve for the industry to grow. And it starts with focusing on golf's current customers.

Where Will Tomorrow's Golfers Come From?

Think about it. There are only about 250,000 golfers alive today that will be living in 2076. Where will the 24.1 million golfers come from to sustain the industry?

There is a leakage within the game. For nearly the past decade more golfers have departed golf than those returning or new entrants to the game, illustrated as follows:

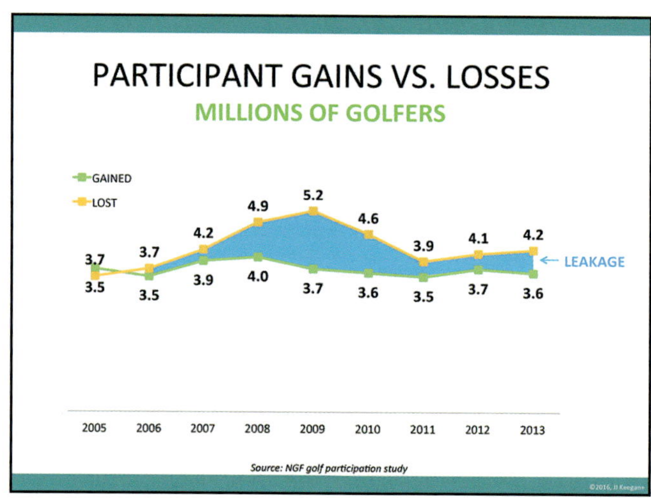

The challenge the game finds itself in is that while attracting women and ethnicities is a desirable goal, the retention of existing players is perhaps an equal challenge.

What does the future of the game and the business of golf hold?

Here is what I believe:

- Golf is a great game and currently an okay business. Both can be really good if a professional effort is made to focus on the business of golf to stimulate the game of golf.
- A golf course requires a clear strategic vision, well-developed tactical plans, and extremely precise and consistent execution. With every course being distinctive, a facility must define and communicate its unique differentiation.

- Success in the business of golf is directly correlated to the extent to which the experience provided equals or exceeds the price assessed. Each golf course needs to understand and benchmark what the value is they are creating versus the price charged. What the competitors is charging is not the answer.
- The historical business models that are based on the status quo need to be radically altered and implemented for the game to thrive. Developing an industry database on which performance of a selective course can be measured, like the Star Reports, in the hospitality industry will provide astute owners the insights to better manage.
- The numerous initiatives recently launched to encourage new entrants to the game (such as Get Golf Ready and Tee It Forward) will have a short-term positive impact on increasing participation that will hopefully stimulate long-term participation.
- Female participation in the sports has declined by over 100,000 players during the past 25 years. The motivating factors that attract women to the game are vastly different than those that attract men. Embracing these differences is essential.
- Tomorrow's golfers will come from those seeking leisure who are welcomed and accorded respect by the industry's professionals. The culture of pro shops must change with employees adopting a hospitality focus and embracing technology featuring mobile tablets, apps, and social media to identify and more effectively serve the customer.

While these offer long-term hope, what are the short-term solutions?

Initiatives Abound

Many positive initiatives are currently being undertaken. Beyond the Drive Chip Putt, Get Golf Ready, PGA Jr. League, and the First Tee and its National Golf in Schools Program featured in Chapter 4, golf is being introduced to new entrants via many other avenues as highlighted on the next page.

FootGolf and 15-inch cups are being presented as an alternative for adaptive use of the land and making the game easy and more fun.

FootGolf is a combination of the popular sports of soccer and golf. The rules largely correspond to the rules of golf and players kick a regulation #5 soccer ball at a golf course facility on shortened holes with 21-inch diameter cups in as few shots as possible. There are 468 golf courses in 48 states that have implemented this alternative[1].

The participants in screen golf is soaring, particularly in Asia. Beach golf, while a novelty, is introducing the sport to an entirely different sector.

There are also new "toys" to make the game more interesting: Arrcos GPS Game Tracking and Game Golf help you track every single shot and create an online community to post and exchange scores.

Perhaps the biggest advances are being seen in transporting and entertaining golfers around a course shown here.

Although the hovercraft is probably not feasible for an entire cart fleet, it is fun to watch. The golf boards that stimulate a surf board and Segways are alternatives to attract a younger set of golfers and create alternative revenue for a

1 http://footgolf.net/

golf course. At Sewaillo in Tucson, Arizona, the golf board surcharge is $25, whereas at Mauna Kea Resort an additional $35 is earned on each of the 12 golf boards in its fleet.

The industry is like a big ship in the ocean that is difficult to turn quickly. What will sustain the industry in the short and intermediate term?

Out with the Old—In with the New

The NGF forecasts that Baby Boomers, as they begin to retire, will represent an increase of 4 million incremental rounds per year, totaling 60 million additional rounds over the next 15 years[2].

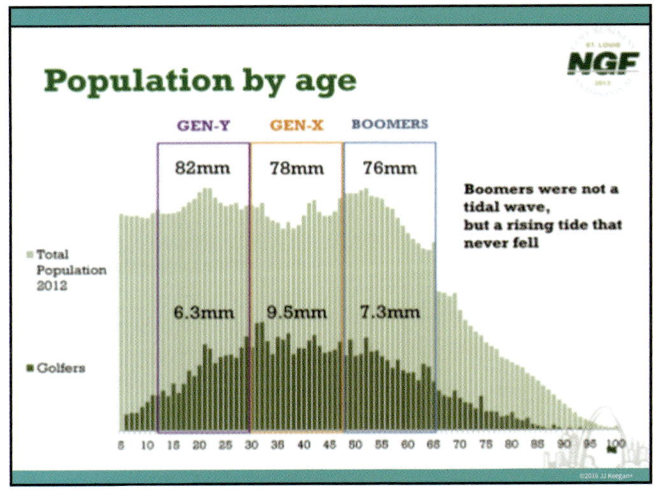

With the Gen-Y (Millennials) and Gen-X representing such a large section of the population, what are the options to attract and retain them? There are currently 6.4 million millennial golfers representing 26% of all golfers playing 90 million rounds per year[3]. In the mid-1990s, roughly 9 million 18- to 34-year-olds were playing golf.

In what direction should the industry turn?

2 National Golf Foundation, "The State of the Industry: the NGF Perspective - 2015," slide 31.

3 Ibid., p. 26.

There Are Two Forks in the Road—Take Both

There are two paths that when jointly pursued can lead to success. Embracing new generations involves respecting the historical foundations on which the game was formed.

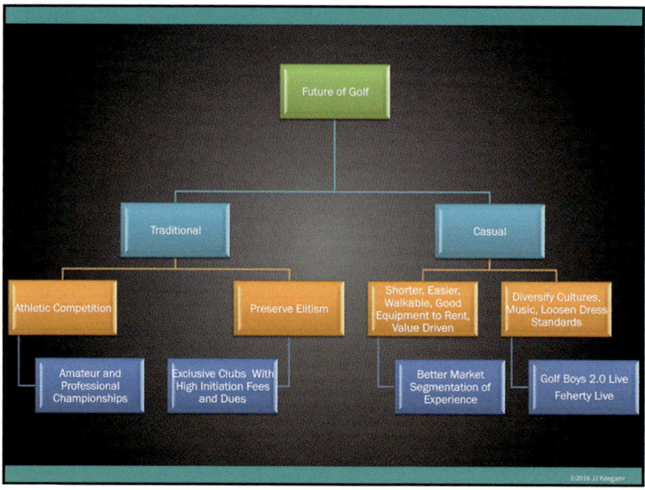

We estimate that 20% of golfers are traditionalists, measured by those who maintain a handicap versus the total number of golfers—about 4 million of the 24.1 million golfers and those like me who are avid golfers with no need for a formal handicap. Tradition comes with a big price tag, and these traditionalists have the financial fortunes to underwrite their hobby.

The historical traditions of the game of golf can evolve nicely through prudent visionary leadership by golf course operators, the media, and golf industry associations.

In Colorado, bastions like Castle Pines Golf Club, with its properly reserved reverence from its founder; Cherry Hills, with its championship pedigree; and Denver Country Club, with its blue-blood orientation as Denver's finest, serving a small segment of society who seek to preserve an aristocratic lifestyle, will continue to maintain and be respected for their celebration of history and tradition.

What about the rest of the population and specifically the millennials?

Attracting and Retaining Millennials

Primary research conducted by NGF resulted in the classifying of millennials into three categories[4].

Throwbackers – Predominantly Caucasian males, most were introduced to golf during their formative years by parents. Most don't think the game needs a serious change, though they're not without concerns. This group is active and successful. They're motivated by competition and challenge, staying fit, and social interaction. When it comes to golf, they're extremely committed to the game and prefer it in the traditional form—most follow the rules closely, keep score, and put work into their game; the majority are fans of professional golf.

Brunch Ballers – These golfers are more likely to have taken up the game on their own—or with the help of a friend—as a late-teen or early 20-something. They're an extremely active group, and more likely to say their schedule is hectic. They're motivated by excitement, adrenaline, and the opportunity to meet new people. Golf for them is not a lifestyle but a social activity, so they're much more likely to enhance the experience with music, alcohol, gambling, and social media engagement. Many take a brunch ball (millennials aren't up in time for breakfast) off the first tee, improve their lie before hitting, take mulligans, and play without keeping score. More than half think golf needs serious reform.

Dabblers – Most don't consider themselves golfers. They play very infrequently and usually only at the urging of someone else. They don't keep score, and are more likely to have been introduced by a spouse or significant other. Only a third say they enjoy golf "very much." These customers are just "dabbling", and without some intervention are not likely to develop into better customers. Many will drift away from the game.

4 Ibid., pp. 16-17.

The frequency of play, spending, loyalty, and enjoyment of golf are as shown here[5]:

BY THE NUMBERS

	THROWBACKERS	BRUNCH BALLERS	DABBLERS
Annual rounds played	18	8	4
% of annual M golf spend	69%	19%	12%
Very likely to continue playing	100%	48%	47%
Consider themselves "golfers"	95%	74%	42%
Very likely to recommend	75%	38%	23%
Enjoy the game "very much"	100%	46%	28%

What the National Golf Foundation study demonstrated was the perception of Generation X and Baby Boomers of millennials was very different than from their self-perception. While perceived as lazy, tech savvy, and not very loyal, millennials perceive themselves as[6]:

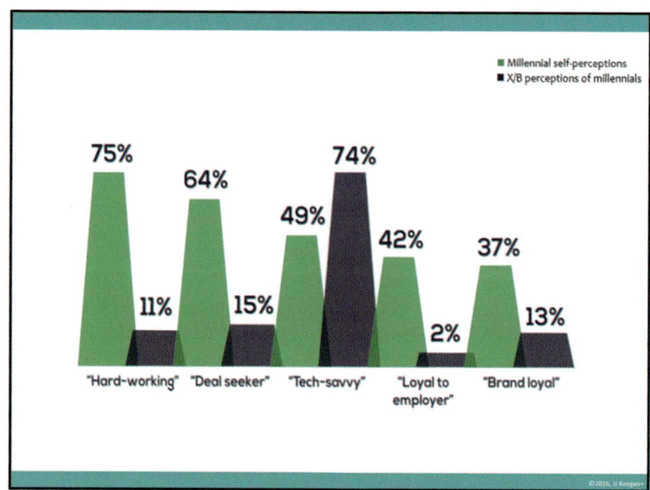

The research presented a series of findings of note:

5 National Golf Foundation, "Project M – Research Findings," slide 20.

6 National Golf Foundation, "Project M – Research Findings," slide 14.

1. Millennials love affordable adventures that give them stories to share.
2. 25% percent play golf for reasons that are unrelated to golf itself.
3. 45% think that golf is elitist and exclusionary.
4. Golf has an invitation problem.
5. When and how they got into golf made a big difference in how likely they are committed to the game.

The observation that when and how one gets into golf is a function of how likely they are committed to the game was corroborated by the U.S. National Physical Activity Council who concluded that individuals who participated in sports during school where far more likely to continue their participation upon entering the workforce as shown here[7]:

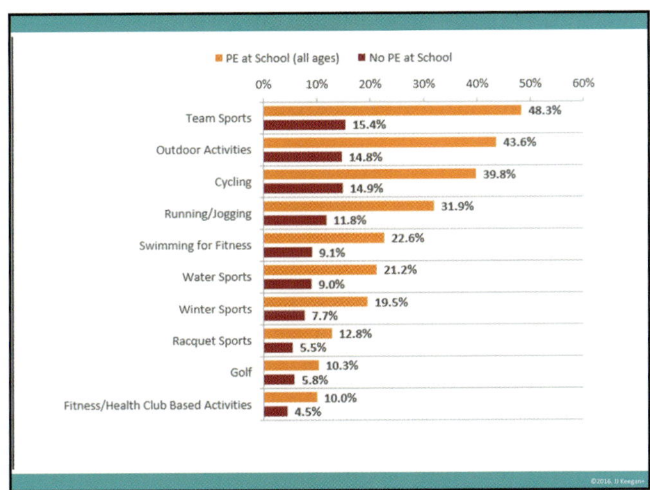

Participation in physical exercise during school had an extreme impact on participation in other activities as 10.3% of the students who play golf did so in school compared to only 5.8% who didn't. This statistic underscores the importance of First-Tee and its National School Golf Program and the Golf in Schools program created and supported by various PGA Sections including Colorado.

The Physical Activity Council, which tracks sports, fitness, and creation in the United States, also provided the golf industry on how to get non-participants in

7 Physical Activity Council, 2016 Participation Report," p. 21.

the sport to become active in it. They found that "having someone to take part in an activity with would be the big push to get them involved. People not only prefer to work out or participate in sports with friends, but it is also a driving force to get them out more and experience different ways to be physically active, as shown here"[8]:

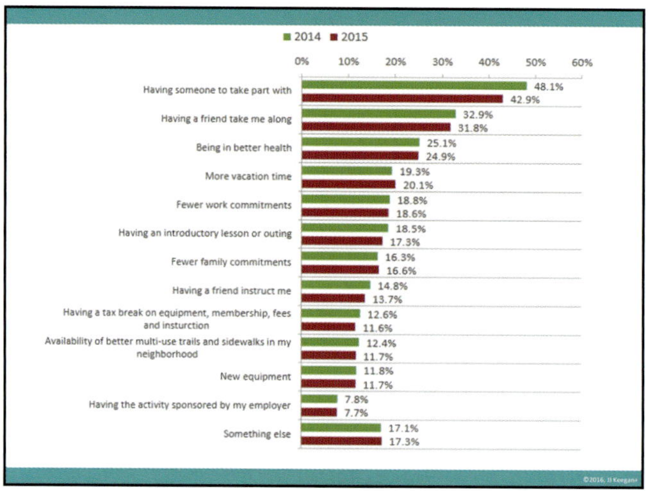

Thus, when all is said and done, hopefully more is done than said and the golf industry will look like this in the coming decades by implementing the concepts contained herein:

8 Physical Activity Council, 2016 Participation Report," p. 20.

Women Off Course

One of the biggest challenges to the long-term success of golf is embracing women, and it remains one of the great hidden barriers to growth in the game.

Three years ago, in publishing *The Business of Golf – Why? How? What?*, I celebrated three initiatives encouraging female participation in the sport: Women on Course, Sassy Golf, and Golf for Cause. In 2016, only Golf for Cause headed by Debbie Waitkus still operates.

Debbie Waitkus believes she has been successful because, in her search through Phoenix/Scottsdale, she found one PGA Professional supportive of her efforts. She commented that finding golf courses willing to host women's or mixed events remains a challenge. Seems hard to believe, but I think it is true.

In 2016, the PGA of America released a study which Jon Last, president of Sports and Leisure Research Group, conducted, titled "Business Golf: The Gender Puzzle." The results were surprising:

- 30% of male golfing execs' business rounds played are played with mixed gender groups.
- 45% of golfing men execs enjoy playing business golf with women.
- 61% of golfing women execs enjoy playing business golf with men.
- 41% of golfing business women have experienced general discrimination on the golf course.

Dana Garmany, president of Troon Golf, shared a story that where he plays golf, his wife is meant to feel unwelcome on the range on Saturday mornings. He commented that:

> "Sixty-nine-year-old board members are likely to want to keep status quo, as ladies days are specified on certain days and men's play is reserved for Saturday morning. It is probably fair to say that than they don't want women on the course at all."

The PGA of America held a committee meeting during the 2016 PGA Merchandise Show to determine how to attract more qualified women to the golf profession. No answers were immediately obvious.

Two years ago, the NGCOA highly recommended to all of the multi-course owners that one of their senior executive women attend the next meeting. Only ClubCorp's Cathy Harbin, then as regional vice president, Public Golf VP, ClubCorp Golf Academy & Programming, was in the meeting. In the succeeding year, even ClubCorp hesitated to have Cathy attend again but recognized the need to be a leader and set the example.

It is Harbin's opinion that, "Everyone is committed to the concept of gender equality on the surface, but companies and much senior management are so focused on daily operations and revenue that it is difficult. We have a way to go to equality."

The efforts of Pam Swensen, chief executive officer of Executive Women's Golf Association and Nancy Berkley, Berkley Golf Consulting, who advocates "more women playing more golf," are laudatory. It is praiseworthy that three women are in the rota to head major trade associations: Diane Murphy, president of USGA; Suzy Whaley, PGA of America; and Jan Bel Jan, American Society of Golf Course Architects.

It is also noteworthy that Topgolf patrons are 32% female, and they are launching at each facility lesson programs to attract new female entrants to the game.

It is my opinion that education of women in the business of golf is sorely lacking. It is my belief that merging the educational aspects of the LPGA with the PGA of America curriculum would benefit the golf industry. Each member of the LPGA would be given a provisional PGA membership contingent on passing the Level 1 Academic Requirements.

Eliminating the professional aptitude test for women would stimulate an increase in membership, but with many PGA Professionals underemployed or relegated to working outside of the industry due to fewer opportunities, would the Association be serving the interests of its current members by welcoming women?

While I realize this will never happen, I believe it should. Golf is about hospitality and entertainment. Women's golf will grow when more women are employed at golf courses and not until.

The Next 20 Years

On that sobering note, there are two signs that the golf industry, while stable in 2016, can flourish in the next 20 years.

We chronicled in Chapter 2 that those between the ages of 6–21 are playing far more rounds today than those within those age groups in 1990. The number of rounds played by those in those group is nearly double that of two decades ago.

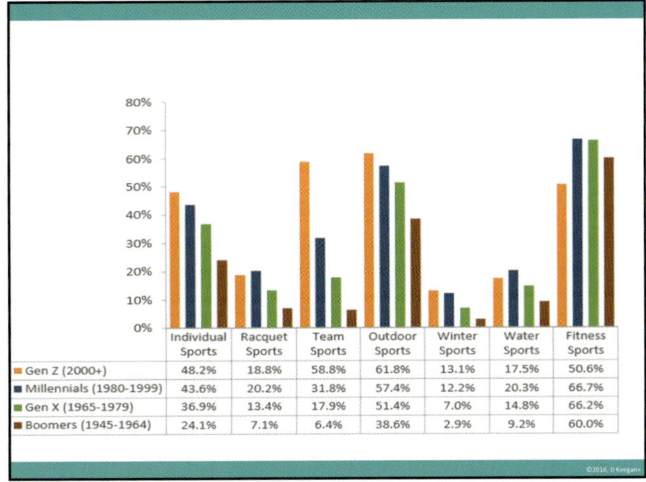

	Individual Sports	Racquet Sports	Team Sports	Outdoor Sports	Winter Sports	Water Sports	Fitness Sports
Gen Z (2000+)	48.2%	18.8%	58.8%	61.8%	13.1%	17.5%	50.6%
Millennials (1980-1999)	43.6%	20.2%	31.8%	57.4%	12.2%	20.3%	66.7%
Gen X (1965-1979)	36.9%	13.4%	17.9%	51.4%	7.0%	14.8%	66.2%
Boomers (1945-1964)	24.1%	7.1%	6.4%	38.6%	2.9%	9.2%	60.0%

What is encouraging is the study by the National Physical Activity Council regarding the trends in participation in individual sports, shown here[9].

The participation rates of Gen Z and Millennials in individual and outdoor sports is a positive sign regarding the game's growth potential.

How do we emphasize the fun and camaraderie that this game brings? How do we create the sizzle that attracts, knowing the game will garner a following? With the adaption of a kinder, gentler, and more embracing environment. Shown here is the focus of Billy Casper Golf Management in transitioning the clubs they manage to a more welcoming environment.

With the industry's future relatively stable, for those who have considered learning the sport, it's a great time to walk through the entry door to the game, and this message should be broadcast widely. Golf course owners and PGA Professionals should emphasize providing value-based entertainment in a warm and welcoming environment. Whether as athletic competition, exercise, or social recreation, golf has many attributes.

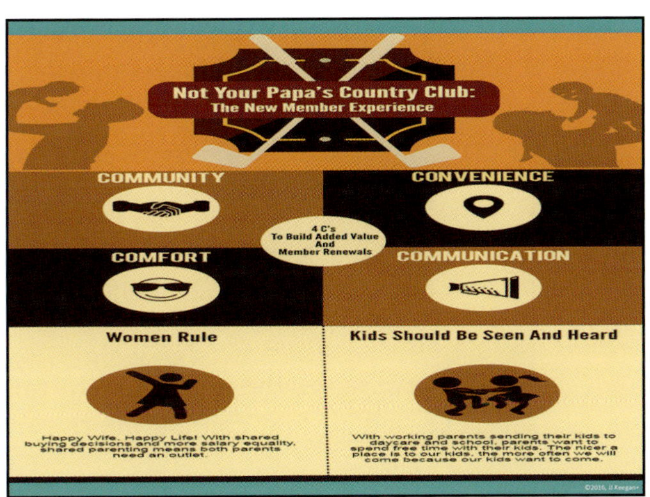

9 Physical Activity Council, "2016 Participation Report," p. 9.

Golf is unique. Only a very small number of individuals have the opportunity to play football at Lambeau Field, basketball at the Garden, baseball at Fenway, or hockey at the Forum. However, everyone can play golf on the course where Tom Watson won the U.S. Open at Pebble Beach Golf Links and attempt the same chip shot on hole 17 that he made to win the tournament. The handicap system allows us to play the game against anyone on an equal basis and have fun—try this with tennis.

Thus, in an industry known for firmly preserving the status quo, in spite of all that is financially negative about the golf industry as it exists today, I believe it can successfully adapt to the changes in our society. In that case, if the golf industry were a common stock, it would make for a wise long-term investment.

Key Points to Remember

For Golf Course Owners

1) Promoting the health benefits of the sport as physical exercise.
2) Shortening golf courses.
3) Ensuring rounds are played in 4 hours or less.
4) Through the course setup, warranting that golf courses play easier.
5) Increasing the emphasis on service that is extremely cordial and accommodating.
6) Simplifying golf operations and the amenities provided.
7) Introducing an alternative scoring format, such as Stableford, as the primary way to keep score.
8) Enhancing the customer experience through technology and simplifying the management of courses through an alert system of guidance.
9) Leveraging the clubhouse to provide alternative functionality focused beyond golf and more comparable to a sports bar or dining club.
10) Segmentation of the functionality of the golf course, emphasizing the game in the morning and entertainment in the afternoon and evening.

11) Ensuring signage conveys a positive message.

12) Adapting dress standards and associated behaviors to the cultural changes in our society.

13) At private clubs, replacing high-equity initiation fees with lower non-refundable deposits, initiation fees, and monthly membership fees based on market pricing.

For the Media

14) Television announcers balancing their commentary between the difficulty of the game and the enjoyment the public derives from it. Make it a sport beginners would like to try rather than one only professionals attempt to master.

For the Trade Associations

15) The USGA bifurcating its advertising message to emphasize both the casual and traditional aspects of the game.

16) Recruiting new players to the game by emphasizing youth, women, and minorities, and motivating former players to return with greater urgency (as with Golf 2.0, Golf Ready, Tee It Forward, Family Golf Monthly, and Play Golf America).

17) The USGA Executive Committee might be proportionally balanced representative to the population in America by gender, ethnicity, and private versus public golfers.

18) The LPGA, at a minimum, should license the PGA Education curriculum, or even more aggressively merge with the PGA to vastly improve the experience of women professionals in the business of golf.

For Equipment Manufacturers

19) Facilitating the use of better equipment through rentals, as the ski industry does.

20) Connecting the manufacturer to the golfer more directly via social media. Ensuring that golfers can easily select for themselves the proper equipment through clearer product descriptions.

Concluding Thoughts

Twenty years from now you will be more disappointed by the things that you didn't do than by any of the ones you did do.

Mark Twain

Conformity is the jailer of freedom and the enemy of growth.

John F. Kennedy

Chapter 18

The Courage to Change

The Final Exam

He has half the deed done who has made a beginning.

Horace

Chapter Highlights

This book has been a journey with a simple purpose—to provide a framework (7 steps) and the tools (21 Excel and PowerPoint files) to enable golf course owners and management teams to create value that will enhance their customers' experiences and therefore ensure the highest potential return on investment for the facility.

This chapter includes a checklist as your "final exam." If you have begun implementing the concepts contained herein, we are confident that the process of managing your golf course will have been simplified and that you will have identified opportunities for higher profits.

It is our suggestion that this checklist become your "dashboard" to ensure your success, so review it frequently to ensure you are "on course."

What Is Your Brand Image?

This book has emphasized the creation of strategic vision, a tactical plan, and operational execution to form a golf course's business plan encased within the facility's brand image.

We all understand what a brand image is: think of Amazon, BMW, Facebook, the NFL, or Nike. Images evolve. Value propositions are well defined. A course's image and value proposition should also be well defined.

The components of a brand are the by-products of the course's name and logo, the facility (the course and clubhouse), the pricing, and the depth and breadth of staff—all controllable factors. A course's brand isn't too different from the brand a rancher puts on his cattle: once it's there, it's all but impossible to change.

The Read Option

Each week from late August to January, college and professional football teams create "game plans" to ensure their victories. Fifty percent of those game plans fail; some fail because of poor strategy, some because their tactics are incorrect, and others because their execution is lacking. Whether because of the lack of attitude or aptitude, their efforts result in teams that fail to achieve their objectives.

As it is with football coaches, every golf course operator who creates a business plan will not win. Without a vision, the course will flounder. With only a great vision and detailed tactical plans, the course will suffer. The finest tactical plans without a talented team are meaningless. It takes all three components: strategic vision, tactical planning, and operational execution to be successful.

A Winning Game Plan: JJ Keegan+ WIN™ Formula

Whether from the lack of resources, time, or adequate leadership skills to train and manage a team or from the constant evolution of a golf course as a living organism, it is estimated that golf courses on average reach only about 60% of their financial potential.

We believe that the fundamental cause for this disappointing level of achievement is the absence of a disciplined approach to the business of golf. It is easy to be overwhelmed with the daily chores and to let slide the crafting of and, more importantly, the adherence to a long-term vision.

Although nearly every golf course creates an annual budget, and many develop marketing or membership plans (private clubs), few develop a strategic plan that serves as the lighthouse for the daily operation of the facility.

The purpose of this book was to create a system for the management of a golf course that would provide a framework by which a golf course could be operated.

This process of strategic planning is rooted in understanding the customers' MOSAIC profile (age, income, and ethnicity) and the number of golfers per 18 holes that reside or work within the competitive local market. Recall that we have developed the Predictive Score Index that defines the potential of your course based on its location, in which we made over 2 million calculations regarding the 15,204 golf courses.

That information allows one to determine the potential niche in which their facility will find success as shown here:

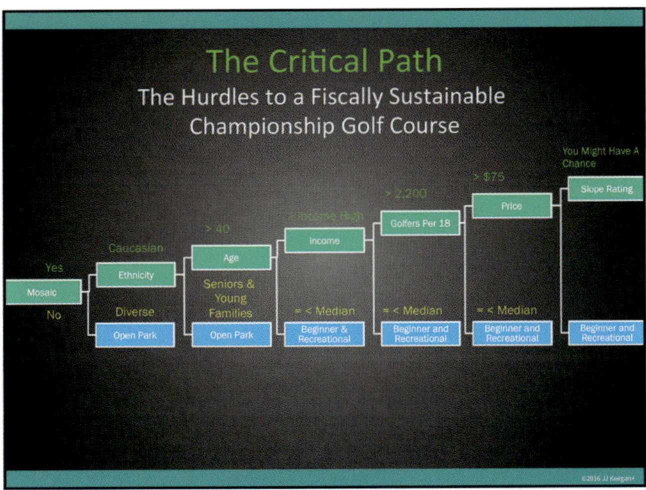

Once the opportunity and the course's likely niche is known, the vision can be defined.

The Business of Golf—What Are You Thinking? provides you with seven steps that will differentiate your facility from local competitors and greatly enhance the probability of financial success. As the saying goes, "luck favors the prepared."

The concepts in this book have been field tested by 20 leading golf course operators that manage over 60 golf courses.

If you answer these post-test questions correctly, I am confident you will know how to use the fundamental principles of successful golf course management.

Post-Test Question 1:

Yes	No	
☐	☐	Have you developed a written strategic plan within the last three years; a plan prepared by management and read by all staff members?

Strategic: It Starts with "Why?"

Each of the world's over 34,000 golf courses is unique. Communicating why you do what you do, rather than focusing on what you offer, is reflected in the vision and mission statements that form your facility's brand.

Post-Test Question 2:

Yes	No	
☐	☐	Does your strategic plan include the "Why?" of your facility?

Post-Test Question 3:

As measured by the experience provided to your customer, what market segment does your facility TARGET?

- ☐ Top 10% (Platinum)
- ☐ Top 25% (Gold)
- ☐ Top 50% (Silver)
- ☐ Top 75% (Bronze)
- ☐ Bottom 25% (Steel)

Post-Test Question 4:

What market niche are you targeting for the majority of golfers who frequent your facility?

- ☐ Accomplished (Championship: 12 handicap or less)
- ☐ Recreational (13 handicap to 25 handicap)
- ☐ Beginners (26 handicap and higher)

Note that it is not our philosophy that every golf course can be ideal for all types of golfers. We believe that differentiating the market is a healthy practice for your course and the game. Having targeted products for different types of current and potential customers is a formula that almost always insures success.

Post-Test Question 5:

Which of the following tools (forecasting methods and reports) do you use to manage your facility?

- ☐ Competitive market share analysis
- ☐ Financial statements
- ☐ Golf Datatech reports
- ☐ Golfer local market analysis (age, income ethnicity, population density, golfers in your market)
- ☐ Mosaic profile (demographic report)
- ☐ Operational budgets

- ☐ Club Benchmarking (private) and Links Insights (public)
- ☐ ORCA reports
- ☐ Rounds—Base-year analysis in the prior year
- ☐ Weather Trends International playable days report
- ☐ Weather Trends International forecasting data

The use of these tools provides a golf course with important perspectives on the controllable and uncontrollable factors influencing its operation.

Post-Test Question 6:

What is your revenue target from activities (tournaments, outings, food and beverage, catering, banquets, etc.), excluding green fees?

- ☐ 10%
- ☐ 25%
- ☐ 50%
- ☐ 75%
- ☐ Over 75%

The lack of dependence solely on golf course revenues (green fees, carts, merchandise, range, etc.) insulates an operation from the vagaries of weather. We learned from studies conducted that creating a certain social atmosphere at a club can develop ongoing business, not directly dependent on the golf course, even though the course may have been the initial draw.

Step 1: Geographic Local Market Analysis

Having defined the strategic plan, the next step is a reality check to determine whether what you have planned is achievable. The answer to that question rests to a certain extent on the location of the golf course.

Post-Test Question 7:

Yes **No**

☐ ☐ Are the median household income and median age within 30 minutes of your golf course (municipal, daily fee, or private club) consistent with your market segment target?

If the answer is "no," as a golf course operator, it is important to import golfers beyond your local market to sustain the facility. The resort areas of Arizona, Florida, and Myrtle Beach come immediately to mind as being dependent on tourists.

Post-Test Question 8:

Yes **No**

☐ ☐ Is the Experian MOSAIC profile supportive of golf within 10 miles of your facility? Your score of the four top categories (sophisticated single, career and family, bourgeois prosperity, and comfortable retired) should exceed 20% compared to the nation.

Post-Test Question 9:

Yes **No**

☐ ☐ For the market niche defined, does the number of golfers that reside within 30 minutes of your golf course exceed 600 avid golfers per 18-hole equivalent (if you are in the public market) or 2,200 avid golfers (if you seek to operate a private club)?

Note that in 2016 while there are 1,626 golfers per 18 holes, the Top 100 core-based statistical areas average 2,288 golfers per 18 holes. The non-core based statistical areas average only 1,046. Golf courses with smaller markets have a daunting challenge ahead.

Step 2: Weather Playable Days

Although the weather is an uncontrollable factor, weather data available today enables a golf course to determine its ideal operating season, to determine if its management is under- or over performing about the number of playable days, and to have the opportunity to plan events in advance and more closely control water expenses.

Post-Test Question 10:

Yes	No	
☐	☐	Do you know how many playable golf days your course has averaged during the past 10 years?

Post-Test Question 11:

Yes	No	
☐	☐	Are you utilizing Weather Trends International forecasting tools to optimize the financial performance of your facility?

Step 3: Technology

Each person comes to the management of a golf course with biases. Admittedly, mine is rooted in the belief that the technology that can generate operating statistics regarding the customer and the facility can be leveraged to increase net income by 20%. While some courses collect data, few use them proactively.

Post-Test Question 12:

Yes	No	
☐	☐	Do you know the customers (19 or more rounds per year) who played your facility in consecutive years?

Post-Test Question 13:

Yes No

☐ ☐ Do you know the customers who played your course for the first time this year?

Post-Test Question 14:

Yes No

☐ ☐ Do you know the customers who played your course last year but not this year?

Post-Test Question 15:

Yes No

☐ ☐ Do you engage in customer relations management by identifying segments (demographics, customer transactions, i.e., frequency, spending, etc.) to send appropriate marketing messages to each group via electronic media (e-mail, website, Facebook, and Twitter) on a periodic basis?

Post-Test Question 16:

Yes No

☐ ☐ Can a customer book a tee time reservation from your home page within three clicks, based on the date, time, and group size of the party (information located in the upper left-hand side of the website home page)?

Post-Test Question 17:

Yes No

☐ ☐ Do you engage in yield management by adjusting prices based on forecasted demand?

Post-Test Question 18:

Yes **No**

☐ ☐ Are your prices (prime time, twilight, specials) consistent through all distribution channels (website, electronic tee sheet, call center, social media)?

Step 4: Financial Benchmarking

The fear that some golf course owners and managers have of participating in national financial benchmarking exercises is surprising. These national data repositories provide meaningful insights into the financial performance of golf courses. With an industry participation rate of less than 20%, when segmented into regional and local markets, the number of respondents is too small to produce meaningful data.

Post-Test Question 19:

Yes **No**

☐ ☐ Do you track revenue per round by customer by year?

Post-Test Question 20:

Yes **No**

☐ ☐ Do you track total spending by customer by year?

Post-Test Question 21:

Yes **No**

☐ ☐ Do you know the utilization rate by hour, by day, by month?

Post-Test Question 22:

Yes **No**

☐ ☐ Do you regularly participate (12 out of 12 months) in the Golf Datatech Rounds and Revenue reporting?

Post-Test Question 23:

Yes **No**

☐ ☐ Do you regularly participate in the ORCA Reports Monthly Analysis?

Post-Test Question 24:

Yes **No**

☐ ☐ Have you participated in the Club Benchmarking or Links Insights Annual Operating Survey?

Post-Test Question 25:

Yes **No**

☐ ☐ Do you regularly participate in Golf Datatech's retail reporting regarding merchandise and equipment sold?

Step 5: Facilities

It is ironic that the asset that draws the golfers to the facility often receives the least attention on the allocation of capital reserves to ensure that as it naturally depreciates, it can be properly updated.

It is also surprising that though golf courses cover about 150 acres, of which 100 are typically maintained, the cost of maintaining such facilities can vary from under $300,000 to over $2 million, with differences in conditioning, obviously noted but often not in harmony with the amounts spent on upkeep and improvement.

Post-Test Question 26:

Yes **No**

☐ ☐ Does your facility allocate at least $200,000 annually to a reserve account for course capital improvements and equipment replacement?

Post-Test Question 27:

Yes **No**

☐ ☐ Is your maintenance labor-hour budget for the year less than 80 hours per playable day?

Post-Test Question 28:

Yes **No**

☐ ☐ Is the appraised value of your facility greater than 1.5 times revenue or 10 times earnings before interest, taxes, depreciation, and amortization?

Step 6: Operations

With touch points on the Assembly Line of Golf ranging from 8 at a military course to at least 14 at elite private clubs, the experience best remembered often involves the lowest paid employee.

Operations are about blocking and tackling—from ensuring that every employee is consistently dressed and identified by name to making sure that the public areas in the clubhouse (including bathrooms) and on the property are neat and tidy.

Post-Test Question 29:

Yes **No**

☐ ☐ Has your facility developed five key benchmarks that are monitored daily to ensure that its financial performance is in line with agreed-upon goals?

Post-Test Question 30:

Yes **No**

☐ ☐ Do you have your golf course secretly shopped?

Post-Test Question 31:

Yes **No**

☐ ☐ Have you developed a formula to determine the fair market value of the experience being provided at your course, independent of competitive local rates?

Post-Test Question 32:

Yes **No**

☐ ☐ Does your advertising, marketing, and public relations budget exceed 5% of forecasted revenue?

Step 7: Customers

With 15% of customers generating 60% of revenue and the annual turnover of those who play and don't return the following year nearing 50%, monitoring customer satisfaction is vital.

The strength of a golf course's customer franchise can be precisely measured. The customer loyalty index serves as an accurate predictor of a golf course's financial success.

Post-Test Question 33:

Yes **No**

☐ ☐ Do you know your facility's customer loyalty score in comparison to that of your leading competitors?

Post-Test Question 34:

Yes **No**

☐ ☐ Are your customers electronically surveyed annually as to their expectations and the experience they have received?

Does the JJ Keegan+ WIN™ Formula Work?

Consider for a moment what happens if the formula doesn't work. At a minimum, what would be obtained from the process would be valuable insights into methods for improved operational performance. Knowing your facility's strategic vision, developing a tactical plan, and forming some commitment to consistent operational execution would produce benefits. In other words, the process of merely working through the formula has substantial value. It represents a methodology and a discipline few achieve.

And what if the formula works? A golf course would significantly enhance its operations in relationship to its competitors, boost its profits in the short term, and increase its value in the long term. Again, great benefits result. We believe, and have proven, that the application of the formula has the potential to increase your EBITDA by 12% of gross revenue.

For over a decade it has been applied successfully at golf courses in Europe and across the United States and Asia.

The business of golf and the game of golf have in common a search for perfection that will probably never be achieved. One day, you think you have found the secret to the game of golf, but it escapes you the next day.

The business of golf is also like that. Any time you gather a group of humans, though the goal of each may be the same, getting consistent execution remains elusive. It is our experience that between the academic theory and the reality of execution, golf courses do well if they implement 70% of these guidelines during the first golf season they are used.

Just before his retirement, John Zobler, assistant city manager for the City of Ocala, stated, "What needed to be accomplished to provide the golf course firm financial footing was identified through this process. While it took five years to navigate the politics and allocate the resources necessary, in the end, what we needed to do was identified in the beginning. The methodology is very sound."

The City of Virginia Beach, due to labor issues and significant deferred capital expenses, went from a $233,000 annual deficit to leasing its golf courses and gaining positive cash flow. As important there is the fact that a talented management company invested over $1 million in the city's best course and is also getting a nice return on investment.

For a daily fee golf course in Sioux Falls, South Dakota, the JJ Keegan+ WIN™ formula suggested that a renovation of this championship golf course with an enhanced database segmentation to facilitate a rebranding would enhance the golfer experience.

For a private club that was transitioning from a developer-owned to a board-managed equity club, the process provided emotional comfort to the board as they navigated the uncharted waters of club management. Customer surveys and member meetings created a solidarity of focus.

The list of examples of where the formula has worked is long. Perhaps unsurprisingly, it is the innovators, early adopters, or the early majority who have embraced this approach while the late majority are too set in their ways to explore new ideas to improve their golf course's lot in life. By the fact that you are reading the book, congratulations. You are in the first group.

The list of success stories is long. Recently we were asked during an interview if the process had created conflict.

At every facility, there are always competing interests—owners who want to judiciously allocate resources, the management team that is seeking more resources to ensure the best customer experience, and the golfers who are always seeking value as illustrated here for the municipal environment.

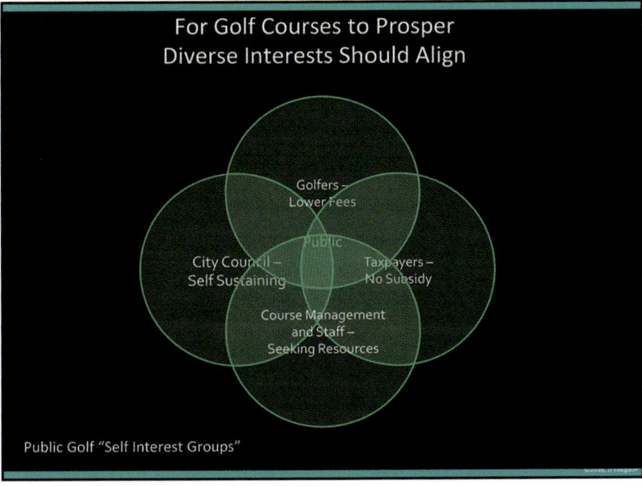

While self-interest dominates, to the extent that a consensus can be built, prosperity can be achieved.

The objective of this methodology is to build a consensus. We have found that good communication is the fundamental path to success. When raising fees, explaining to the golfers where the incremental money is to be invested usually achieves support. Providing management a capital budget that is funded gives them hope that they will be able to keep the customer experience at the level desired.

And for the owner, success is achieved when the steps outlined here are executed.

Challenges Beyond the Grasp of One

While the primary focus of golf course owners and managers should be their facilities, such focus should come with a broad perspective on understanding what the game of golf is and what it represents to our society.

There are major themes to the game of golf that each person active in the industry should comprehend. These themes direct us to the future of the golf business:

1. **Industry:** The game of golf is currently largely dominated by male, well-to-do Caucasians who are in their forties. That mirrors those who are employed in the industry. As of 2014, of the 23,152 members of the PGA, only 854 are minorities (3.68%). There are 364 minorities among the 4,081 apprentices. Minorities in the United States comprise 27.6% of the population. The imbalance of minorities in the sport must be corrected for the industry to grow.

   The LPGA has 1,500 members representing 5.5% of the operational workforce at golf courses. Women who play the game represent 22% of golfers. The imbalance in gender employment and participation in the sport must be corrected for the sport to grow.

   Diversity is the key to the future of the game.

2. **The Game:** It is expensive to play golf, and unless you are good, frankly, it isn't much fun. Golf provides recreation and entertainment, but its real benefit is in the values developed in those who participate. Failure to attract new golfers is serious, but Public Enemy Number One is attrition. Participation rates continue to decline.

3. **Environment:** Water is a critical resource, and its threatened supply greatly affects the golf industry. Many courses should focus on reducing the size

of the playing field, thereby reducing the requirements for irrigation and fertilization. Curtailing water consumption would also reduce expenses. The industry needs to transition from emphasizing a manicured experience to allowing a natural experience.

4. **Clubhouse Facilities:** Consistent with these trends is the construction of large clubhouses exceeding 40,000 square feet, which are expensive to operate. The cost to maintain these facilities is exorbitant, and the costs are passed on to the golfers; this is another negative influence on the adoption of golf by the masses.

5. **Management and Staff:** To remain relevant, individuals within the profession and those entering the profession need to acquire the requisite business skills in accounting, management, marketing, and technology to appreciate the complexities of successfully running a golf enterprise.

   Successful business operators are never satisfied with the status quo. Tomorrow's leaders will share their information, provide expertise, and clearly articulate their values and standards.

   The axiom is, "Is it easy for customers to do business with us?" If not, let's change it, for the best operations will be both high touch and high tech.

6. **Technology:** The most effective way of connecting with customers to build brand loyalty is communicating via the adroit use of websites, e-mail, text messaging and social media. The golf industry has historically lagged in the adoption of technology.

   This is a short-term fix that will solve a long-term problem.

7. **The Golf Course:** During the past two decades, the courses that have been built are more difficult, more expensive, and more time-consuming. One way to measure difficulty follows is via the slope rating shown on the next page.

   Prior to 1990, the average slope rating was 120. Post-1990 the average slope rate is 127 with a median of 129.

The daily fee course should create an experience through which golfers feel they have been challenged, but one that through their efforts they have conquered. Golf courses should be made to look hard and play easy. Courses for the vast majority need to become kinder and gentler to and for the masses.

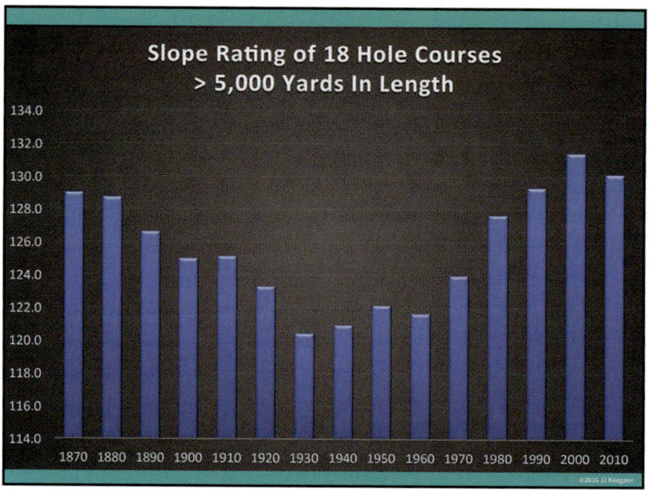

This Is the End . . .

The end is the beginning, and the beginning starts with focusing on your customers. When you create a value-based experience, the foundation for your success is set.

Understanding why golfers make choices and what factors impact those choices is necessary. The factors of cost and time so often quoted as negative factors for golf are not identified as the leading factors that impact golfer choice. Engagement with the facility, as emphasized in the Simon Sinek video, provides the key to the future successful operation of a golf course.

This analysis of the golf industry and the explanation of the formula that leads to the successful operation of a golf course have been presented in a way that hopefully will lighten the spirits of the professionals who serve the business of golf.

I have written with the hope and understanding that course owners who take these words to heart and head and hands and feet will have the opportunity to bolster their investment return.

Golf is a great game, and it can be a fabulous business. It is my wish that your goals in life, as well as the goals you set for your golf course, are achieved.

Thank you for taking the time to read this book. And, as I hope you say to all of your departing customers, "I appreciate your support, and I look forward to serving you again. Best wishes."

Path to Success: Your Final Grade

1) In the post-test presented in this chapter, for the 30 "yes" and "no" answers, most golf courses would answer "no" to over 20 of those questions. If you answered "yes" to:

   Less than 15: You have lots of company.

   15–20: Progress is being made. There is hope.

   21–25: You are clearly ahead of your peers.

   26–30: You are one of the industry's leaders. Congratulations.

2) For multiple choice questions 3–6, if you know precisely the answers for your facility, you are absolutely on the path to success. Way to go!

Concluding Thought

YIN-YANG: In the black, there is some white; In the wrong, there is some right; In the dark, there is some light; In the blind, there is some sight.

Ven Abhinyana

It is not the critic who counts; not the man who points out how the strong man stumbles, or where the doer of deeds could have done them better. The credit belongs to the man who is actually in the arena, whose face is marred by dust and sweat and blood; who strives valiantly; who errs, who comes short again and again, because there is no effort without error and shortcoming; but who does actually strive to do the deeds; who knows great enthusiasms, the great devotions; who spends himself in a worthy cause; who at the best knows in the end the triumph of high achievement, and who at the worst, if he fails, at least fails while daring greatly, so that his place shall never be with those cold and timid souls who neither know victory nor defeat.

Theodore Roosevelt

Index